From Independence to Statehood

From Independence
to Statehood

Managing Ethnic Conflict
in Five African and Asian States

Edited by

Robert B. Goldmann
and
A. Jeyaratnam Wilson

St. Martin's Press, New York

Library of Congress Cataloging in Publication Data

Main entry under title:

From independence to statehood.

    1. Underdeveloped areas—Social conditions—Addresses,
       essays, lectures.
    2. Ethnic relations—Addresses, essays, lectures.
    3. Social conflict—Addresses, essays, lectures.
    I. Goldmann, Robert, 1921–
    II. Wilson, A. Jeyaratnam.

HN980F76   1983   305.8′009172′4   83–6663

ISBN 0-312-30723-3

CONTENTS

PREFACE

This book is about one of the scourges of this century. It has to do with ethnic conflicts in selected states, which have caused more problems of a global nature and more human suffering than can be attributed to any other single source of violence. The word *ethnic*, in the context of this volume, covers a wide range of communal or group interactions—racial, tribal, religious, linguistic, or any other characteristic that distinguishes groups from each other—that often lead to struggle and which can be violent or non-violent. It can be a conflict between an ethnic or religious majority and minorities, or a dispute between ethnic or religious minorities. In many cases, such disputes have caused widespread violence or serious and costly disorders. They are always sources of political instability, at times threatening the cohesion of a country; often, they menace peace among nations. One need think only of the civil war in Nigeria, the situations in Cyprus, Lebanon, or in the Indian sub-continent to understand how ethnic warfare within a country can disturb or disrupt relations among countries.

From Northern Ireland to Southeast Asia, Quebec to Sri Lanka or Yugoslavia to Burundi, ethnic groups assert their identity, rights, and needs. Sometimes they clash violently, often politically, economically or socially, with others within the same nation. Many of these nations became independent sovereign states after World War II, inheriting the boundaries of a colonial past which disregarded or re-enforced differences. Today, the governments of these countries must defend their boundaries and attempt to forge into nations with common goals and aspirations people of different races, tribal origins, religions, languages, and cultural backgrounds. These governments must breathe life into a society whose constituent groups find little meaning in nationhood and which feel primary kinship and loyalty to fellow members of their particular ethnic groups. The internal conflicts governments are grappling with are all the more harmful because these societies are, at the same time, seeking to speed up their economic and social development. Every time an ethnic conflict breaks out in a developing society, every time ethnic tensions result in governments taking steps or introducing policies that promote the economic and social progress of any one group to the detriment of the other, the main objective of a society is set back.

Against this background, the Ford Foundation, over several years, has explored ways to contribute to efforts in the developing world to easing, mediating, or reducing conflict and sources of tension. Consultations with scores of individuals in academic and public life in eight African and Asian states yielded a consensus that can be helpful in the exchange of experience in respect of policies and programmes designed to ease group tensions while those countries move toward higher levels of social and economic justice.

This consensus led to the design and development of two workshops, one held in Taita Hills, Kenya and the other in Trincomalee, Sri Lanka. The first workshop dealt with structural approaches, for example, constitutional, federal, and regional autonomy systems; the second focused on affirmative action or equalisation policies. The material presented in this volume was prepared for these meetings. The authors were asked to write policy-orientated papers reflecting either their direct involvement with processes relevant to the topic or their assessment of the policies and their impact. Therefore, some of the contributors chose not to follow the pattern of academic monographs; they carried few footnotes and only limited bibliographical data.

Professor Myron Weiner provides a broad panorama of the issues, with specific examples from the United States and India, and raises some fundamental policy questions inherent in all public policies seeking to deal with these highly complex, emotionally charged and therefore extremely sensitive issues.

From Nigeria, there is the personal experience of Dr Uma Eleazu as a member of the commission that drafted the 1979 Constitution, a document forged in the wake of a bloody civil war and which explicitly addressed itself to bridging the ethnic gaps that were tearing this large African state apart. Professor Sam. Egite Oyovbaire views the same facts and developments from an observer's perspective and in light of the historical antecedents so important to understanding modern Nigeria.

Upendra Baxi provides a provocative assessment of India's reservations' policy for scheduled castes, tribes and backward groups. Professor Chitnis focuses on the area of reservations for scheduled castes and tribes and backward groups in India—regarding education—and assesses their design and effects. Like Chitnis and Mavis Puthucheary, Professor Tai Yoke Lin focuses on a particular area of policy (in Malaysia it is called the New Economic Policy). Their papers review the content and impact of the NEP in the employment field. Professor Benno Ndulu deals with yet another approach to reducing disparities between groups: Tanzania's regional equalisation policy. In many cases, he explains, that 'region' is almost synonymous with ethnic group, so that this Tanzanian concept also addresses itself, albeit implicitly, to ethnic tensions and differences.

The Sri Lankan contributors illustrate how discrimination against ethnic minorities have, since independence in 1948, damaged national unity. The disfranchisement in 1948-9 of the Indian Tamil plantation workers, who produce the major share of the country's national wealth; the declaration in 1956 of Sinhala as the only official language with the other language, Tamil, consigned to an inferior status, a language spoken by some 20 per cent of the population; and the enshrinement of Buddhism in 1972 as an article of a new autochthonous constitution whereby the state is required to give special protection to it and foster it in every way— when more than 30 per cent of people are Hindu, Muslim, and Christian— provide evidence of a hesitancy of leadership.

The economic solutions to these problems are given by Neelan Tiruchelvam in his 'Ethnicity and Resource Allocation', by C. R. de Silva and K. M. de Silva in their chapters on discrimination against Tamils in the matter of university admissions, and by S. W. R. de A. Samarasinghe in his follow-up of the way discrimination in education has affected the recruitment of Tamils to the service of the central government.

The overpoliticisation of an electorate has accelerated the process whereby a state with the potential for national unification at the time of Britain's departure is now virtually a state at risk. There can therefore be no certainty about the island's future. Neelan Tiruchelvam's chapter on district development councils tells us how the flood of Ceylon Tamil militant resentment has to some extent been dammed by the executive president of the republic, J. R. Jayewardene. There are insurmountable obstacles—a sceptical Sinhala political elite—at the top, middle, and lower echelons, as well as a Sinhala bureaucracy that is unwilling to delegate power either for bureaucratic or communal reasons, or both.

C. R. de Silva's Sinhala-Tamil rivalry is a starting point. At the risk of being thought unduly pessimistic, can a quarrel and wars that run through a recorded history of more than 2,500 years be brought to an amicable conclusion in only a few years? A state with so much promise, one prone to the slogans of race, religion, and possibly caste (very much in undertones these days in contemporary Sri Lanka), makes the task of sewing a patchwork quilt immeasurably difficult. Can we, in such circumstances, adopt strategies for nation-building? The auguries do not seem good. This is but one of the problems that the International Institute for Ethnic Studies proposes to study with a view to providing frameworks for possible future solutions.

The two workshops yielded precisely the exchange of experience they were designed to elicit. Participants questioned each other and responded, both at formal sessions and in informal gatherings between and after meetings. From the workshops emerged a strong desire to sustain this kind of contact on a more organised basis. The Sri Lankan group responded with a proposal to establish an institute in Sri Lanka for that purpose. In the summer of 1982, with a grant from the Ford Foundation, the International Centre for Ethnic Studies was established in Colombo, with a research department in Kandy, near Sri Lanka's Peradeniya University, with its extensive library and documentation facilities. The Centre is organising workshops; stimulating and co-ordinating comparative policy-oriented research; developing a library and documentation section that can serve as a catalyst for exchanging written materials; and attempting to facilitate practical co-operation between individuals and institutions in countries with comparable problems and different ways of dealing with them.

Readers interested in pursuing any issue touched on in this book or, albeit inadequately, described in this preface, are invited to contact the International Centre for Ethnic Studies, 8 Kynsey Terrace, Colombo 8, Sri Lanka.

Robert B. Goldmann
A. Jeyaratnam Wilson

1 STRUCTURAL CHANGE AND THE PROBLEMS OF NATIONAL COHESION: THE NIGERIAN EXPERIENCE

Sam. Egite Oyovbaire

In this chapter the basis of recent structural changes in Nigeria in terms of their contributions and limitations to the enhancement of national cohesion will be examined. This will be done in three related ways: (1) as national cohesion is not an end in itself, its conceptual value will be sketched particularly as it is related to the building of authority and community in Nigeria; (2) contemporary communal structures of the Nigerian state are examined in terms of their pre-colonial and colonial origins; and (3) structural designs of the Constitution of the Second Republic are identified and evaluated from the point of view of national cohesion.

I

The term *national cohesion* has been employed rather than *national integration* to avoid some of the pitfalls in studies of African politics when we discuss such matters as 'social change and modernisation' and 'development and underdevelopment'. The concept of national integration in theories and studies of social change and modernisation carries premises and meanings that are not always clear. It is often assumed that political parties, leadership and bureaucracies actually function either to integrate or disintegrate, that a 'nationally integrated political community' necessarily serves the interests of citizens, and vice versa, that we can actually feel or measure the extent to which a political community is really integrated, that national integration is the same as national homogeneity, national harmony, peace and stability.

In real life, the essence of national integration is embodied in the dominant structures and values of productive and distributive activities—in the manner in which these activities serve or harm class interests. National integration is not, and cannot, 'bridge' the economic interests in the society. National integration is therefore either a contradiction in terms or it reflects the strengthening of those class interests dominant in the production and distribution processes.

When the concept of national integration is viewed against the background of Nigeria's colonial origins and its political economy, one encounters enormous difficulties trying to identify *elite* and *mass*, in determining whose 'gap' is being bridged, which cultural and territorial tensions and discontinuities of 'communities' and 'ethnic groups' are being reduced, what social conditions and class interests are dominant in the economy, and in identifying this dominance with national integration. In short, to what extent does the increase in the power of some class interests serve to describe prevailing cultural and territorial tensions and discontinuities among ethnic groups?

There is ample evidence of these factors in the history and functioning of the Nigerian political system. It is these elements that the new constitution is designed to come to grips with. To understand what has been and is being attempted, the more straightforward and less complex term *national cohesion* (rather than 'national integration') is a more helpful tool. Unlike 'national integration', *national cohesion* does not presume harmonised or integrated interests, at least as a point of departure for the attainment of higher welfare. Regardless of how people came together in the first place or were brought together, national cohesion is simply an acknowledgment of the minimum need to resolve the problems of social existence.

The concept of national cohesion also provides a better basis for evaluating the way in which successive governing classes in Nigeria have come to view and articulate politics and the country's political process. Modern Nigerian political aspirations are characterised by the values and structures of capitalism and liberal democracy, with a commitment to some notion of federalism.[1] Nigeria's leadership has consistently articulated and cultivated that framework of politics and government— from the decades of anti-colonial nationalism through the politics of the First Republic and military rule to the emergence of the experiment of the Second Republic. The point here is not whether this framework has allowed the growth and development of the Nigerian political system, but whether the leadership has operated from the premiss of this basic minimum of national cohesion. Such a framework reflects three dominant structural characteristics: (1) the plurality of subcultures or communal groups in rivalry among themselves, and the tensions between these communal groups, on the one hand, and the emergent Nigerian national culture or community, on the other; (2) a political life that is elitist or class-conscious in concept, recruitment and organisation; and (3) political cleavages which, while dominated by class interests, revolve around the country's multiple subcultures or communities.

It is these features of the Nigerian political system that delimit the patterns of political authority and the emerging Nigerian community that the country's constitution and leadership have attempted to identify and provide for in forming and operating the Second Republic, at least from the point of view of the problems of national cohesion. Because these features are products of historical development, it is appropriate to review the antecedents briefly in order to appreciate their salience in the operation of the current political process.

II

Until this century, Nigeria was composed of entities or communities described variously as empire, caliphate, kingdom, chiefdom, city-state or village republic. For now, and for some time to come, no one can claim knowledge of the actual number of these communities in Nigeria. In recent times, as demand for the creation of new states and local government areas increased, so 'new communities' emerged in the forefront of the political process. We begin to appreciate that the 'kingdoms, caliphates, and chiefdoms' were themselves superficial entities. Be that as it may, the pre-colonial systems varied in size—in productive, distributive and exchange organisation and in degrees of autonomy from, and dependence upon, each other. The territories of some, such as the Sokoto Caliphate and the Yoruba and Benin empires, went beyond Nigeria's present borders. Two important points should be made about this geo-political configuration of the 'Nigerian region' before colonial domination. The first point concerns the nature of inter-relationships among the various pre-colonial communities, the second, the character of the social formations in each community.[2]

Until Britain established and consolidated its control over the boundaries of the country after 1914, no ruler or set of rulers, social class or regime had any claims on the pre-colonial state systems. The largest of these systems was the Sokoto caliphate, only a century old when it was made part of the new Nigerian entity. Even the imperialism of that caliphate, however, had great difficulty in expanding beyond the kingdom of Borno, parts of present-day Gongola State, the Benue valley and the forest regions south of the Benue–Niger confluence. Other would-be imperialist systems, such as the old Oyo and Benin empires, were constrained to limit their expansionist objectives; they seemed aware of the dangers of disintegration and disaffection within each empire, due largely to their limited military and economic resources.

Prior to 1900, slavery, serfdom and other semi-feudal characteristics manifested themselves in such systems as those of the Kanuri, the Hausa-Fulani emirates post-jihad, Yoruba, Nupe, Igala, Jukun and Benin. In the Benin system, for example, the organisation of resource production, distribution and exchange reflected the interests and world view of a ruling class, with the Oba as the kingpin of the social structure. The strength of the Benin empire (the existence of non-toiling classes of Oba, chiefs, priests, warriors and protection of the elderly, weak and infants) meant a heavy burden for the working masses.

As in Benin, so it was in the Sokoto caliphate, Borno and their neighbouring states. Here, the flourishing system of slavery and serfdom was firmly grafted on to the largely peasant mode of production. Well into the first decade of the twentieth century, the output went chiefly to the tribute-collecting, semi-feudal aristocracies in Yola, Sokoto, Kano, Borno and Zaria. This type of system characterised most of the political entities of the Nigerian region.

In such places as Lagos, Badagry and the city-states of the Niger Delta, however, foreign trade with Western Europe for more than two centuries had left its mark on the domestic economies of these Nigerian states. The evidence was everywhere: freed and resettled slaves and their offspring between 1850 and 1900; the 'civilising activities' of Christian missions; the growth and effect of West European education, skills and organisation, etc. By the turn of the century, these influences had produced a distinct new social structure with a class of 'proto-bourgeois and maritime merchants' as its pivot. While this new elite exploited the peasants, it also developed a commercial system of property rights.

In many areas, such as the valleys of the Niger and Benue rivers, the Jos Plateau, the village republics of Gwari, Igbo, Tiv and the Idoma societies, there was little formal governance or state structure. These communities were essentially peasant groups when they were incorporated into the colonial system.

Against this background of varied and largely weak organisation, Britain removed all African and rival European opposition to the building and consolidation of its colonial empire. Colonialism, however, did not completely destroy the pre-colonial social relations of production, distribution and exchange, or the patterns of authority and culture. By 1914, the rudimentary boundaries and contours of the contemporary Nigerian state had emerged, developing clear trends toward cohesion and historical and cultural legitimacy.

Thus, in the Nigerian system, pre-colonial social formations continue to be an effective, usable basis for social and structural changes. In this sense, Nigeria is an amalgam of many distinctive local communities and a nationwide community of interests. Colonial domination forged strong links *vis-à-vis* the rest of the world and the trading and other economic and technological opportunities it offered.

British colonial control and repression ensured, within the institutional devices of 'indirect rule', that the pre-colonial arrangements were re-ordered around a strategy of mutual hostility yet co-existing under the colonial system. The amalgamation of 1914 did not create a unitary or uniform system of politics and administration.

As a beginning, a confederation of two groups of colonial provinces was created—one in the north and the other in the south. Propelled by colonial and post-colonial requirements, changes were made in 1938, 1954, 1963, 1967 and 1976. For example, the federation of the unevenly developed regions of 1954 was eventually transformed into the nineteen relatively evenly sized units of 1976. Similarly, by 1976/77 about 300 local government units had been established, cutting across colonial boundaries of 'native authorities' yet retaining the structural sensitivities of pre-colonial communities.

The intended effect of these changes was to promote the growth and development of the political process and to foster homogenisation of the culture of politics and administration. As has been indicated, however, the same effects generated heightened communalism along the ethnic lines of the pre-colonial period. The major consequence of these effects was the chain of events that led to the collapse of the First Republic in 1966 and to the civil war. The logic of restructuring the 'federated colonial units' is the logic of ethnicity as an autonomous social force operating in the context of the inclusive colonial and post-colonial state. Ethnicity provides usable approaches for the allocation of resources among unequal individuals, unequal social groups or communities, and unequal political or administrative regions.

For decades, the system of colonial rule shielded some communities from and exposed others to the traumatic effects of colonial capitalism, patterns of education and colonial administration. At the same time, some communities increasingly participated in urbanisation and the acquisition of European values, skills and techniques of social organisation. While some communities were brought into the modernisation process early in the colonial period, others were kept out. Colonial domination delayed critical consciousness and social organisation in those communities with whom colonial administrators cultivated affinity.[3]

The manifestations of colonial protection and disjunction did not change after independence. In fact, they were extended by the system and operation of party and competitive politics. Communal pluralism continued to pose problems for the cohesion of the political system. Contradictions persisted between the ideology of regionalism or communalism, on the one hand, and nationalism or centralism, on the other; between communities that dominated the political system through the possession of 'technological' and administrative power and those that sought domination through the use of political power based on numerical strength; between 'majority ethnic groups' that sought to dominate the structures of power, status and wealth, and minority ethnic groups which deliberately protested their subordinate status.[4]

The 1979 Constitution was unequivocal in these matters. In inaugurating the drafting committee on 18 October 1975, the Military Head of State suggested these basic approaches to the problems of national cohesion:

The major political parties of the past emerged with regional and ethnic support.

The main political parties of the past were in fact little more than (regional or ethnic) armies organised for fighting elections in the regions for the regional and federal legislatures.

So vile was the abuse of the electoral process in the past that this has raised the question as to whether we need continue to accept simple majorities as a basis for political selection especially at the centre.

Given our commitment to a Federal System of Government; to a free democratic and lawful system which guarantees fundamental human rights; and to the emergence of a stable system through constitutional law, the creation of viable political consensus and orderly succession to political power. We should:

    seek to eliminate cut-throat competition in the political process; discourage institutionalised opposition to the government in power, and instead develop consensus politics and government based on a community of all interests rather than interest of sections of the country;

    eliminate over-centralisation of power and as a matter of principle decentralise power wherever possible as a means of diffusing tensions;

    evolve an electoral system which is free and fair and ensures adequate representation of our peoples;

    evolve a system from which will emerge genuine and truly national political parties;

    recommend the establishment of an executive presidential system of government in which the president and vice-president are assigned clearly defined powers and made accountable directly to the people, and in which the making of the president, the vice-president and the members of the executive council deliberately reflect the federal character of the country.

Finally, the Head of the Military Government advised the CDC and the country:

Past events have shown that we cannot build a future for this country on a rigid political ideology. Such an approach would be unrealistic. The evolution of a doctrinal concept is usually predicated upon the general acceptance by the people of a national political philosophy ... consequently, until all of our people, or a large majority of them, have acknowledged a common ideological motivation, it would be fruitless to proclaim any particular philosophy or ideology in our Constitution.[5]

These fundamental elements of Nigeria's origins, growth and development provide the framework for analysing how this vast, complex system has survived and intends to continue its cohesion in the future. What follows is an analysis of elements of the 1979 Constitution, which is the concrete expression of that aspiration.

III

It is quite clear from the debate in the Constitution Drafting Committee and the proceedings of the Constituent Assembly that there was a consensus on the objectionable aspects of the country's past political life as indicated by the chief spokesman of the Supreme Military Council; the commitment to the basic tenets of capitalist development, liberal democracy and federalism; and the outlines of a Constitution to cope with the problems of national cohesion.[6]

Chapter II of the Constitution re-states the country's commitment to the principles of federalism, republicanism, democracy and social justice; the fostering of 'national integration' together with the directive that the Nigerian State should 'promote or encourage the formation of associations that cut across ethnic, linguistic, religious or other sectional barriers . . . foster a feeling of belonging and of involvement among the various peoples of the Federation, to the end that loyalty to the (Nigerian) nation shall override sectional loyalties'. Having acknowledged the cultural pluralism of Nigeria, Section 20 of the Constitution directs that 'The State shall protect and enhance Nigerian culture'.

Section 14 (3) and (4) is even more compelling:

The composition of the Government of the Federation or any of its agencies and the conduct of its affairs shall be carried out in such a manner as to reflect the federal character of Nigeria and the need to promote national unity, and also to command national loyalty, thereby ensuring that there shall be no predominance of persons from a few states or from a few ethnic or other sectional groups in that government or in any of its agencies.

The composition of the Government of a State, a local government council, or any of the agencies of such government or. council, and the conduct of the affairs of the government or council shall be carried out in such manner as to recognise the diversity of the peoples within its area of authority and the need to promote a sense of belonging and loyalty among all the peoples of the Federation.

The preceding citations from the provisions of the 1979 Constitution illustrate the many objectives and intentions in the Constitution designed to relate constitutional structures to the problems of national cohesion. Five public agencies carry major responsibilities to consolidate national cohesion: the executive agencies (presidency and governorships); political parties; the electoral system; the public services; and agencies responsible for resource allocation. This list does not by any means exhaust the structures pertinent to the future of national cohesion, and discussion of each can only be brief in the context of this chapter.

The Executive

The country learned a fundamental lesson from military rule. Against the background of the collapse of the 1963 Constitution, the 1966/67 national crisis, and the civil war, military rule succeeded in establishing structures (state and local government units) which responded to the country's communal diversity. But it also succeeded in nationalising the political system and thereby curbed the excesses of the politics of a plural federal system. The new Constitution charged the President with sustaining and further developing this process of building national cohesiveness. In the words of the Report of the CDC:

we want to be able to develop our economy, to modernise and *integrate our society, to secure and promote stability in the* [Nigerian] community and safeguard civil liberty. [The Presidency] would be imbued with energy, unity, *cohesion and despatch* in grappling with the day to day affairs of government.

Two sets of constitutional provisions are intended to enable the President of the Federation or the Governor of a state to take due advantage of existing national cohesion so as to further promote it. The provisions are related to his election and the choice of key people to assist him in discharging the duties of his office.

Chapter VI of the Constitution contains various provisions relating to the emergence and performance in office of the President (or Governor). The Executive will be elected directly. Although a presidential nominee of a political party, the requirements for election put a premium on a programme with national appeal. There is the additional requirement that in the event of more than two candidates, the elected candidate shall be the one who has obtained a majority of the votes cast at the election and has 'not less than one-quarter of the votes cast in each of at least two-thirds of all the States in the Federation'. In a heterogeneous and communally complex society like Nigeria, these requirements of the Constitution clearly undergird elements of unity and consensus and strengthen national cohesion.

In the 1979 elections for President, the five registered parties actually carried their appeals and campaigns across the entire country. The outcome of these elections—of the President and each of the nineteen Governors—clearly reflected the constitutional spirit of the need to forge national cohesion. For the first time in the history of electoral politics in Nigeria, the President, unlike the Prime Minister in the First Republic, was solidly elected by a majority vote from at least ten states of the Federation and not less than one-quarter of the votes in thirteen states.[7] Interestingly, of the thirteen states that solidly voted for the northern-born-and-based President, three (Rivers, Cross Rivers and Bendel) are in the southern geo-political regions, whereas five can be declared traditionally 'minority states' (Rivers, Cross Rivers, Bendel, Plateau and Benue). The President was therefore elected on a wide geo-political basis, a significant experience for the historical dichotomy of north–south in Nigerian colonial and post-colonial politics. The same thing can be said of the elections of the governors. In the interesting case of Kaduna State, where the political party that overwhelmingly won the legislative elections but narrowly lost the governorship, the problems of national cohesion at the level of the state were immediately transformed from communal diversity and cultural/religious complexity into those of class interests and class struggle. These at least are the terms in which the victorious party interpreted its mandate.

With respect to the formation of executive councils and other political appointments, the President or Governor is required to comply with the provisions of Chapter II of the Constitution, those on 'Federal character' and 'the diversity of the peoples and the need to promote a sense of belonging and loyalty among all the peoples of the Federation'. In addition, it is mandatory upon the President to 'appoint at least one Minister from each State who shall be an indigene of such State' (Section 135).

These constitutional provisions have, by and large, been upheld by the actions of the President and state Governors; because these appointments must be approved by the national Senate and state assemblies, strict observance has been insisted upon since October 1979. In fact, group interests built around these provisions have had to ensure that even non-ministerial appointments, though political in nature, are carried out in compliance with the 'federal character' and the 'diversity of the peoples'. In other words, communities or geo-political groups are made to feel through these appointments a sense of attachment to governments both at the centre and in the states.

On the negative side, two major problems have arisen in operating the new political system. First is excessive partisanship. Appointments make membership in the party or alliance of parties which controls the government virtually the only criterion, and this has led to the exclusion of people who either belong to rival parties or have not professed commitment to the ruling party or coalition. The second problem is the inclination to promote bureaucratic and even technocratic mediocrity in the name of reflecting the 'federal character' of appointments. The desire to balance appointments geographically is so pervasive that it becomes difficult to name people to fill the vacancies on management boards of quasi-public enterprises, and to insist on competence and experience of those on the professional and technical levels.

Federalism

Although they are conscious of the risk of establishing too many governmental units, both the CDC and the Constituent Assembly felt that an essential element for enhancing national cohesion is the broadening and deepening of Nigerian federalism. Section 7 of the Constitution guarantees the existence of the system of 'democratically elected local government councils', together with properly defined structures, composition, functions and sources of finance. Section 8 provides the processes, though cumbersome politically, for the creation of new states in the country.

While governmental operations under the Constitution since October 1979 leave much to be desired, no one doubts that these clauses of the Constitution have given rise to increasing demands for further subdividing and decentralising the country's governmental structure. Some suggestions go as far as to call for increasing the number of local government councils from the present 301 to almost 1,000, and new states from the present nineteen to as many as fifty.[8] The precise optimum number of states and local government units may be debated, yet two deeply rooted features emerge clearly from an examination of history and of Nigerian politics: (1) the anchor of Nigerian federalism is the village, not the state and local government council; and (2) national cohesion cannot be achieved until the political system has moved away from the excessive use of ethnic categorisation and the prejudice and conflict often associated with it. In all this, I believe that as a structural arrangement of politics and government, federalism, especially in an underdeveloped and communally complex society, is a means and not an end—a means for sustaining national cohesion and achieving a new statehood (and nationhood) over and above the existing sense of national community.

Structures of Representation

As a liberal capitalist democratic document, the 1979 Constitution explicitly or implicitly stipulated particular structures and processes within or through which conflicts are to be mediated and cooperation promoted.

For the first time in the history of constitution-making in Nigeria, the formation, role and operation of political parties are covered in the basic document governing the nation's political life. Parties and the electoral system date from the 1920s. Political parties were largely responsible for the pernicious and destructive politics of the 1940s, 1950s and 1960s. Curiously, however, the effects of their activities on the development of the Nigerian state and community were hardly discussed by the politicians and the makers of previous constitutions.

For the first time, the CDC and Constituent Assembly came to grips with the role of political parties. They did so at the behest of the Military Head of State, who not only forcefully drew attention to their baneful practices but specifically asked the CDC to make recommendations on how the country could develop and operate 'genuine and truly national parties'.

These matters were discussed at the CDC and the Constituent

Assembly, then translated into specific provisions in the Constitution.[9] The areas pertinent to this chapter include:

The membership of an association seeking registration as a political party must be open to every citizen of Nigeria irrespective of his place of origin, sex, religion or ethnic grouping.

The name of the association, its emblem or motto, contains no ethnic or religious connotations, nor does it give the appearance that the activities of the association are confined only to a part of the geographical entity Nigeria.

The headquarters of the association is situated in the capital territory of Nigeria.

The Constitution and rules of a political party shall ensure that the members of the executive committee or other governing body of the political party reflect the federal character of Nigeria.

The members of the Executive Committee or other governing body of the political party shall be deemed to reflect the federal character of Nigeria only if the members thereof belong to different states not being less than two-thirds of all the states comprising the Federation.

The programme, as well as the aims of and objects of a political party, shall conform to the provisions of Chapter II of the Constitution ('Fundamental Objectives' and 'Directive Principles of State Policy').

No association shall retain, organise, train or equip any person or group of persons for the purpose of enabling them to be employed for the use or display of physical force or coercion in promoting a political objective or interest or in such manner as to arouse reasonable apprehension that they are organised and trained or equipped for that purpose.

No association by whatever name shall function as a political party unless registered by the Federal Electoral Commission.

The conduct of elections to the offices of President and Governor of a State and of National and State Assemblies shall be conducted by the Federal Electoral Commission, and to Local Government councils by State Electoral Commissions.

There are debates and doubts whether each of the five political parties registered in 1978 and allowed to contest the 1979 elections actually satisfied these rules; whether those refused registration actually failed to meet the criteria laid down; whether the parties were 'genuine and truly national'; whether the electoral system was fair and free from mal-practices; whether the Federal Electoral Commission will be able to register new parties (provided for in the 1981 Electoral Bill); and whether the Commission can actually conduct free and fair elections at the expiration of the present tenure of the executives and legislatures.

With the benefit of hindsight, it is clear from these provisions, and even the perversions that attended their operation in the 1979 elections, that they remain far superior to the party and electoral system of the First Republic. For they clearly point the country toward national cohesion. Furthermore, whatever the fate of Nigerian politics in the future, the national political process which these parties and electoral systems have helped shape is bound to create a more wholesome environment for dealing with conflicting interests and developing cooperative relationships than was possible under the dominance of communalism and regionalism.

Structures of Recruitment

I have already drawn attention to the nature of political recruitment especially as projected by the offices of the President and State Governor, and to the extended misuse and abuse of these structures in the civil services and other organisations and enterprises, thus limiting the process of national cohesion. One area in particular is singled out here for a separate, brief discussion, and that is the field of education and the manpower-development needs associated with it; for education is crucial both in the development of individual skills and of a national sense of community.

The aim of national education policy has been to allocate more resources for accelerating the educational process of less developed areas without slowing the development of already relatively advanced areas. Thus the Federal Government in the 1970s assisted eleven states considered less developed educationally to establish schools of basic studies (higher schools) to prepare students of those states for entry into universities. With regard to admission to federal institutions of education and training, there are clear directives on quotas. Thus, 20 per cent of all admissions are allocated on national merit, while 80 per cent are equally distributed among the states for admission to technical colleges, schools of arts and science, teachers colleges and polytechnic institutes. As for the secondary schools, 20 per cent of admissions are on national merit, 50 per cent are equally distributed among the states and 30 per cent are based on residence (rather than state of origin). In the case of admission to universities, the application of the rules is required but is generally left to the university authorities to implement.

In principle, these policies are consistent with the commitment to promoting national cohesion. In practice, however, the effects of quotas on admission to educational institutions have been counterproductive. The historical forces of uneven development have thrown forward many more candidates for admission from communities already educationally advanced, regions and states than can be supported by their quota or by federal allocation. This situation has resulted in falsification of data as well as doubts about the system as a whole. Occasionally, reactions to these problems have given rise to violence.

In addition to the issues of fairness and justice, the policy has had an impact on the quality of education. While it is desirable for more people to benefit from education, it has become increasingly difficult to determine with reasonable objectivity who is capable of benefiting from a university education. In short, the effort to give all areas of the country their fair share and thereby strengthen the federal character and national cohesion has led to a tendency to lower or abandon minimum admission standards for candidates from less developed communities.

As to manpower, four development plans since independence have consistently drawn attention to the debilitating constraints from short-falls in the number and quality of Nigerian skilled manpower in all sectors and subsectors of the economy, including administrative and clerical skills. All the more disturbing is the communal or geo-political spread or concentration of the extremely limited number of skilled people. States and communities with low educational development are also the ones with abundant manpower. Ideally, a capitalist economy should have adjusted the discrepancy through labour mobility, but in fact political blockages arising from the need to keep jobs for people indigenous to those states have worked against such mobility. Generally, non-Nigerians, often called expatriates, are recruited for employment for which Nigerians, though 'non-indigenes', are available. Where such 'non-indigene Nigerians' have been recruited, the practice has been to recruit them on contract.[10]

Against these tendencies has been the development since the military regime of two institutions to promote cohesion—the National Youth Service Corps scheme (NYSC) and the National Institute for Policy and Strategic Studies (NIPSS). This is not the place to engage in details about their origins or to evaluate their performance.[11] Two conclusions drawn by Otwin Marenin from a study of the first few years of the NYSC are pertinent here: 'The effective aspects of the [NYSC] programme are those related to increasing interaction among people—the impact on the participants seems to be related to their enforced exposure to other people'; but while contact or interaction 'reinforces the awareness of ethnic distinctions, [it] also raises the levels of positive attitudes towards fellow Nigerians, and the belief that cultural distinctions are not necessarily detrimental to national unity'.[12] Otwin Marenin continues: 'The phenomenon of national consciousness is multi-dimensional, and its relationship to national unity is indirect. National consciousness does not exist in a vacuum, but within the wider context of group politics and governmental performance.'[13] These findings on the NYSC conform with the objectives of the scheme and the expectations of its founders.

As to NIPSS, the overriding goal is that of providing a national forum to close 'the problem of communication gap' between and among structures and members of Nigerian governing classes. The philosophy and objectives of NIPSS are that it 'aims to be a model institution for inculcating the highest national ideals and achieving the best results from rational deployment of resources, serves as a high-level centre for reflection, research and dialogue . . . on ideas and great issues of society'.[14] Established in September 1979, NIPSS is still grappling with infra-structural problems, but with both the participants at the Institute and its activities up-to-date, the hopes of its initiators that it will be a structure for enhancing national cohesion seem to be justified.

Structures of Resource Allocation

The structures mentioned above are the components of Nigeria's unique federal system. Three prominent aspects are the constitutional arrangement for allocation of the federation's revenue, the politics of development planning and the politics of 'federal presence' or of the socio-economic activities of the Federal Government in each state. As to the first aspect, the 1981 Revenue Act that enabled the activation of the relevant clauses of the Constitution allocated revenue on the following basis:

> Federal Government 58.5 per cent
> State governments   31.5 per cent
> Local governments   10.0 per cent

The Act also insisted that (a) allocation to the local government councils be made directly to those councils and not through the states; (b) 3.5 per cent of the Federal Government allocation be shared between the Federal Capital Territory (2.5 per cent) and areas with ecological problems (1 per cent); and (c) of the 31.5 per cent going to the states, 5 per cent be deducted for the direct benefit of mineral-producing states on the principle of derivation. These matters are highly contentious and at least one of them—direct disbursement to local government councils—has been challenged in the courts. The point of interest in the allocation of revenue is the claim by the Federal Government that national cohesion would be enhanced by the present formulas of revenue allocation.

The same is true of both development planning (as fragmented as it is nationalised) and the system of direct grants to the states. Although each matter touches upon the politics of a dependent capitalist system grappling with problems of underdevelopment, the point needs to be repeated that the twin existence of a pluralised socio-cultural base and a centralising authority of the Federal Government provides Nigeria with structures for coping with building a national community over and above the multi-communal base.

Conclusion

The burden of the analysis in this chapter is to suggest that one significant development in the Nigerian political system since it was brought together under British colonial domination and expatriate capitalism is the way (or ways) in which the 1979 Constitution has been designed consciously to respond to the problems generated by:

The communal pluralism and complexity of the society.

The factor of class interests founded by the growth and development of capitalism.

The need to adopt an ideology of politics (liberal democracy) to cushion the first two sets of forces.

What is important in these forces is that the Nigerian political system has continued to adjust to their imperatives. It is in their interplay that we can seek to understand the problems of national cohesion. If this conclusion is tenable from the preceding analysis, the best observation in these matters is the one made in 1977 by the former chief of staff, Supreme Headquarters, General (now retired) Shehu Musa Yar'Adua in the heat of the public debate of the draft constitution:

The movement from a predominantly agrarian to an industrial society is bound to affect people's values, relationships and outlook on life. Already, the indigenisation decree is producing a class of the new rich. A shift in the balance between agricultural pursuits and industry may breed new insecurities and new tensions in society. Ethnicity may very well become less salient in our political life, and social stratification may emerge. What impact this will have on the political system is yet unpredictable.[15]

While the problems of national cohesion in Nigeria and countries with similar colonial origins, inheritances and development must begin with communal pluralism and complexity, these problems are bound, over time, to be transcended by those of class coalescence and class issues.

Notes

1. S. E. Oyovbaire, ed., *Democratic Experiment in Nigeria—Interpretative Essays*, manuscript, 1981.
2. The details of the analytical value of these matters are dealt with in my two articles, 'The Nigerian Political System in the Perspective of History', in W. Graf, ed., *Towards a Political Economy of Nigeria—Critical Essays*, Koda Publishers and Oleander Press, Nigeria and the United Kingdom, forthcoming; and 'The Nigerian State as a Conceptual Variable', *Proceedings of the 1980 Conference of the Nigerian Political Science Association,* School of Social Sciences, University of Port Harcourt.
3. See James O'Connel, 'Political Integration: The Nigerian Case', in A. Hazlewood, ed., *African Integration and Disintegration*, Oxford, Oxford University Press, 1967; and K. W. J. Post and M. Vickers, *Structure and Conflict in Nigeria*, London, Heinemann, 1973.
4. Ibid., among other sources.
5. Address by the Head of the Federal Military Government, Commander-in-Chief of the Nigerian Armed Forces at the opening session of the Constitution Drafting Committee, on 18 October 1975.
6. See the following documents, among others: (i) *Report of the CDC,* containing the Draft Constitution, vols. I and II; (ii) *Proceedings of the*

Constituent Assembly, vols. I, II, III; (iii) The Constitution of the Federal Republic of Nigeria, 1979; (iv) *The Great Debate—Nigerian Viewpoint on the Draft Constitution*, a *Daily Times* publication; (v) O. Marenin, 'Class Structure and Democracy in Nigeria', in S. E. Oyovbaire, ed., *Democratic Experiment in Nigeria—Interpretative Essays.*

7. The issue of whether the President actually won two-thirds of the nineteen states in accordance with the provisions of the Constitution was tested in the Supreme Court, and the contestant lost. There is no intention here of entering into an analysis of the issue and the Court's decision.

8. For elaboration of these justifications, see *Report of the Panel to Investigate the Issue of the Creation of More States and Boundary Adjustments in Nigeria,* December 1975.

9. These provisions of the Constitution (sections 201–202) have been incorporated in an enabling bill and enacted by (September 1981) the National Assembly: *Electoral Bill 1981.*

10. The details of these matters were discussed exhaustively at an in-house seminar in Jos in July 1980; see S. E. Oyovbaire, *Report of the National Integration,* NIPSS, Jos.

11. A good, easily accessible account of the NYSC is O. Marenin, 'National Service and National Consciousness in Nigeria', *Journal of Modern African Studies*, vol. 17, no. 4 (1978), 629–54. No open account or study of NIPSS has been undertaken.

12. Marenin, 'Class Structure', op. cit.

13. Ibid.

14. NIPSS Brochure, January 1980.

15. Address of the Chief of Staff, Supreme Headquarters, Brigadier Shehu M. Yar'Adua, at the opening of the National Conference on the Draft Constitution, Nigerian Institute for Social and Economic Research, University of Ibadan, 3 April 1977, *New Nigerian,* 16 April 1977.

2 THE CONSTITUTIONAL STRUCTURE AND DEVELOPMENT OF NIGERIA

Uma O. Eleazu

It is the bad side that produces the movement that makes history, by providing a struggle.   Karl Marx, *The Poverty of Philosophy*

I

Nigeria's political history has been plagued by ethnic tension. This tension led now and then to open confrontation and conflict because the stressful condition of the body politic raised questions that challenged the very basis on which the political community—the modern state of Nigeria—is organised. This confrontation and conflict led to four *coups d'état*, a thirty-month civil war and thirteen years of military rule. The civil war was fought between those who wanted a united Nigeria and those who had come to believe that separation was the only solution. The war settled only one issue: that Nigeria will remain a single political entity. Beyond that, nothing is certain.

After the change in leadership of the Federal Military Government in July 1975, Nigeria's military rulers reasoned that the other questions still unsettled could be resolved only by involving a wider spectrum of opinion in the country. Therefore they adopted a political programme designed to return the country to civilian rule. A major point in this programme was the drafting of a constitution setting forth the ground rules for another attempt at democratic, constitutional government. Thus, on 18 October 1975, then head of state General Murtala Mohammed inaugurated the Constitution Drafting Committee (CDC). In his opening speech, he underscored the need for structural change and for a review of the country's political process: 'While it is evident that some of our difficulties may have been created by political leaders who operated the constitution, it is clear also that some of the provisions of the constitution facilitated the periodic political crises this country went through'.[1]

What must be kept in mind, he said, is that any new constitution must 'reflect our past experience' and it must 'be capable of influencing the nature and orderly development of the politics of people'.[2]

One aspect of the old constitution that came under severe criticism was the lopsided nature of the states (then called 'regions'), where one was larger than all the others put together, in both area and population. K. C. Wheare was continually being quoted in support of the contention that if, in any federation, one of the federating units was so large as to dominate the others, federalism was bound to fail.[3]

In Nigeria, fear of domination of the country by one region was a potent issue. The fact that there was also a dominant ethnic group in each of the three original regions made domination of the federal government by one ethnic group almost inevitable. If that had been the only problem, it could have been dealt with, as the head of state said, 'by the simple constitutional act of creating more states'. But in fact, the military administration under General Gowon had divided the country into twelve states, which did not satisfy certain ethnic groups, and a further exercise under the Murtala/Obasanjo regime created seven more states, bringing the total to nineteen.[4]

Then, however, both the Supreme Military Council (SMC) and the members of the CDC realised that such a structural adjustment was itself not enough. The new constitution was intended to help solve other problems as well.[5] According to the SMC, it would transform politics 'from its previous scenario of bitter personal wrangles into a healthy game of political argument and discussion'.

In addition, the CDC was enjoined to create viable political institutions that would:

ensure maximum participation and consensus, as well as the orderly succession to political power;

eliminate cut-throat political competition based on a system of winner-takes-all;

eliminate over-centralisation of power in a few hands and, as a matter of principle, decentralise power wherever possible, as a means of diffusing tension.[6]

These objectives reflected the bitter political experience of the First Republic, and it is against this background that one should view some of the provisions in the present constitution.

In speech after speech in the CDC, it became clear that the members were not motivated by abstract principles or theories but by the need to find practical, workable solutions to concrete and perennial political problems. Every proposal was examined from the point of view of its usefulness in solving the problem it addressed.

The drafters of the constitution operated on the premise that ethnic politics was not going to be wished away, nor could it be legally proscribed. Rather, it was to be seen as a potent force that needed to be faced and contained; otherwise, it would destroy Nigerian society. Thus, the drafters attempted to provide incentives that would encourage would-be politicians to transcend localism and parochial sentiments by making it impossible for them to attain high office riding on the wave-crest of ethnic jingoism.

Fundamental Objectives and Directive Principles

A long debate ensued in the CDC whether to recommend an ideology for Nigeria. Many argued that without such an ideology as a binding force, people were likely to fall back on ethnic and tribal sentiments. On the other hand, it was argued with equal force that an ideology or political path was the province of political parties, that as a nation, Nigerians should not be subjected to the tyranny of such phrases as 'democratic centralism', 'socialism' or 'communism'; rather, they should confine themselves to broad principles and objectives of national policy. One such fundamental objective was:

National integration through free mobility of people, goods and services throughout the country, full residence rights for all citizens in all parts of the country, inter-marriage, associations that cut across ethnic [and] linguistic ties, religion, etc., shall be actively encouraged, while parochial, ethnic or religious prejudice shall be discouraged.

The State shall foster a feeling of belonging and of involvement among the various peoples of the country, to the end that loyalty to the nation shall override sectional loyalties.[7]

Given the ethnic and religious heterogeneity of the country, and the endemic problems they have caused, it was not difficult to adopt these objectives. When it came to defining the 'directive principles' to implement the objectives, however, opinions differed. The sub-committee that had recommended the objectives also recommended this directive principle:

The domination of the government by one State or ethnic grouping or combination of them shall be avoided; also, the affairs of the State shall be so conducted as to ensure that the component states and ethnic groupings are accorded equal treatment but without prejudice to special safeguards designed to protect the position of minority groups.[8]

As we have noted, opinions differed. According to one view, such a provision would, in fact, give special recognition to ethnicity in a way that could only perpetuate ethnic consciousness. Any ethnic grouping that imagined itself not receiving 'equal treatment' was bound to organise on that basis to protect its members. What would emerge would be pockets of ethnic pressure. Further, the proponents of this view said that it would be unwieldy and impractical to expect every ethnic and linguistic group to participate in the federal government. Some preferred to split hairs over what was meant by 'equal treatment' and 'participation'. This group favoured a more general provision, for example, 'The composition of the Federal Government and the conduct of its affairs shall be carried out in such a manner as to ensure fair and equitable treatment for all the component states and ethnic groups in the country'.[9]

Others argued with equal force that inter-ethnic rivalry was not only rife at the federal level but at the state level too. Even when a state was made up of people of the same ethnic/linguistic group, new cleavages could emerge to create sub-ethnics. What was necessary, in their view, was not to enshrine pious words such as 'fair' and 'equitable' but to be quite categorical in stating that no group should be excluded, and that what applied at the federal level should, in principle, apply to every level of government. This group was equally afraid of majority ethnic groups perpetually monopolising such offices as president or governor. So they proposed a provision to preclude

the predominance in the Federal Government or any of its agencies of persons from some states, ethnic or other sectional groupings, *to the exclusion of persons* from other states, ethnic or other sectional groups, or the monopoly of the office of the president by persons from any state or ethnic group. . . .[10]

The third group merely argued that a person should be seen first as a human being in relation to the nation. That person's ethnic origin should be irrelevant to his or her qualifications as a citizen of the country. Members of these groups would rather play down the ethnic and sectional approach in favour of a more universal approach. Thus they proposed that 'the composition of every government in the federation and the conduct of its affairs shall be carried out in such manner as to recognise the need for national integration and the promotion of national unity'.[11]

As can be seen, the various proposals were all variations on a theme of tribalism and ethnic tensions, as well as how to write ground rules that would help lower tensions. Many speakers kept returning to a phrase that had occurred in the head of state's speech to the CDC, when he said:

We [the SMC] feel that there should be legal provisions to ensure that the [president and vice-president] are brought into office in such a manner as to reflect the *federal character of the country*; the choice of members of the cabinet should also be such as would *reflect the federal character of the country*.[12]

Gradually, the theme 'federal character of Nigeria' gained acceptance and came to embody, however hazily, what we were groping to achieve—a provision to the effect that in both theory and practice of government, people should be made to feel a sense of belonging and have the opportunity to participate in the affairs of the country. The first two views gradually merged into what one might call the predominant realistic view, and it was accepted by a majority of the members in the following form, which eventually was sent to the Constituent Assembly:

The Constitution of the Federal Government or any of its agencies and the conduct of their affairs shall be carried out in such manner as to recognise the federal character of Nigeria and the need to promote national unity and to command national loyalty.

Accordingly, the predominance in that Government or its agencies of persons from a few States, or from a few ethnic or other sectional groups shall be avoided.

In addition to this elaborate provision, the term 'federal character of Nigeria' was defined as

the distinctive desire of the peoples of Nigeria to promote national unity, foster national loyalty and give every citizen of Nigeria a sense of belonging to the nation, notwithstanding the diversities of ethnic origin, culture, language or religion which may exist and which it is their desire to nourish and harness to the enrichment of the Federal Republic of Nigeria.[13]

Fundamental Rights

In the chapter on fundamental rights, there is a provision to ensure non-discriminatory treatment of people on grounds of ethnic origin. Section 39(1) states:

A citizen of Nigeria of a particular community ethnic group, place of origin, sex, religion or political opinion shall not, by reason only that he is such a person—
  (a) be subjected either expressly by, or in the practical application of, any law in force in Nigeria or any executive or administrative action of the government to disabilities or restrictions to which citizens of Nigeria of other communities, ethnic groups, places of origin, sex, religions, or political opinions are not made subject; or
  (b) be accorded either expressly by, or in the practical application of, any law in force in Nigeria such executive or administrative action, any privilege or advantage that is not accorded to citizens of Nigeria of other communities, ethnic groups, places of origin, sex, religions or political opinion.

It is instructive, however, to note that this same provision was in the 1963 constitution as Section 28. The only difference is the change of the word *tribe* to *ethnic group*.

The Executive and How It Is to Be Constituted

Much of what causes friction in any society is the way officials of the government interact with or treat members of the public. In a country rife with corruption and nepotism, people tend to assume that to get anything out of any government department, one must 'know some-body' or develop 'long legs'. In such a situation, to elevate one man as supreme over everyone else is similar to giving him power over life and death.

The sub-committee that reported on the nature and type of executive needed in the new constitution stated: 'What has been uppermost in our minds is how to provide for an effective leadership that expresses our aspirations for national unity without at the same time building up a Leviathan whose power may be difficult to curb'.[14]

Election of the President

The sub-committee on the executive came up with a proposal (which was rejected) that involved balancing the ticket, zoning the country and rotating the office of the President from zone to zone. The system would have grouped the nineteen states into A (North) and B (South), producing: Zone 1A (Sokoto, Niger, Kwara and Kaduna states); Zone 2A (Kano, Plateau, Benue, Borno, Bauchi and Gongola states); Zone 3B (Lagos, Oyo, Ogun, Ondo and Bendel); and Zone 4B (Anambra, Imo, Rivers and Cross River). Each presidential ticket must be balanced between Group A and Group B. If a president were elected from any zone no candidate from that zone would be accepted for nomination after his term of office. The presidency would have to rotate to another zone, as would the vice-president.

The sub-committee thought this system would ensure that no one state or section of the country would monopolise the high office of the presidency to the exclusion of others. Besides, each state would know that sooner or later, it would send a president to the capital. The snag was that, given a four-year term and assuming no second term, it would take the last state seventy-six years to provide a president. During the debate on the report, it was pointed out that the grouping of the states would most likely re-create the old north–south cleavage. On the other hand, two principles, or criteria, introduced by the sub-committee were accepted: if the President were to be popularly elected, he had to show that he was a nationally accepted, popular figure by not merely winning a majority of the total votes cast but also by showing an adequate geographical spread of that popularity.

Having rejected zoning and rotation, the CDC decided on popular election of the President, and required that the winning ticket must have:

(a) the highest number of votes cast at the election (national popularity); and

(b) not less than one quarter of all the votes cast at the election in each of at least two-thirds of all the states in the federation (territorial spread).

The objective was to avoid the kind of situation we had in the First Republic, where a national leader could emerge by winning just a seat in a tiny federal constituency, or form a political party made up largely of his ethnic kinspeople. The principle of territorial spread was designed to ensure that aspirants to such high office, in their campaign and in their basic attitude, transcend ethnic lines and actively and convincingly seek support from areas outside their home base.

The Appointment of Ministers

In carrying out his functions as the Chief Executive, the President is allowed to appoint ministers who will be confirmed by the Senate before taking office. In making such appointments, however, the constitution provided, in Section 153(3) that:

Any appointment under sub-section (2) of this Section by the President shall be in conformity with the provisions of Section 14(B) of this constitution: provided that in giving effect to the provision aforesaid, the President shall appoint at least one minister from each state who shall be an indigene of such state.

Similarly, the appointment of commissioners by the governor of a state 'shall conform with the provisions of Section 14(4) of this constitution' (Section 173(2)). The specification in the case of ministers at the federal level that at least every state be represented was to ensure that no section of the country or a state would feel completely left out of the federal cabinet.

It was not enough just to say that the Cabinet should reflect the federal character. The constitution had to spell it out—by prescribing at least one minister from each state. Likewise, commissioners in the states were to be chosen so as to ensure that all local government areas were represented.

Providing for Political Parties

Nigeria's experience with political parties during the First Republic was a far cry from the theoretical models of mass parties, mobilising and social-ising citizens for nation-building. In an attempt to develop grass-roots support, each party leadership fell back on their ethnic kinspeople. Tribal sentiments were whipped up to the extent that parties at the national level were little more than ethnic fronts for fighting (literally) elections. Since opinions differ as to what, in fact, a genuine 'national political party' is, the CDC was left to work out criteria for determining that, as well as establishing criteria for limiting the number of such parties. The CDC recommended as general principles that, to be regarded as a national party, an association must:

—reflect a national outlook and appeal to a cross section of the population;
—reflect a federal character in its leadership;
—declare sources of all funds, which must be 'federal';
—be open to all citizens.

These principles were followed up with specific provisions relating to open membership, the barring of ethnic emblems, and representation of different regions of the country in the parties' governing bodies.

It was a novel experiment to include in the constitution such details of the regulation of political parties. Many felt that never again would tribal chieftains be allowed to promote themselves as national leaders unless they first demonstrated that they could conduct themselves accordingly. Never again would ethnic parties be allowed to turn themselves into private armies to harass innocent citizens for no other reason than that such citizens were from a different ethnic group.

The Armed Forces

The spate of coups in Africa and the pattern of violence they initiated led many observers to doubt the theory of unified command and cohesion that the officer corps is supposed to acquire during training. It was not realistic to expect that the constitution could effectively prevent military officers from leaping into the political arena. After all, coups, by their very nature, are *un*constitutional; the only cure is a good, stable government. Therefore, the CDC took the view that what was necessary was to ensure that the military was national in outlook. 'The process of developing a national army would demand that the armed forces be open to all. Selective recruitment into the armed forces will have to be stopped, and no particular tribe should be dominant in the forces or a particular arm of it.'[15] This principle found expression in the provision in Section 197(2): 'The composition of the officer corps and other ranks of the armed forces of the Federation shall reflect the federal character of Nigeria'.

Thus it can be seen that all hope of lowering ethnic tension hinged on the interpretation and application of the phrase 'federal character of Nigeria'.

II

To a certain extent, the creation of more states helped assuage the bitter tone of politics. Table 2.1 shows the major ethnic composition of the nineteen states. So far, the interpretation of the federal character has come to place more emphasis on state government and power than on ethnicity.

On the other hand, it has been discovered that the notion of 'indigene of a state' is not easy to apply; for what are the criteria for determining when a community is indigenous to a place? In the final analysis, we fall back on socio-cultural and linguistic criteria. In the line-up of nineteen states, five are predominantly Yoruba-speaking, six are Hausa-Fulani, and two are Igbo; the remaining six have varying degrees of ethnic, socio-cultural and linguistic mix. In the circumstance, application of the federal character has been quite difficult.

Table 2.1. Ethnic Composition of States

State	Major ethnic group
Anambra	Igbo
Bauchi	Hausa (Fulani)
Bendel	Edo, Urhobo, Igbo
Benue	Tiv, Idoma
Borno	Kanuri (Hausa)
Cross River	Efik-Ibibio, Ekoi
Gongola	Hausa, Jukun
Imo	Igbo
Kaduna	Hausa-Fulani
Kano	Hausa-Fulani
Kwara	Yoruba (Igala/Igbira)
Lagos	Yoruba
Niger	Nupe, Gwari
Ogun	Yoruba
Ondo	Yoruba
Oyo	Yoruba
Plateau	Hausa, Birom
Rivers	Ijaw, Kalabari
Sokoto	Fulani (Hausa)

Voting Behaviour and the Formation of Parties

With the lifting of the ban on party politics, the Federal Electoral Commission (FEDECO), which was given the task of registering political parties that are truly national, added one more requirement to those already in the constitution: to be regarded as *national*, a political association must have field offices and must be physically present and operating in at least two-thirds (or thirteen) states. When the register opened, there were more than fifty political associations that had applied to be registered as political parties. Given the stringent requirements of the constitution and of FEDECO, only five associations qualified:

Peoples Redemption Party (PRP);
Nigerian Peoples Party (NPP);

Unity Party of Nigeria (UPN);
National Party of Nigeria (NPN);
Great Nigeria Peoples Party (GNPP).

Unlike the situation in the First Republic, here, each party made a genuine effort to ensure an ethnic mix in their party executive and established offices in various states. Only the NPN and the UPN had offices in all nineteen states. The pattern of leadership and following, however, did not reflect the same broad representation. Each party tended to be identified with the ethnic group of its presidential candidate, as in Table 2.2.

Table 2.2. Party Leadership and Following

Party	Leader	Following
PRP	Alhaji Aminu Kano	Hausa
NPP	Dr Nnamdi Azikiwe	Igbo
UPN	Chief Obafemi Awolowo	Yoruba
NPN	Alhaji Shehu Shagari	Hausa-Fulani
GNPP	Alhaji Waziri Ibrahim	Kanuri

Although each presidential candidate chose his running mate from a different ethnic group, the usual pattern of voting for the ethnic notables did not change, as can be seen in Table 2.3. The GNPP candidate received the greatest number of votes from the home state of the leader—Borno; 54 per cent. The PRP candidate, Alhaji Aminu Kano, polled 76.4 per cent of the vote in Kano. Chief Awolowo, the UPN candidate, carried all the Yoruba states. Dr Azikiwe carried the two Igbo states, while Alhaji Shagari, who emerged the winner, drew much support from the Hausa-Fulani states. He made a strong showing in states outside the Hausa-Fulani areas. He won seven states and was second in six, thus satisfying the twin principle of popular majority support and a good territorial spread. The appearance of the old guard—Zik, Awolowo and Aminu Kano—probably gave the election the old look and must have influenced many voters. It remains to be seen whether the withdrawal of these ethnic notables of the First Republic will make any difference in voting behaviour.

Still, voting behaviour in 1979 reflected changes in the direction sought by the CDC:

1. There was widespread support for the winning ticket. The lowest appeal it had was in Ondo State, where the NPN polled 4.9 per cent of the votes cast.
2. Each candidate made a showing in all states—an indication of the development of a national image.

Table 2.3. Votes Cast in Each State in 1979

State/total votes cast		GNPP–Waziri		UPN–Awolowo		NPN–Shagari		PRP–Aminu		NPP–Azikiwe	
Anambra	1,209,038	20,228	(1.67%)	9,063	(0.75%)	163,164	(13.5%)	14,500	(1.2%)	1,002,083	(82.88)
Bauchi	998,683	154,218	(16.44)	29,960	(0.3)	623,989	(62.48)	143,202	(14.34)	47,314	(4.74)
Bendel	669,511	8,242	(1.2)	356,381	(53.2)	242,320	(36.20)	4,939	(0.70)	57,629	(8.60)
Benue	538,879	42,993	(7.97)	13,864	(2.57)	411,648	(76.38)	7,277	(1.35)	63,097	(11.77)
Borno	710,968	384,278	(54.04)	23,885	(3.35)	246,778	(34.71)	46,385	(6.52)	9,642	(1.35)
C. River	661,103	100,105	(15.14)	77,775	(11.76)	425,815	(64.40)	6,737	(1.01)	50,671	(7.66)
Gongola	639,138	217,914	(34.09)	138,561	(21.67)	327,057	(35.52)	27,750	(4.34)	27,856	(4.35)
Imo	1,153,355	34,616	(3.00)	7,335	(0.64)	101,516	(8.80)	10,252	(0.59)	999,636	(84.69)
Kaduna	1,382,712	190,936	(14.00)	92,382	(7.00)	596,302	(43.00)	437,771	(31.00)	65,321	(5.00)
Kano	1,195,136	18,482	(1.54)	14,973	(1.23)	243,423	(19.94)	932,803	(76.41)	11,081	(0.91)
Kwara	354,605	20,251	(5.71)	140,006	(37.48)	190,142	(53.62)	2,376	(0.67)	1,830	(0.52)
Lagos	828,414	3,943	(0.48)	681,762	(82.30)	59,515	(7.18)	3,874	(0.47)	79,320	(9.57)
Niger	383,347	63,273	(16.6)	14,155	(3.67)	287,072	(74.88)	14,555	(3.77)	45,292	(1.11)
Ogun	744,668	3,974	(0.53)	689,655	(92.61)	46,358	(6.23)	2,338	(0.31)	2,343	(0.32)
Ondo	1,384,788	3,561	(0.26)	1,294,666	(94.50)	57,361	(4.19)	2,500	(0.18)	11,752	(0.86)
Oyo	1,396,547	8,029	(0.57)	1,197,983	(85.78)	177,999	(12.75)	4,804	(0.32)	7,732	(0.55)
Plateau	548,405	37,400	(6.82)	29,029	(5.29)	190,458	(34.73)	21,852	(3.98)	269,666	(49.70)
Rivers	687,951	15,025	(2.18)	71,114	(10.33)	499,846	(72.65)	3,312	(0.46)	98,754	(14.35)
Sokoto	1,348,697	359,021	(26.61)	34,102	(2.52)	898,094	(66.58)	44,977	(3.33)	12,503	(0.92)
Total	16,846,633	1,686,489		4,916,651		5,688,857		1,732,113		2,822,523	

3. Major officeholders in the party machine still reflect broad ethnic support even for the parties that lost the presidency.
4. Because each party was in control in at least one state, the relative openness of the Shagari administration gave the impression of easy access.

Appointments to ministerial and other high offices. In the appointment of ministers, the President did more than the minimum required by the constitution. There were at least two ministers from each state. Inevitably, however, the most desirable ministries went to states that voted solidly for the President's party (NPN). Nevertheless, by the very presence of someone from each state, the Shagari cabinet does communicate an image of 'national' government.

On the other hand, the situation in individual states is less satisfactory. In the mono-ethnic states, complaints have been made that certain areas were being neglected, especially where the ruling party did not fare well in the previous election. The complaints were not made on ethnic grounds but on partisan political lines. In states that are mixed, one still hears of discrimination on ethnic grounds, Hence, there have been several demands for the creation of more states.

The public services and the armed forces. The phrase 'composition of the Federal Government or any of its agencies' has been interpreted to mean that not only the political offices but the permanent services should reflect the federal character. Here, application of the principle is somewhat more difficult; for these reasons: (a) the differential impact of Western education on various sections of the country; (b) the extent of adaptation of various groups to modernisation; (c) the effect of the civil war, which kept out one section of the country from certain arms of the public service, a position they have been unable to step back into.

The net effect is the predominance of the Yoruba ethnic group in the public services of the federation. At the same time, there are civil service rules against dismissal or removal of civil servants from office. Does one wait for the normal retirement and renewal process to redress the imbalance, or does one change the entire structure in one fell swoop? In the army, for instance, a large group of officers from the Eastern Region—Igbo, Efiks, Ibibio—were either killed during the war or dismissed after it; thus, in the higher echelons one seldom finds officers from that region. The same is true of the police force. The real day-to-day dealings of the government with the people is at the level of civil servants and lower-level officials. Much of the high-handedness or discrimination that ordinary citizens suffer is meted out at this level, a level difficult to federalise. There is hope, however, that in time, this situation will gradually be corrected. Some argue, though, that there is a danger of breeding a self-perpetuating oligarchy via the Civil Service Commission and the internal promotion process—that something more drastic should be done, at least at the top, to balance things out.

Conclusion

The search for ways to lower ethnic tension is an ongoing one; there is nothing conclusive or final about the presentation above. It is entirely an experiment at this point, which some people are sanguine enough to believe will succeed—only if (and it is a big *if*) we have patience with ourselves and allow the new arrangements to be tried and amended if need be. One encouraging sign is the way the idea of 'federal character' is being accepted.

A recent cartoon showed a Muslim politician caught embracing an urban coquette. Embarrassed by the cartoon, the wife of the politician muttered, 'It may be that my husband wants to reflect the federal character in this household, too!'

Notes

1. Address by the Head of the Federal Military Government, Commander-in-Chief of the Nigerian Armed Forces at the opening session of the Constitution Drafting Committee, Saturday, 18 October 1975. Reproduced in the Report of the Constitution Drafting Committee, vol. pp. xli–xliii, Federal Ministry of Information, Lagos, 1976. Henceforth, this report will be cited as *Report of the CDC*.
2. Ibid.
3. K. C. Wheare, *Federal Government*, New York, Oxford University Press, 1964. See also, Thomas M. Franck, ed., *Why Federations Fail: An Inquiry into Requisites for Successful Federation*, New York, New York University Press, 1968.
4. From the original East, West and Northern regions in 1963, a Midwest Region was formed, becoming the fourth Region. Just before the outbreak of the civil war, in 1967, Gowon announced the creation of twelve states from the four regions; thus:

1 Western Region	2 Midwest	3 Northern Region	4 Eastern Region
Western State Lagos State	Midwest State	North Eastern State North Western State North Central State Kwara State Benue Plateau Kano	East Central South Eastern Rivers

The Irikefe Commission on the creation of new states reported while the CDC was meeting and recommended the creation of seven more states, which were arrived at by splitting East Central State into Imo and Anambra, Western State into Oyo, Ogun and Ondo States; North Western State was broken into Sokoto and Niger States while North Eastern became Borno and Gongola States. The following states were untouched: Lagos; Midwest (renamed Bendel); Rivers; South Eastern State (renamed Cross River State); Kwara; and Kano.

5. Address by the Head of the Federal Military Government.
6. Ibid.
7. Ibid.
8. *Report of the CDC*, vol. 1, para. 3.2.3.
9. Ibid.
10. Ibid.
11. *Report of the CDC*, vol. 2, article 3, p. 37.
12. Ibid.
13. Ibid.
14. Ibid., para. 3.5–3.
15. Ibid., para. 3.5–4.

3 POSITIVE DISCRIMINATION IN INDIA WITH REFERENCE TO EDUCATION

Suma Chitnis

The struggle for social equality has been difficult and long drawn out. Efforts to reduce inequalities in wealth, income, social prestige, political power and access to education or to prestigious occupations have, no doubt, resulted in relatively more thresholds of equality in these spheres. Around the world, however, such achievements have been accompanied by the emergence of new inequalities and the surfacing of constraints on equality that once went unnoticed. Thus the goal seems to recede, and the struggle continues—making it necessary at each successive threshold to probe further into the sources of inequality, to reconsider and redefine the concept of equality and to review strategies for action.

One of the most significant outcomes of this process, and one that marks the high point of achievement in the struggle for equality in this century, is the acceptance by several nations of the policy of positive discrimination over the last three or four decades. Known by different labels in different countries,[1] the policy basically refers to provisions and programmes that aim at direct intervention through a system of quotas and reservations, for individuals from groups formerly discrim-inated against, in public and political office, education, administration and employment. The policy may also be extended to describe special con-cessions granted to ethnic or cultural groups in danger of extinction, suppression or exploitation. The core of the policy is an open admission of the premise that 'selective discrimination' is not only compatible with but necessary for social equality. As such, the policy marks the achieve-ment of a distinctly new threshold in the concept of equality.

Fresh Challenges

The policy also involves a new range of conceptual, administrative, ethical and political problems. The definition of criteria in terms of which *domina-tion, discrimination* and *disadvantage* are to be determined for eligibility for preferential treatment, and the fixing of limits on discrimination are difficult tasks. So too, programmes must be administered in a manner which ensures that vested interests/existing power groups do not gain ascendancy and dislocate efforts and that the 'disadvantaged' actually receive the intended benefits. A far different order of problems arises from the fact that quotas and reservations are frequently occupied by persons not adequately equipped to fulfil the functions expected of them. In an age when competence is prized, this situation inevitably leads to the criticism that positive discrimination negates the principle of equal liability and exempts a sector of the population from the obligation of fulfilling its responsibilities.

Feelings against the policy build up as those in danger of being dislocated from their positions of privilege press to retain their advantage. Meanwhile, the beneficiaries of the policy begin to look upon positive discrimination as a right, an obligation that the larger society owes them in atonement for injustice and discrimination inflicted earlier. Inevitably, the issue becomes highly politicised. The basic, underlying moral and ethical issues begin to be questioned, and implementation of the policy becomes a delicate task of harmonising the rival claims and interests of various groups, balancing some of the finer issues of social justice, and containing conflict.

This chapter presents the Indian experience with respect to the use of positive discrimination as a strategy for achieving equality in and through education. It tries to identify some conceptual, administrative, ethical and political problems involved in implementing the policy. Its purpose is to clarify issues, identify sources of tension and help determine the direction the effort must move in.

The Beneficiaries

In India, positive discrimination for education is provided to four major categories of beneficiaries. First are the religious 'minorities' (all non-Hindus) and the linguistic 'minorities' that exist in each state due to the administrative division of the country into states, territorially defined in terms of the majority language of a region.[2] Second are the former untouchable or nearly untouchable castes (now known as Scheduled Castes) who were denied the right to formal education and are categorically excluded from practice of any but the most demeaning of occupations by virtue of the caste system. Third are the tribals (now known as Scheduled Tribes) who have been physically and culturally isolated from the mainstream of Indian life and who therefore have not only been excluded from formal education but are confined to the periphery of the relatively more advanced urban and rural economies. They are restricted to such occupations as fishing, subsistence farming, forestry and food-gathering. In the fourth category are the 'other backward classes', a heterogeneous group comprised mainly of castes and some non-Hindu communities low in the hierarchy of castes, as well as the secular social hierarchy (though not so low as the Scheduled Castes).

The Provisions and their Objectives

Positive discrimination for religious minorities is inspired by a concern that they have the freedom and ability to practise, conserve, develop and propagate their beliefs, faith and culture. The provision for linguistic minorities was motivated by a related commitment to ensure that minority linguistic groups and cultures within a region are not smothered by the majority culture. Both minority categories are protected by a consti-tutional 'right to establish and to administer educational institutions of their own choice' (Article 30) and a constitutional safeguard that 'every State and every local authority in the State shall endeavour to provide adequate facilities for instruction in the mother tongue at the primary stage'. The latter provision, however, is merely a corollary to the greater obligation to provide all the children in the country with school-education in their mother tongues; only the former provision may actually be viewed as discriminatory.

Basically, positive discrimination for the Scheduled Castes, Scheduled Tribes[3] and other backward classes is provided in the form of reserved admissions to institutions of higher education.[4] Reservations are supple-mented by a series of supportive facilities—for example, scholarships, bursaries, special hostels at school and post-school levels.[5] Because all three categories of beneficiaries suffer from poverty, political powerless-ness, low social status and vulnerability to continued exploitation, positive discrimination may be viewed basically as a measure for securing their economic, political and social equality. The policy, however, also aims at the more specific objectives of eradicating the caste inequalities suffered by the Scheduled Castes and at obtaining the assimilation and integration of the tribals.

Minority Rights to Establish and Administer Educational Institutions

Viewed in the context of the constitutional emphasis on secularism, the provision that guarantees minorities in India the right to establish and administer their own educational institutions is a bold, graceful expression of the commitment to cultural freedom and human rights. To appreciate the ethical and political significance of this provision, it is necessary to recognise that decades of bitter communal conflict in the pre-independence period, culminating in the violent partition of the country, made for great insecurity among the minorities when independence began.

The provision of special rights in education was designed to soothe their fears.

So far, the provision has served well. Minorities freely nurture their religions and culture in their educational institutions; their right to do so has hardly been contested. In fact, an analysis of the points of contention underlying thirty-six cases quoted in a fairly comprehensive listing of court cases fought over the issue of minority rights in education in 1954–1980 reveals only one case in which the religious exclusiveness of a minority institution was challenged as incompatible with the constitutional commitment to secularism.[6]

That the right to exclusive practice of a minority religion in an educational institution has rarely been contested shows that the social climate in the country is relatively free of religious tension. It also indicates that the managements of minority educational institutions have carefully refrained from religious activism or separatism. It would be naïve, however, to assume that this situation will last. India has a long and painful history of communal strife. The tolerance seen in the past three decades was probably generated by a sense of attrition caused by the horrors of partition and by the martyrdom of Gandhi. The tolerance is beginning to wear out; Hindu and Sikh fundamentalism are creeping into Indian politics.[7] The winds of Muslim fundamentalism are blowing in from other parts of the world. The 'oil' conversions to Islam, particularly among the Scheduled Castes, in Kerala and in some other states have upset the other religious groups, posing a distinct threat to communal peace. So too does the fact that the decadal growth rate of Muslims and Christians in the country is consistently larger than that of the Hindus.[8]

The existing equilibrium could easily be disturbed. If it is, minority educational institutions inevitably will be drawn into religious activism, and the protective discrimination they now enjoy could be explosive.

Autonomy in Administration: The Dangers of Misuse and Incipient Conflict

There is yet another point at which minority rights in education could become abrasive. The post-independence expansion of education in India was accompanied by a high degree of governmental control over education. State education departments, universities and other regulatory bodies minutely define academic and administrative practices and procedures to be followed. Under the circumstances, the autonomy available to minorities to administer their educational institutions stands out as a special prerogative.

Minority leaders can use, and have been using, this prerogative to retain autonomy *vis-à-vis* the state, the universities and other authorities in matters ranging from syllabuses, language, and procedural requirements to such crucial matters as the composition and operation of management governing boards. They have even contested—and won—autonomy *vis-à-vis* the regulatory control of University Acts.[9] Indeed, analysis of the cases in the document in question indicates that twenty-nine out of the thirty-six cases listed centre on the issue of administrative autonomy.

It is significant that both the high courts and the Supreme Court generally have seen fit to uphold the autonomy of the minority institutions in the disputes contested. This is acceptable as long as autonomy is honestly used and as long as the managements of minority institutions remain sensitive to their larger moral obligations as Indians. In fact, the autonomy available to minority educators is generally valued in the country; several minority institutions that have upheld their autonomy happen to be quality institutions that have deliberately used their minority rights to slow the deterioration of standards.

A scanning of the issues contested, however, suggests that autonomy can easily be misused. In at least two cases, minority institutions contested the obligation to maintain the required quota of reservations for scheduled caste/tribe students. In two other cases, minority managements operating village schools tried to prevent the establishment of other schools in the same villages, with a view to gaining exclusive control over education in the villages. The managements used the argument that a rival school would draw away their students and thus interfere with their right to 'establish and administer' educational institutions.

Confronted with this evidence, one is apprehensive about the abuse of a well-meant provision. Throughout the country today, serious malpractice is evident in the administration of education. Complaints are frequently made that minority managements use minority rights to get away with such malpractice. Because this behaviour is not only unethical *per se* but in the long run damaging to the interests of the minorities, the government will likely have to find a way to curb it, gently but firmly, before it gets out of hand.

Reservations and Other Supportive Facilities for the Scheduled Castes and Scheduled Tribes

From the outset, the policy of reservations for the Scheduled Castes and Scheduled Tribes was opposed. Immediately after its promulgation it was contested in the Madras High Court as a 'communal award'.[10] No less a figure than Pandit Jawaharlal Nehru proposed a constitutional amendment to deal with the objections put forward.[11] While this took care of the issue's legality, it did not obtain for the commitment from the leaders, the bureaucracy and the people that the architects of the Constitution hoped to arouse.

An Attempt to Fight Casteism and Bypass the Barriers to Performance

According to instructions issued by the Union Ministry of Education to all state governments and Union Territory administrations, 20 per cent of the seats in all educational and technical institutions had to be reserved for Scheduled Castes (15 per cent) and Scheduled Tribes (5 per cent). The reservations must be interchangeable. Where admissions were restricted to candidates who obtained a certain percentage of marks, and did not merely pass a certain examination, a reduction of 5 per cent for the Scheduled Castes and the Scheduled Tribes was recommended, provided the lower percentage prescribed did not fall below the minimum required for passing the examination. These provisions were designed to alleviate two problems: the practice of caste discrimination by admission authorities, resulting in exclusion, on purely caste considerations, of persons otherwise qualified; and the 'failure' of low caste/tribal candidates to meet the qualifying requirements.

Poor Implementation

Three decades after the establishment of reservations as a statutory requirement, at least fifteen out of 115 universities in India have no reservations at the undergraduate level.[12] Several other universities have failed to provide it at the post-graduate level. Moreover, in institutions of higher education throughout the country, there is a massive gap between the number of seats reserved and the number occupied (Table 3.1). Further, data with reference to individual institutions within universities indicate that scheduled caste/tribe students are clustered in relatively inferior non-prestigious institutions and crowded into 'low status' courses that do not lead to lucrative or high-ranking occupations.[13] The situation was particularly bad during the first two decades after implementation of the policy began. This situation has improved somewhat since the 1970s, due mainly to frequent complaints against the poor administration of the policy of reservations by the Commission on Scheduled Castes and Scheduled Tribes in its annual reports, the sharp criticism of special committees and commissions appointed periodically to examine the situation of these communities, and the repeated discussion of the issue in state legislatures and Parliament.

Apathy or Discrimination?

For the major part, poor implementation of the policy of reservations seems to be a consequence of apathy and social inertia. This, in turn,

Table 3.1. Size of Reservation for Admission of Scheduled
Castes/Scheduled Tribes to Undergraduate
Courses and Actual Coverage: 1977-78

Name of state	Total No. of universities in state*	Total percentage of	
		Reservation allowed	Actual coverage
Andhra Pradesh	9	18	7.08
Assam ·	3	20	12.32
Bihar	9	20	6.74
Gujarat	8	20	9.87
Haryana	3	20	4.73
Himachal Pradesh	1	20	6.95
Jammu and Kashmir	2	8	1.98
Karnataka	5	18	6.48
Kerala	4	20	4.31
Madhya Pradesh	10	33	7.04
Maharashtra	11	20	11.38
Meghalaya	1	40	58.86
Orissa	4	20	6.58
Punjab	4	25	8.83
Rajasthan	4	20	7.55
Tamil Nadu	5	18	7.90
Uttar Pradesh	20	20	10.98
West Bengal	8	20	12.19
Delhi	4	20	5.54
All India	115	20	9.01

* Includes institutions classified as universities.

reflects the fact that the cause of the scheduled castes/tribes has not become a major social movement. Efforts in this direction witnessed early in this century were diluted by politicisation of the issue before independence. The movement has almost been extinguished by the post-independence inclination to assign responsibility for social action to the welfare state.

Poor Organization and Lack of Leadership

Scheduled Castes and Tribes are not adequately organised for self-help. Lack of leadership is the main obstacle to effective organisation. Members of the SC/ST communities who gain economic and social mobility may foster the advancement of individuals from their own families, but they do not work for their group. Meanwhile, the movement towards equality is hampered because most leaders are unconcerned with the struggle for equality. The leaders suffer from a displacement of goals, in the sense that they strive for continued concessions rather than for achievement of capacities that render concessions redundant.

The Problem of Standards

The problem of standards is exacerbated by the fact that the policy itself fails to recognise the gap between the performance level of the SC/ST·and others. The initial requirement that a 5 per cent reduction be made in the marks required to qualify for admission assumes only a small gap between the performance of SC/ST candidates and others.[14] The failure to support reservation of admissions with provisions for compensatory education further indicates the belief that once admitted, students will somehow adapt to academic requirements. Experience has shown both assumptions invalid. At prestigious centres of higher education there is often a 25–30 per cent gap. Students who are admitted regardless of this gap rarely manage to come through.

The Surfacing of Vested Interests and the Beginning of Resentment

Regardless of the problems described above, admissions in higher education have thus far been fairly well accepted. The 1981 caste riots over reservations for medical education in Gujarat and the earlier violence over renaming a university in Maharashtra indicate the onset of resentment.[15] It is significant that both Gujarat and Maharashtra are states in which the Scheduled Castes are visibly advancing—educationally, economically and politically. It is even more significant that this resentment has occurred despite the fact that, regardless of their advance, the SC/ST are far behind the others.[16] Obviously those hitherto advantaged feel threatened and have decided to regain lost ground.

The Next Move

Under the circumstances, it is important for those who are interested in the advancement of the SC/ST to consider their next move. Urgent action seems required in at least the following five areas:

1. There is an immediate need to remedy the academic inadequacy of SC/ST students—in fact, to attack the problem where it starts: early at school. This is most important, not only because poor academic performance provides vested interests with valid ground for criticism of reservations but becuase it also alienates people who are otherwise sympathetic to the cause of the SC/ST. Moreover, improvement in academic standards is necessary for the SC/ST to qualify for the posts

Table 3.2. School Enrolment Ratios of Students Belonging to General Population, Scheduled Castes and Scheduled Tribes in Classes I-V and VI-VIII to their Populations in the Corresponding Age Group for the Year 1977-78

Name of the State/ Union Territory	General population		Scheduled Castes		Scheduled Tribes	
	I – V	VI – VIII	I – V	VI –VIII	I – V	VI –VIII
Andhra Pradesh	71.7	25.8	81.1	66.7	62.8	9.3
Assam	70.3	34.1	105.8*	19.2	85.4	31.6
Bihar	67.3	27.1	46.0	9.4	75.8	32.4
Gujarat	95.5	42.8	108.4*	41.6	71.8	20.3
Haryana	69.1	42.4	50.7	22.3	–	–
Himachal Pradesh	96.9	53.6	81.1	32.2	78.2	32.7
Jammu & Kashmir	62.0	39.5	40.4	53.7	–	–
Kerala	107.1	87.6	114.8*	87.5	67.7	40.1
Karnataka	86.6	39.0	73.0	25.4	105.7	38.8
Madhya Pradesh	60.6	27.2	80.4	20.5	46.6	10.2
Maharashtra	102.7	45.0	152.4	50.3	76.3	16.1
Manipur	140.6	51.3	180.0*	56.4	164.9	40.7
Meghalaya	120.7	41.4	586.5	138.5	132.7	42.6
Nagaland	165.3	70.8	–	–	155.9	116.7
Orissa	81.2	25.7	77.0	14.6	61.1	9.0
Punjab	110.9	55.5	127.3	40.0	–	–
Rajasthan	54.7	26.3	42.8	14.8	35.5	11.1
Tamil Nadu	106.7	49.6	115.3	40.4	59.9	15.5
Tripura	75.5	33.9	93.8	26.4	55.8	14.8
Uttar Pradesh	91.2	36.4	63.3	21.7	75.5	30.9
West Bengal	83.7	32.8	58.3	19.3	48.7	13.4
Andaman & Nicobar	120.5	63.3	–	–	78.9	27.8
Arunachal Pradesh	70.5	17.3	–	–	70.2	15.9
Chandigarh	63.5	64.5	88.7	25.0	N.A.	–
Dadra & Nagar Haveli	84.6	22.8	–	474.0	–	155.6
Delhi	94.8	74.2	136.2	43.7	–	–
Goa, Daman & Diu	112.5	64.8	115.8	54.7	73.4	15.6
Lakshadweep	154.4	84.6	–	–	159.2	86.3
Mizoram	–	–	–	–	–	–
Pondicherry	103.6	64.8	98.2	40.2	–	–
India,	82.8	37.9	75.5	25.5	66.1	17.7

* Percentage above 100 denote enrolment in all schools of even higher age groups while population is only for specified age group.

Table 3.3. State-wise Undergraduate and Postgraduate Enrolment of SC and ST Students in Universities and Colleges during 1977-78

Name of the State/Union Territory	SC pop. as a % of the total pop. of the State	SC students enrolled at the graduate level as a % of the total pop. of students enrolled at this level	SC students enrolled at the Post-Grad. level as a % of the total pop. of students enrolled at this level	ST pop. as a % of the total pop. of the State	ST students enrolled at the grad. level as a % of the total pop. of students enrolled at this level	ST students enrolled at the Post-Grad. level as a % of the total pop. of students enrolled at this level
Andhra Pradesh	13.27	7.1	7.1	3.81	0.7	0.4
Assam	6.10	4.6	4.5	12.84	7.7	5.6
Bihar	14.11	3.6	1.5	8.75	3.1	N.A.
Gujarat	6.84	6.0	2.4	13.99	3.9	1.5
Haryana	18.89	4.6	4.6	—	0.1	1.6
Himachal Pradesh	22.24	4.1	N.A.	4.09	2.9	N.A.
Jammu & Kashmir	8.26	2.0	1.1	—	—	—
Karnataka	13.14	5.9	4.3	0.79	0.6	0.5
Kerala	8.30	3.8	6.4	1.26	0.5	0.5
Madhya Pradesh	13.09	6.0	5.5	20.14	1.1	2.2
Maharashtra	6.00	9.4	11.4	5.86	2.0	2.4
Meghalaya	0.38	2.6	0.5	80.48	56.3	35.8
Orissa	15.09	3.5	3.5	23.11	3.1	2.1
Punjab	24.71	8.7	5.8	—	0.1	—
Rajasthan	15.82	4.8	5.2	12.13	2.8	4.9
Tamil Nadu	17.76	7.4	6.5	0.76	0.5	0.8
Uttar Pradesh	21.00	10.8	10.9	0.22	0.2	0.2
West Bengal	19.90	11.0	6.2	5.72	1.2	0.1
Delhi	15.64	5.0	3.3	0.12	0.5	1.1
All India	14.60	7.5	7.5	6.94	1.6	1.3

SC/ST graduate students as a percentage of total enrolment by faculty (1977-78)

	Arts	Science	Commerce	Education	Eng./Tech.	Medicine	Law	Agriculture	Vet.Sc.	Other
SC*	10.4	4.4	4.7	6.1	6.1	8.4	6	5.6	6.8	13.5
ST*	2.0	0.8	1.3	2.0	0.9	1.9	0.4	1.4	1.9	0.5

* Size of Reservations 15 per cent for SC and 5 per cent for ST.

reserved for them in the higher cadres of employment. The annual reports of the commissioner of SC/ST continuously complain that not enough SC/ST candidates are available to fill the posts reserved for them in higher employment levels. As against a 15 per cent reservation for the SC and a 7.5 per cent reservation for ST, only 4.75 per cent of Class I posts and 7.37 per cent of the Class II posts are filled by the Scheduled Castes. The corresponding figures for the Scheduled Tribes are even lower—0.94 per cent and 1.03 per cent respectively.[17]

2. It is important to make the public aware of the facts concerning the true situation of the SC/ST. Spot studies done at the time of the Gujarat riots reveal that the public was ignorant of facts and was acting on the basis of the false impression that the SC/ST has advanced quite far.[18]

3. It is necessary to arouse and organise public interest and sympathy and to support the cause of the SC/ST.

4. It is necessary to promote the organisation of the SC/ST for self-help. There are limits to how far legal action and government intervention will be effective.

5. It is necessary to improve the administration of reservations and of the supportive facilities provided SC/ST students at school and college. National and state-level studies on the education of the SC/ST reveal anomalies that urgently need to be removed. First, there is a serious imbalance between the Scheduled Castes, on the one hand, and the Scheduled Tribes on the other (Tables 3.2 and 3.3). Secondly, sharp inter-state, inter-district, inter-caste, inter-tribe, rural-urban and gender disparities exist in advances made within each of these communities.

Balancing Rival Claims and the Finer Points of Social Justice

Will social justice eventually determine the course of positive discrimination? Or will political expediency, the over-riding concern to pre-empt conflict, finally prevail? Some examples of the prevalence of politics are the failure to 'deschedule' the castes and tribes that have advanced over the years, to otherwise deal with the new emerging inequalities, the two extensions of the reservations over the years (initially provided as a short-term measure for ten years). Today, the challenge is to restore the balance between politics and social justice.

Notes

1. The labels used consist of different combinations of the terms *affirmative*, *protective*, *compensatory*, *differential* and *preferential*, on the one hand, and *action*, *policy*, *programmes*, *treatments* and *discrimination*, on the other.
2. The Eighth Schedule of the Indian constitution officially recognises

fourteen languages, though a fifteenth has been added. But there are several languages besides those officially listed, and each language has several dialects.

3. There is no definition of *Scheduled Caste* and *Scheduled Tribe* in the Constitution. The President, however, is empowered to draw, in consultation with the governor of each state subject to revision by Parliament (articles 341–342) a list of castes identified as Scheduled Castes and Scheduled Tribes. The former constitute 15.1 per cent of the population and the latter 7.5 per cent.

4. It is important to note that reservations in education are only part of a much larger programme of positive discrimination for the SC/ST, consisting of reserved seats in Parliament and state legislatures, reserved employment promotion in government, quasi-government and public-sector jobs and a series of economic and social benefits.

5. Included in the supportive facilities provided for the advancement of education among scheduled castes and tribes are residential schools (known as Ashram schools, for children of Scheduled Tribes living in sparsely populated tribal areas), special hostels for SC/ST students, reservation of seats for SC/ST students in general hostels, a special hostel for SC/ST girls, pre-matric and post-matric scholarships for SC/ST students, book banks for SC/ST students in engineering and medical colleges, reservation of seats in various educational and technical institutions and National Overseas Scholarships for SC/ST students. (For details regarding these facilities, see Government of India, 'Report of the Commissioner for Scheduled Castes and Scheduled Tribes 1978–79', pp. 163–79.)

6. *Judgements on Minority Educational Rights*, published by Catholic Bishops' Conference of India, CBCI Centre, Ashok Place, New Delhi, 1980.

7. *India Today*, 31 October 1981.

8. The growth rate among Hindus in 1961–71 was 23.73; among Muslims, 30.85; and among Christians, 32.64 (Census of India, Series I, India Paper 2 of 1972, Religion P. III, New Delhi.) See also, (i) Census of India, Series I, Paper 2 of 1972, Religion, New Delhi, pp. 2–4; (ii) A. Bhende and T. Kanitkar, *Principles of Population Studies*, Bombay, Himalaya Publishing House, 1978, p. 190.

9. *Judgements,* St. Xavier's College, Ahmedabad vs. University of Gujarat, pp. 49–260.

10. Suma Chitnis, 'Reservation in Education, The Policy and the Practice, in Shah, P., Vimal, *Proceedings of the Seminar on Removal of Untouchability*, Dept. of Sociology, Gujarat University, Ahmedabad, 1980.

11. Ibid.

12. University Grants Commission, New Delhi, December 1981.

13. Suma Chitnis, 'Education for Equality', *Economic and Political Weekly*, vol. VII (31–3), special number, 1972.

14. By 1970, the notion of relative performance implied in 'reductions'

had been abandoned. Today, all SC/ST students who pass the relevant qualifying examination are eligible for reserved admission.

15. For details, see P. K. Bose, 'Social Mobility and Caste Violence: A Study of the Gujarat Riots', *Economic and Political Weekly*, vol. XVI, no. 16, 1981, pp. 713–16; I. P. Desai, 'Anti-Reservation Agitation and the Structure of Gujarat Society', *Economic and Political Weekly*, vol. XVI, no. 18, 1981, pp. 819–23; A. Yagnik, 'Spectre of Caste War', *Economic and Political Weekly*, vol. XVI, no. 13, 1981, pp. 553–5.

16. Of 25 per cent of the seats reserved for SC/ST students in the five medical colleges of Gujarat, less than 5 per cent have actually been filled by the reserved castes. And only a little more than 3 per cent of the teaching posts in medical colleges have been filled by all the SC/ST teachers combined (S. Yagnik, 'Spectre of Caste War', *Economic and Political Weekly*, vol. XVI, No. 13; 1981, pp. 553–4).

17. Government of India, Report of the Commissioner for Scheduled Castes and Scheduled Tribes, 1978–79.

18. Ibid., Yagnik, 17 above, p. 555

4 INTER-ETHNIC RESTRUCTURING IN MALAYSIA, 1970–80: THE EMPLOYMENT PERSPECTIVE

Tai Yoke Lin

Introduction

The New Economic Policy (NEP) was launched in 1970 in the aftermath of the racial riots of May 1969, which were widely seen as an expression of the deep discontent felt among Malays over domination of the Malaysian economy by the Chinese minority. Under this new strategy more rapid 'Malayanisation' of society was planned and a commitment was made to 'restructure' the economy so as to give Malays equivalent, or equal, economic status with non-Malays. This extended from increasing Malay equity participation in industry and upgrading Malays in employment to reducing the extent of Malay poverty, notably in the rural areas where most Malays live. The target date for completion of the process was 1990, but before that date a series of detailed plans were developed in order to reach the goal.

Vast resources have been devoted to the NEP, and behind the scenes controversy has raged about the objectives themselves, about the most appropriate means of achieving them, whether they were being realised, and about the social and economic costs and benefits of doing so.

It is in that context that this chapter examines the main trends in the employment structure over the past quarter century. To the extent that available data allow, its purpose is to determine how much ethnic restructuring has occurred and where it has occurred.

Historical Background

Aside from foreign dominance of the economy, there were at the time of independence in 1957 three important economic groups in Malaya—the politically powerful Malays, the economically dominant Chinese and the ambiguously situated Indians. With relatively few exceptions, each group operated in separate economic enclaves of the economy. Throughout the colonial period, the Malay masses were treated as outside the mainstream of the commercial and industrial life of the country. By supporting a Malay elite based on the traditional aristocracy, the British had preserved Malay culture and customs, along with the rural orientation of Malay economic activities. The immigrant Chinese, for their part, had been at the forefront of tin mining (having come mainly as coolie labourers) and, since the nineteenth century, had dominated local commerce. Indians, too, had been imported in large numbers, some as civil servants and technicians but mainly as indentured labourers for the rubber estates.

By the time of independence, the ethnic division of labour had been accentuated, which was reflected in sharp inequalities in income, asset ownership, skills, schooling and living standards. In the context of post-independence communal politics, deep-rooted fears of Chinese encroachment on Malay rights and fears of Malay threats to Chinese economic freedom grew. Rapid economic growth kept these fears from exploding until 1969, when a recession and an upset result in the general election helped spark racial riots. From this experience emerged the New Economic Policy, designed to 'reduce poverty and restructure Malaysian society so that identification of race with economic function and geographical location is reduced and eventually eliminated.'[1] Specifically, it set a target: 'within a period of twenty years, Malays and other indigenous people (Bumiputras* or 'sons of the soil') will manage and own at least 30 per cent of the total commercial and industrial activities in all categories and scales of operation'. In terms of employment the NEP provides that 'the employment pattern at all levels and in all sectors, particularly the Modern Rural and Modern Urban sectors, must reflect the racial composition of the population'.[2]

In part, the problem arose because the government neglected rural development in the early years of independence. Developmental expenditures were chiefly allocated to additional infrastructure facilities, particularly roads and irrigation canals. Between 1965 and 1970, with rubber prices at their lowest in several decades and development expenditures virtually stagnant (hovering at around M$850 million annually), the economic plight of the Malay population worsened. Thus the Malays felt they were unable to enjoy the fruits of development, because they were not participating adequately in the most productive and dynamic sectors of the economy.

Table 4.1 gives the employment pattern among the ethnic groups at independence and at the start of the NEP. It is clear that between 1957 and 1970, Malays remained locked in agriculture, their population within the sector having increased by approximately 200,000 over thirteen years. The same period was marked by the movement of Chinese and Indians out of agriculture, so that the Malay share of agricultural employment increased from 61 to 68 per cent. Not only did Malay employment not

*This term includes Malays as well as other groups. Throughout this chapter, 'Malay' and 'Bumiputra' are used interchangeably.

Table 4.1. Employment Among Races by Industry, 1957, 1970

	1957 No. ('000)				1957 % share of employment			1970 No. ('000)				1970 % share of employment		
	Total	Malays	Chinese	Indians	Malays	Chinese	Indians	Total	Malays	Chinese	Indians	Malays	Chinese	Indians
Agriculture, forestry, fishing	1,223	752	303	151	61	25	12	1,406	951	301	142	68	21	10
Rubber estates	264	50	79	137	19	30	51	226	63	70	93	28	31	41
Rubber smallholdings	332	206	116	7	63	35	2	350	228	98	21	65	28	6
Padi	398	386	12	—	97	3	—	300	294	6	—	98	2	—
Fishing	61	41	19	1	68	31	1	68	37	31	0.2	54	46	—
Forestry	19	8	11	0.2	40	59	1	48	16	24	—	40	60	—
Other agriculture*	149	61	66	6	41	44	4	422	313	72	27	74	17	6
Industry	288	63	182	40	22	64	14	427	113	285	26	26	67	6
Mining & quarrying	60	11	43	7	18	70	12	85	21	56	7	25	66	8
Manufacturing	160	30	109	21	19	68	13	264	76	173	14	29	65	5
Construction	68	22	32	12	33	47	18	78	16	56	5	22	72	6
Commerce	195	33	129	31	17	67	16	351	83	229	38	24	65	11
Transport & communications	78	29	32	16	37	41	22	119	51	47	20	43	40	17
Services	354	159	102	57	45	29	16	474	230	169	66	49	36	14
Government services	167	95	18	23	57	11	14	240	139	50	46	58	21	19
Other services (personal & community services, utilities etc.)	187	64	84	34	34	45	18	251	103	122	25	41	48	1
Total	2,149	1,039	748	295	48	35	13.7	2,794	1,437	1,034	298	51	37	11

Sources: Third Malaysia Plan 1976–1980, pp. 164, 187; Snodgrass (1980), pp. 86, 87, 96; *Rubber Statistics Handbook* (1973).
* Racial composition of 'other agriculture' calculated as a residual quantity in 1970; so caution should be exercised in trying to compare it with figures for 1957.

reflect the changing structure of the economy, but Malay participation within the rural sector was also characterised by the more traditional categories. It was concentrated in the padi, rubber small-holding and fishing sectors in which poverty remained widespread. In 1970, in each group specified, poverty incidence exceeded 60 per cent (padi farmers registered 88.1 per cent), whereas, in the Indian- and Chinese-dominated sectors—for example, mining, manufacturing and construction—the incidence of poverty was typically half that level.[3] In 1970, after thirteen years of independence, the Malays, in whose hands lay the reins of political power, still comprised three-quarters of the number of poor in the country, while foreigners and immigrant Chinese dominated the existing economic order. Hence, it was not surprising that major efforts would be made to rectify incongruity between economic and political power within the country and that the new policy would entail a much greater degree of state intervention.

Policies and Progress, 1970–80

The employment strategy during the first decade of the NEP's existence rested on four major components:

(a) expansion of the services sector;
(b) rapid growth of the manufacturing sector, particularly labour-intensive industries;
(c) land development;
(d) rapid expansion of higher-education facilities.

Government policies aimed at restructuring were designed to alter both the demand for and the supply of Bumiputra labour. They ranged from preferential recruitment and training of Bumiputras to regulation and intervention in the industries in which Malays were under-represented.

Preferential Recruitment

Preferential recruitment was a central feature of the employment restructuring strategy, especially in the services sector, in land-development schemes (part of the 'modern rural' sector) and in institutions of higher learning.

Within the services sector, preferential recruitment was most marked in government, where, over the period 1970–80, a total of 260,000 additional Bumiputra workers were employed. Table 4.2 shows the net employment change in the public sector for the period 1970–77 and for each consecutive year thereafter. It can be observed that the proportion of public sector jobs created that accrued to Bumiputras showed progressively higher levels with the advance of the NEP. Over 1970–77, Malays comprised 68 per cent of the increase in the number of workers employed in the government; by 1977–8, this proportion had increased to 73 per cent, and by 1979–80 to 93 per cent. Meanwhile, in the same period (1970–80), the public sector undertook three major upward revisions of salaries, making it not only the largest employer but one of the highest paying ones as well. Thus, in its efforts to employ Bumiputra labour in the public sector and increase the attractiveness of the public service, the government brought about a significant inter-ethnic transfer of resources, public services becoming a major redistributive mechanism. The same trend in recruitment was observed in the military and the police (Table 4.3). Together, the high intake of Bumiputras into the government and the military and police effectively consolidated Bumiputra political supremacy in the country.

Table 4.2. Bumiputra Employment in Public Sector, 1970–80

	1970–77	1977–78	1978–79	1979–80
Government jobs created ('000)	162.2	28.0	32.1	31.7
Number Malays employed ('000)	109.6	20.4	25.9	29.6
Share of jobs created	68%	73%	81%	93%

Source: Central Personnel Records, PSD, Kuala Lumpur, and author's estimates based on them.

Table 4.3. Ethnic Composition of Armed Forces and Police
1969–70 and 1979–80

	1969–70			1979–80		
	Total no.	% Malays	% non-Malays	Total no.	% Malays	% non-Malays
Armed forces	44,750	75	25	64,500	90	10
Police	39,000	65	35	50,000	80	20
Total	83,750	70	30	114,500	86	14

Source: The Military Balance (1969/70), p. 47 (1979/80), p. 69, and author's estimates.

To combat the shortage of trained Bumiputra personnel, Bumiputra intake into vocational institutes and institutions of higher learning was accelerated. Table 4.4 shows the levels of enrolment of the various ethnic

Table 4.4. Malaysia: Enrolment in Tertiary Education by Race and Levels of Education 1970, 1980*

	1970					1980				
	Total no.	Bumiputra %	Chinese %	Indians %	Others %	Total no.	Malay %	Chinese %	Indians %	Others %
Diploma and certificate courses										
Politeknik Kuantan	—	—	—	—	—	461	74.2	19.7	4.7	1.3
Universiti Pertanian Malaysia	545	84.0	13.2	0.6	2.2	1,680	93.2	4.2	2.5	0.1
Universiti Teknologi Malaysia	822	60.6	35.3	2.9	1.2	3,346	89.3	7.7	2.2	0.7
Institut Teknologi MARA	1,902	100.0	—	—	—	7,854	100.0	—	—	—
Politeknik Ungku Omar	418	39.2	57.4	3.4	—	1,817	74.3	20.0	4.4	1.3
Kolej Tunku Abdul Rahman	—	—	—	—	—	2,203	0.3	96.9	2.8	—
Subtotal	3,687	81.9	16.3	1.1	0.6	17,361	81.2	16.8	1.6	0.4
Degree courses										
Institut Teknologi MARA	7,267	39.1	49.8	7.2	3.9	719	100.0	—	—	—
Universiti Malaya	231	27.0	57.1	13.9	2.0	8,045	50.3	39.3	8.4	2.0
Universiti Sains Malaysia	179	97.0	2.4	0.6	—	3,597	54.4	37.6	7.5	0.5
Universiti Kebangsaan Malaysia	—	—	—	—	—	5,807	86.1	10.7	3.1	0.2
Universiti Pertanian Malaysia	—	—	—	—	—	1,783	81.9	12.5	4.9	0.7
Universiti Teknologi Malaysia	—	—	—	—	—	813	83.6	11.1	4.2	1.1
Subtotal	7,677	40.2	48.9	7.3	3.6	20,764	66.7	26.2	6.0	1.0
Total	11,364	53.5	38.4	5.3	2.7	38,125	73.4	21.8	4.0	0.7

Source: Based on *Fourth Malaysia Plan*, p. 351–2, Table 21–3.

* Figures do not include students pursuing courses overseas and in local private institutions. In 1980, the number of students in institutions overseas numbered 29,731 (FMP, p. 351, 352), 75 per cent of whom were non-Malays. Students in local private institutions numbered 10,060 of whom 88.8 per cent were non-Malays.

groups in higher education in 1970 and 1980. Within the decade, total enrolment multiplied more than threefold, and overall Bumiputra intake increased from 53.5 per cent to 73.4. Bumiputra enrolment in the institutes offering certificate and diploma courses remained largely unchanged, at 81 per cent, but the increase in Bumiputra intake into the universities was significant. In 1969, Bumiputras comprised 35.6 per cent of the 7,677 students in degree courses.[4] By 1980, this percentage had increased to 66.7, of 20,764 students. At the University of Malaya, preferential recruitment resulted in a decrease in the absolute number of Chinese enrolled between 1970 and 1980; but on the whole, the increase in Bumiputra enrolment was achieved through rapid expansion of total intake rather than displacement of other ethnic groups. The available evidence indicates that the shortage of higher education places among non-Bumiputras was acute, with the result that many turned to education abroad. Official statistics show that, of 29,731 students in institutions abroad in 1980, 75 per cent were non-Malays, while 88.8 per cent of 10,060 students in local private institutions were non-Malay.[5]

In agriculture, the most prominent aspect of employment restructuring was the establishment of land-development schemes. These schemes probably helped alleviate pressure for more fundamental reform in the agrarian sector while giving a portion of the landless population the chance to engage in high-income, modern agricultural activity. During 1970–80, 92,300 jobs were created by federal and state land-development schemes, of which approximately 95 per cent were taken by Bumiputras.[6]

There are indications that the desired movement of Bumiputras into the 'modern rural sector' occurred as a natural economic process unaided by the government. Table 4.5 shows the ethnic composition of estate labour in 1970 and 1980. Even as estate labour experienced a reduction, there

Table 4.5. Ethnic Composition of Estate Workers

	1970	(%)	1980	(%)
Malays	74,279	(27)	95,830	(38)
Chinese	85,648	(31)	35,500	(14)
Indians	116,703	(42)	121,120	(48)
Others	650		720	
Total	277,280	(100)	253,170	(100)

Source: Labour and Manpower Report, 1980, p. 30.

was a significant increase in Malay employment in that sector. It was coupled, however, with a 50 per cent fall in the number of Chinese estate workers. (The number of Indian estate workers remained largely unchanged.) Whether preferential recruitment played a role in these shifts is unclear, but it is probable that 'pull' factors were strongly at work, with Chinese labour moving into higher-income employment in the construction and services sectors, and Malays moving out of the villages into estate labour. New wage agreements and high rubber prices were additional factors in hastening the entry of Malay labour into the estates.

Outside the government and the modern rural sectors, Bumiputra employment did not proceed with the same speed. Partly due to the strong family orientation of the traditional Chinese enterprises, low pay and, to some extent, cultural barriers and discrimination, Malay penetration of Chinese enterprises (beyond that of being production workers in some manufacturing industries) was negligible. Even in the less traditionally orientated enterprises, the rate of Bumiputra absorption was slow, so that pressure for a faster rate of change began to grow in the ranks of the political leadership. Thus, in the 1970s, various pieces of legislation were passed with the aim of better monitoring of NEP's progress, especially in industry.

Direct Regulation

Of the new regulations affecting the industrial sector, some were highly industry-specific (for example, the Petroleum Development Act (1974) and the Palm Oil Registration and Licensing Authority Act (1976)) and appear to have been designed more for the purpose of restructuring ownership and increasing government control of the operations of these industries than for changes in the employment structure.

Employment restructuring is potentially more effectively brought about by the Industrial Co-ordination Act of 1975, because it covers all employment and carries specific provisions for policy implementation. The act requires the manufacturer to furnish the government with 'returns or other information (excepting trade secrets) pertaining to any manufacturing activity of the manufacturer',[7] and provides the government with full powers in issuing, extending, revoking or imposing conditions on licenses. No clear indications are provided as to what those conditions might be or what criteria would be used in the licensing process. In the few years that the act has existed, however, it has become apparent that employment restructuring and ownership redistribution (non-Bumiputra to Bumiputra, foreign to local) are important considerations. The manufacturing sector thus has shown some progress in achieving NEP targets in the last half of the 1970s. It can be seen in Table 4.6 that in thirteen of seventeen manufacturing industries employing 25 employees or more, the percentage of Bumiputra workers was higher than that of the other groups. In eight of these industries, Bumiputra participation

Table 4.6. Employment Structure in the Manufacturing Sector by Industries Employing 25 Employees and Above

Industry	(1979) Employment			
	Bumiputra (%)	Chinese (%)	Indian (%)	Others (%)
1. Food Manufacturing	47.9	37.3	12.7	2.1
2. Beverages & tobacco	40.6	46.2	8.9	4.3
3. Textile & textile products	48.9	36.6	13.7	0.8
4. Leather & leather products	50.4	39.1	10.3	0.2
5. Wood & wood products	57.7	32.1	8.9	1.3
6. Furniture & fixtures	48.1	35.5	15.7	0.7
7. Paper, printing and publishing	36.7	50.8	11.7	0.8
8. Chemical & chemical products	47.1	40.1	10.9	1.9
9. Petroleum & coal	48.2	34.8	15.4	1.6
10. Rubber products	50.8	31.5	16.8	0.9
11. Plastic products	52.2	31.4	15.8	0.6
12. Non-metallic products	50.9	29.3	17.9	1.9
13. Basic metal industries	41.7	45.3	12.2	0.8
14. Fabricated metal products	50.2	34.6	13.9	1.3
15. Machinery manufacturing	38.1	48.5	11.9	1.5
16. Electrical & electronics	59.9	24.9	14.4	0.8
17. Transport equipment	51.6	35.3	12.3	0.8

Source: Labour and Manpower Report, p. 32.

was greater than 50 per cent, and in sixteen of the seventeen, Bumiputras made up more than 40 per cent of the labour force. It is not clear, however, that, in NEP terms, they are sufficiently represented at the higher levels of the hierarchy in industrial enterprises. Such information was to be made available under the new regulations of the Industrial Co-ordination Act, which remains potentially one of the most powerful tools for inter-ethnic employment restructuring.

Direct Participation—Public Enterprises

Confronted with an apparent Bumiputra inability to take up shares in commerce and industry, the public enterprise emerged as a new instrument in ownership restructuring, buying up shares in trust for Bumiputras, to be re-sold to Bumiputras later. Table 4.7 shows the net income and ethnic composition of public enterprises in 1976 in terms of government ownership. It can be observed that Bumiputra employment at both higher and

Table 4.7. Net Income and Employment in Public Enterprises According to Government Ownership 1976

% Govt. ownership	Total net profit or loss		Employment						Total
	1976 ($ mill.)	Cumulative ($ mill.)	Managerial, professional Technical, supervisory			Others			
			Bumiputra No. (%)	Others	Total	Bumiputra No. (%)	Others	Total	
100	653.4	−133.0	2,225 (63.1)	1,300	3,525	15,682 (91.2)	1,509	17,191	20,716
50–99	0.7	−48.2	1,227 (40.8)	1,784	3,011	7,494 (68.1)	3,503	10,997	14,008
0–49	46.4	53.3	620 (29.9)	1,452	2,072	7,948 (27.4)	5,181	13,129	15,201
Total	700.5	−127.9	4,072 (47.3)	4,536	8,608	31,124 (62.3)	10,193	41,317	49,925

Source: Report on Guidelines for Public Enterprises in the Fourth Malaysia Plan.

lower levels (but more so at the latter) is directly proportional to the level of government ownership in the enterprises. The figures for net income also indicate that the restructuring process via Bumiputra participation in public-owned enterprises has involved substantial 'costs of learning'. There appears to be a close relationship between higher costs and higher degrees of government ownership. Public enterprises with 100 per cent government ownership showed cumulative losses amounting to M$786.4 million by 1975, but their performance improved markedly the next year. However, this has to be interpreted with some caution since the reversal was almost entirely due to profits from a single petroleum enterprise.

Overall progress in employment restructuring, both in terms of sectoral distribution of ethnic groups and occupational levels, is shown in Tables 4.8 and 4.9. It is clear that employment creation took place predominantly in the services and manufacturing sectors, which together accounted for approximately 60 per cent of new jobs created between 1970 and 1980. Agriculture, though it employed more than half the country's labour force, contributed to a mere 8.9 per cent of new employment in the economy (and approximately 70 per cent of the additional jobs were directly attributable to the public land-development schemes of Felda and Felcra).[8] Table 4.8 shows that in mining and quarrying there was a 'displacement' of Chinese by Bumiputras. This was the result of the closure of many marginal mines owned by Chinese, coupled with

Table 4.8. Net Employment Changes by Industry and Ethnic Group 1970–80

Sector	Increase in total no. employed ('000)	Contribution of sector to total employment increase (%)	Contribution of racial group to increase (%)		
			M	C	I
Agricultural, forestry, fishing	+133.1	9.0	40.6	10.8	48.3
Industry					
Mining, quarrying	+ 0.6	–	–	–	–
Manufacturing	+498.7	33.5	45.5	45.0	8.5
Construction	+149.2	10.0	42.6	51.5	5.2
Commerce	+272.9	18.3	47.4	47.2	4.8
Transport and communication	+ 50.2	3.4	70.5	14.5	14.9
Services	+382.7	25.7	68.6	23.0	8.3
Total	+1,487.4	100.0	52.1	35.2	10.9

Source: Distribution Section, EPU.

Table 4.9. Employment by Occupation and Race 1970-80

Occupation ('000)	1970					1980				
	Malay	Chinese	Indian	Others	Total	Malay	Chinese	Indian	Others	Total
Professional and technical	64.2	54.0	14.8	3.7	136.7	118.2	87.1	26.9	4.0	236.2
(%)	(47.0)	(39.5)	(10.8)	(2.7)	(100.0)	(50.0)	(36.9)	(11.4)	(1.7)	(100.0)
Administrative and managerial	7.4	19.3	2.4	1.6	30.7	16.2	29.2	3.1	2.7	51.2
(%)	(24.1)	(62.9)	(7.8)	(5.2)	(100.0)	(31.6)	(57.0)	(6.1)	(5.3)	(100.0)
Clerical related workers	50.4	65.4	24.5	2.2	142.5	169.4	110.8	21.0	5.3	306.5
(%)	(35.4)	(45.9)	(17.2)	(1.5)	(100.0)	(55.3)	(36.2)	(6.9)	(1.7)	(100.0)
Sales and related workers	69.1	159.6	28.7	1.1	258.5	99.8	299.0	32.7	0.8	432.3
(%)	(26.7)	(61.7)	(11.1)	(0.4)	(100.0)	(23.1)	(69.2)	(7.6)	(0.2)	(100.0)
Service workers	100.0	89.5	32.7	3.4	225.8	168.4	140.1	40.7	2.1	351.3
(%)	(44.3)	(39.6)	(14.6)	(1.5)	(100.0)	(47.9)	(39.9)	(11.6)	(0.6)	(100.0)
Agricultural workers	920.5	221.3	123.7	13.2	1,278.7	998.9	289.9	175.4	10.6	1,474.8
(%)	(72.0)	(17.3)	(9.7)	(1.0)	(100.0)	(67.7)	(19.7)	(11.9)	(0.7)	(100.0)
Production, transport and other workers	266.0	434.5	74.4	2.5	777.4	640.6	601.9	160.9	8.7	1,412.1
(%)	(34.2)	(55.9)	(9.6)	(0.3)	(100.0)	(45.4)	(42.6)	(11.4)	(0.6)	(100.0)
Total	1,477.6	1,043.6	301.4	27.7	2,850.3	2,211.5	1,558.0	460.7	34.2	4,264.4
(%)	(51.8)	(36.6)	(10.6)	(1.0)	(100.0)	(51.9)	(36.5)	(10.8)	(0.8)	(100.0)

Source: Fourth Malaysia Plan, p. 59, Table 3.11.

government entry into large-scale mining operations, especially during 1975–80. The table also shows the extent to which Bumiputras were able to capture additional jobs in transport and communication; the services sectors exceeded their proportional representation in the population. Bumiputra employment in these two sectors was 43 and 49 per cent, respectively, in 1970, reflecting major progress in these non-agricultural sectors toward the employment targets of the NEP.

As to occupational groups, Bumiputra employment in production and transport showed a highly significant increase. More than half of the increase in overall Bumiputra employment was in this category. It amounted to an increase of 375,000 Bumiputra workers, which alone was one and a half times the size of the group in 1970. The effects of such an increase in the ranks of the Malay 'proletariat' are not yet clear, but they will be important to watch in future.

Another feature of the 1970–80 period is the large increase of Bumiputras in the ranks of professional and technical personnel. In these and the clerical and agricultural categories, Bumiputra participation in 1980 was 50 per cent or higher. At the same time, there was a large influx of Chinese into sales and related occupations in the decade 1970–80, reflecting perhaps the constraints on non-Bumiputra entry into other occupations. Administrative and managerial positions continued to be dominated by the Chinese in 1980 (57 per cent), although admittedly, their share of employment in this category declined from 63 to 57 per cent over the ten-year period considered.

Problems and Prospects

It appears from all available data that progress towards achievement of NEP employment targets is well under way. On closer examination, however, one cannot be sure that all is as well as it seems. In the first place, while it is true that Bumiputra participation has risen sharply outside agriculture, it is also clear that it has been achieved mainly in selected areas. The entire process of the nurture and absorption of Bumiputra labour, especially in the middle and higher ranks, has been one involving much 'protection' by the government. The author's estimates (Table 4.10) show that between 1970 and 1980, 47.3 per cent of additional Bumiputra employment was generated in government, defence and the public enterprises alone. Although it may be a defensible strategy in the short run, such unevenness in the direction of growth of the Bumiputra labour force gives rise to the very real problems of integration and cost in the long run. There is a danger that the Bumiputra community may, in the face of continued government protection, be spared the need to constantly upgrade and compete with other segments of the population.

Table 4.10. Contribution of Government Services, Defence and Public Enterprises to Bumiputra Employment in Non-Agricultural Activities, 1970–80

	Change in no. of Bumiputras employed	Contribution to increase in Bumiputra employment in non-agriculture 1970–80
Government services	210,400	32.8%
Military and police	39,800	6.1%
Public enterprises	55,000	8.4%
Total	305,200	47.3%

Sources: Central Personal Records Office, PSD; *The Military Balance* (1969 to 1980), author's estimates based on *Report on Guidelines for Public Enterprises*.

Various divergences are showing up in patterns of participation. So far, the rise of an alliance between foreign interest, state (hence, Bumiputra) capital and a handful of favoured Chinese capitalists in managing the 'commanding heights' of the Malaysian economy is apparent. Below this tip of the pyramid, the labour market appears broadly segmented along Bumiputra government-protected and non-Bumiputra non-government-protected lines. An employment policy based on the creation of a separate labour market for Bumiputras, in the long run, is inherently detrimental to inter-ethnic relations, besides which it may also stifle the much needed development of a dynamic Bumiputra labour force.

Moreover, it is not clear that preferential absorption can continue at the same rate, given the predicted performance of the Malaysian economy over the next decade. Already, there are signs of an 'absorption fatigue' within the government sector, and, given the youthfulness of its composition (71 per cent of government employees are below 40 years of age),[9] the attrition rate will be lower than in the past. All this does not augur well for the expectation that somehow the state will provide. It is clear that in the long-term interests of efficiency and growth, avenues of absorption other than a swollen bureaucracy must be found. Whether this will involve even tighter regulation to enforce higher absorption rates of Bumiputras in the non-government sectors is unclear, though the signals of such a policy are apparent. Already, some reaction in the form of the emigration of non-Bumiputra professionals and the outflow of Chinese capital (both large and medium-size) has been noted. Given the probable decline in the expansion of labour-intensive industries, lower commodity prices and depleting reserves of mineral deposits, the costs of a tighter squeeze, especially on middle- and lower-income non-Bumiputra groups, will lead to escalation of ethnic dissatisfaction.

The process of employment restructuring in the 1970s has also created new problems within the Bumiputra community. In a situation where demand for government benefits—whether in terms of land, higher education or jobs—increasingly outstrips the available supply, the entire question of 'Who benefits?' among Bumiputras comes to the fore. Increasingly, segments of the Bumiputra poor claim that benefits are tied to allegiance to the ruling party or in any case accrue to the newly created Bumiputra elites of the towns. Due to limited access of the poor to visible benefits, new divisions have begun to emerge in the Bumiputra community. Support for Bumiputra opposition parties reportedly is growing among non-beneficiaries and even among groups of beneficiaries (Felda settlers in Johore are said to have turned to the opposition in greater numbers in recent years). Bearing in mind the existence of a potentially powerful 'Malay proletariat' in the urban and modern rural sectors (whose loyalties in the future are unpredictable), it may become difficult for the government to meet the demands of these groups. The next arena of conflict may well be within the Malay community, since the other groups have been losing much of their political and economic clout in the last decade.

Table 4.11. Net Employment Changes by Industry and Ethnic Group 1980-90

Industry	Increase in total no. employed ('000)	Share in new job creation (%)	Required contribution of racial groups to increase (%)		
			M	C	I
Forestry, agriculture, fishing	692.2	33.2	35.3	64.0	2.4
Industry					
Mining, quarrying	7.0	0.3	271.4	-168.6	2.9
Manufacturing	303.4	14.6	93.6	- 11.5	16.6
Construction	- 1.1	- 0.1	-	-	-
Commerce	427.5	20.5	88.0	- 0.1	12.6
Transport and communications	110.5	5.3	63.5	36.9	0.4
Services	498.6	23.9	58.5	28.8	8.4
Total	2,083.3	100.0	65.2	30.3	6.0

Source: EPU, Distribution Section *Third Malaysia Plan*, p. 68, *Fourth Malaysia Plan*, p. 219.

Note: Percentages may add up to more or less than 100 because of non-inclusion of 'Others'.

Expectedly, the NEP restructuring process has taken its toll of inter-ethnic unity. The last decade of restructuring dealt with the issues along Bumiputra-non-Bumiputra lines, at the same time, underplaying the divisions between rich and poor in the country. While inter-ethnic sentiments can perhaps be improved again, it would be unduly optimistic to expect this to happen within the next decade. To achieve strictly proportional ethnic representation, Bumiputras will have to take up 93.6 per cent of the additional jobs in manufacturing, 88 per cent of those in commerce and 58.5 per cent in services (these sectors are expected to be the three largest sources of employment in the next decade). Achievement of restructuring targets would also involve significant adjustments at the administrative and managerial levels—84.9 per cent of the additional jobs at that level (Table 4.12) must accrue to Bumiputras. If the Chinese are to be represented proportionally in agriculture, absolute decreases in the number of Bumiputra and Indian agricultural workers must occur by 1990. In the absence of any indication that the government intends to increase substantially Chinese participation in land-development schemes, and in view of the restricted access of Chinese to agricultural land, it is difficult to see how this can occur. In fact, all these targets (with the exception of that in services) appear out of range. Apparently aware of this, the government has downgraded the achievement levels for most categories for 1990. The Fourth Malaysia Plan thus provides that Bumiputras will comprise 46 to 51 per cent of the labour force for most occupation levels (compared with 55 per cent, which is the estimated proportion of Bumiputras in the population, by 1990).[10] They will remain underrepresented in the sales occupations and overrepresented in the agricultural labour force.

Conclusion

The process of employment restructuring in Malaysia, while it has not lacked resources and governmental commitment, has proceeded along more or less segmented channels, with the Bumiputra labour force nurtured and absorbed into markets protected from competition with other ethnic groups. As a result, progress has been concentrated mainly in government and government-related sectors or, in the case of private industry, among production workers. Such dependence on government and a few selected job fields seems untenable over the long run. Restructuring has also created negative ethnic sentiments, especially among the poor and middle classes. In the face of leaner years expected ahead, it can be anticipated that these ethnic dissatisfactions will sharpen, though to what extent they will do so, and the particular form they will take, is open to conjecture. To manage the problem, continued rapid growth is

Table 4.12. Employment by Occupational Groups and Shares in New Employment Creation 1970-80, 1980-90

Occupation	1970-80					1980-90				
	Increase in no. employed ('000)	Share in new job creation (%)	Contribution to increase (%)			Increase in no. employed ('000)	Share in new job creation (%)	Required contribution to increase (%)		
			M	C	I			M	C	I
Professional and technical	99.5	7.0	54.3	33.3	12.2	156.0	9.8	46.2	39.0	13.3
Administrative and managerial	20.5	1.4	42.9	48.3	3.4	22.5	1.4	84.9	0.9	20.0
Clerical and related workers	164.0	11.6	72.6	27.7	-2.1	129.4	8.1	25.6	46.7	28.0
Sales and related workers	173.8	12.3	17.7	80.2	2.3	197.2	12.4	63.2	15.8	20.1
Service workers	125.5	8.9	54.5	40.3	6.2	215.4	13.5	55.6	29.8	12.8
Production transport and other workers	634.7	44.9	59.0	26.4	13.6	766.7	48.1	60.3	31.6	7.9
Agricultural workers	196.1	13.9	40.0	35.0	26.4	105.7	6.6	-33.1	151.0	-20.5
Total	1,414.1	100.0	51.9	36.4	11.3	1,592.9	100.0	50.0	38.8	10.6

Source: *Fourth Malaysia Plan*, p. 59, Table 3-11. *Fourth Malaysia Plan*, p. 175, Table 9-6.

Note: Required ethnic shares in jobs to be created over 1980-90 were calculated based on the assumption that ethnic employment will reflect the racial composition of the population in 1990. The latter was estimated to be 55 per cent Bumiputras, 34 per cent Chinese and 10 per cent Indians.

crucial. The particular form of employment restructuring must, therefore, be managed with dynamic growth in mind, and a move must be made away from high subsidisation and protection, which, in the long run, could be detrimental to the Bumiputra community and to national unity as a whole.

Notes

1. *Second Malaysia Plan*, p. 1.
2. Ibid., pp. 41, 42.
3. *Fourth Malaysia Plan*, p. 33.
4. *Report of the Committee Appointed by the National Operations Council to Study Campus Life of Students of the University of Malaya*, p. 33.
5. *Fourth Malaysia Plan*, pp. 351, 352.
6. Ibid., p. 265.
7. Industrial Co-ordination Act (Amendment) Act, 1979, p. 7.
8. Calculated from the *Fourth Malaysia Plan*, p. 265, and Table 4.7 of text.
9. *Labour and Manpower Report*, 1980, p. 35.
10. *Fourth Malaysia Plan*, p. 175.

Bibliography

Official Documents

Fourth Malaysia Plan, 1981–1985, National Printing Department, Kuala Lumpur, 1981.
Industrial Co-ordination Act, 1975.
Industrial Co-ordination (Amendment) Act, 1979.
Labour and Manpower Report, 1980, Ministry of Labour and Manpower, Kuala Lumpur, Malaysia.
Mid-Term Review of the Second Malaysia Plan, 1971–1975, Government Printers, Kuala Lumpur, 1973.
Report of the Committee Appointed by the National Operations Council to Study Campus Life of Students of the University of Malaya, Government Printers, Kuala Lumpur, 1971.
Second Malaysia Plan, 1971–1975, Government Printers, Kuala Lumpur, 1971.
Third Malaysia Plan, 1976–1980, Government Press, Kuala Lumpur, 1976.

Other References

Khoo, P. 'Impact of Industrial Policies on Growth and Redistribution', paper presented at Fifth Malaysian Economic Convention, 1978.
Lim, L. L. 'Income Distribution, Employment and Poverty in the Process

of Economic Growth in West Malaysia, 1957–1970.' Ph.D. thesis, University of Malaya, 1978.

Mehmet, O. 'Manpower Planning and Labour Markets in Developing Countries: A Case Study of West Malaysia', *Journal of Development Studies*, January 1972.

Pekerjaan dan Tenaga Kerja dan Latihan, paper presented at Bumiputra Economic Congress, 1980.

Snodgrass, D. *Inequality and Economic Development in Malaysia*, Kuala Lumpur, Oxford University Press, 1980.

Thillainathan, R. 'The Twenty-Year Plan for Restructuring Employment in Peninsular Malaysia: A Quarterly Assessment'. *Kajian Ekonomi'* Malaysia, December 1977.

Young, K., *et al.*, *Malaysia, Growth and Equity in a Multiracial Society*, World Bank Country Economic Report, 1980.

5 THE PURSUIT OF ETHNIC EQUALITY THROUGH PREFERENTIAL POLICIES: A COMPARATIVE PUBLIC POLICY PERSPECTIVE

Myron Weiner

I

Virtually everywhere in the world there is now a demand for greater equality among ethnic groups. Whether it is India or the United States, Sri Lanka or Belgium, Malaysia or Canada, educationally and economically disadvantaged ethnic groups are demanding governmental intervention on their behalf. Most governments have responded, either out of a concern for social justice or to mitigate political conflict. Preferential policies—or affirmative action programmes, reservations, or compensatory discrimination, as these policies are variously called—are one such governmental response. Of the various policies intended to reduce ethnic differences, preferential policies are among the most controversial, opposed even by many who subscribe to the goal of reducing ethnic differences. Why preferential policies are so controversial, what new policy questions they raise once a government is committed to their use, what the assumptions underlying these policies are, and how these questions look when viewed from a comparative perspective cutting across developed and developing countries—this is the theme of this chapter.

In any assessment of impact, it is equally important to look at the kind of political process and the policy disputes produced by such policies. My intent is to present these public policy controversies as sharply as I can, even at the risk of appearing to be unduly provocative. To sharpen the issues while at the same time keeping us close to the actual experiences of countries, I shall draw my analysis from the American and Indian experiences, two cases which at one level are quite different but which, at another, have much in common.

Precisely because the subject before us is so controversial, it is especially important to start with a common conceptual language. For example, such words as *ethnicity, ethnic equality* and *preferential policies* often have different meanings to different users.

By *ethnicity*, I mean the way individuals and groups characterise themselves on the basis of their language, race, religion, place of origin, shared culture, values and history. Ethnicity is generally, but not always, a matter of birth. Many people collectively may redefine their identity; government policies often are important in shaping the identity of an ethnic group and determining who is a member.

Ethnic equality can refer to equality of opportunity, equality of results or equality of treatment. By 'equality of opportunity' we mean that individuals, irrespective of the ethnic group they belong to, are considered for education and employment, as well as other public and private goods, on the basis of their ability and skills or their needs. When there is equality of opportunity, individuals are not discriminated against because of their religion, race, sex, place of birth, caste or any other ethnic category.

Equality of results, as it relates to ethnicity, means that the distribution of income, wealth and occupations among individuals is in proportion to the population of each ethnic group in the country.

Equality of treatment suggests that citizens, regardless of the ethnic group they belong to, are treated alike, that people with more money are entitled to more material goods but are not entitled to degrade others because of the latter's lower income or ethnic group.

Preferential policies refer to laws, regulations, administrative rules, court orders and other public interventions to provide certain public and private goods, such as admission into schools and colleges, jobs, promotions, business loans, and rights to buy and sell land on the basis of membership in a particular ethnic group.

Why is there a demand for ethnic equality, and how does ethnic equality differ from other forms of equality?

The Ethnic Division of Labour

First, let us note the universality of ethnic inequality. All multi-ethnic societies exhibit a tendency for ethnic groups to engage in different occupations, have different levels (and, often, types) of education, receive different incomes, and occupy a different place in the social hierarchy. One explanation for this ethnic division of labour is that the differences reflect domination by one ethnic group of another through the imposition of its economic power, control over the state, and assertion of central legitimising principles and symbols intended to justify the domination. Thus, in India, the upper castes, especially the Brahmins, monopolised political and economic power, further consolidated their position by moving into education and government services offered by the British, opposed the extension of mass education, and advocated a religious ideology that emphasises merit in the performance of caste duties and obedience to caste rules as the essence of *dharma*. Hierarchy was thus the basis of social organisation, religious ideology and a system of economic and political power.

In the United States, public policies over the past thirty years have reflected the view that a system of brutal repression had subordinated the Indian tribes, and a system of slavery discriminated against a black population forcibly imported from Africa to do menial work. Even with the end of slavery, white domination persisted, imposed by legal barriers in the American South and by subtler barriers to education, employment and equal housing in the North. In the United States, in the view of some social scientists and political figures, a liberal ideology that emphasised equality of opportunity and achievement through individual merit led to and sanctioned inequality of results as the natural consequence of unequal performance.

An alternative theory explaining an ethnic division of labour emphasises the different values, preferences and ambitions of ethnic groups. According to this theory, differences in education, occupation, income, and status can in part be understood as a consequence of cultural differences. One group, for example, may have little regard for education, whereas another values education highly. One group may prefer entrepreneurial activities, another the professions, and still another physical labour. One group consists of high achievers who seek to move up to whatever occupations are most valued or best paid, while members of another group have less ambition, prefer to live as they have in the past and are less willing to venture forth from the community or into new occupations.

The ancient debate—between those who see differences as a result of societal constraints and those who see them as a result of individual or group cultures, values and preferences, between those who 'blame society' and those who 'blame the victim', between the socio-political determinists and cultural/individual behaviourists—is often at the root of different policy perspectives. The policy lever one pulls depends in part on how one explains ethnic differences. It hardly needs to be argued that in most societies both sets of explanations may be at work: groups may be both the victims of societal discrimination and lack initiative and drive; there may be barriers to education as well as indifference to education; groups kept out of certain occupations may also have occupational preferences.

Both perspectives grow out of the contemporary debate over how best to remove educational, income and occupational differences among ethnic groups. Until recently, however, most societies did not view these differences as a problem. That particular religions, castes or linguistic groups in India predominated in the military, the bureaucracy, trade and commerce, as landowners, tenant-cultivators, landless labourers or artisans seemed to many to be a 'natural' order reflecting, if not innate differences in ability, at least innate differences in culture. In the United States it struck no one as a problem that in New York City the Irish dominated the police, the Jews the school system, that particular ethnic groups were disproportionately represented among municipal garbage collectors, postal workers, textile workers and, for that matter, corporate, university and foundation presidents.

The contemporary concern over inequalities between ethnic groups in part is a reflection of a broad concern over income inequalities between classes. Large income gaps between social classes and between peoples who live in different regions of the same country have led to a veritable industry of studies concerned with determinants and solutions to these inequalities. One school, dominated primarily by economists, has focused on policies likeliest to bring about a more equitable distribution of income within society without regard for race, religion or ethnic group—policies centring on sectoral and regional investments, incomes policies, tax policies, social welfare programmes, land reforms, and so forth. The concern of this group is how to achieve greater distributive justice in the allocation of society's benefits, to minimise income differences and maximise opportunities.

Another approach focuses on the maldistribution of benefits among ethnic groups. The concern here is with whether each ethnic group is represented proportionately among the rich and the poor, among the employed and the unemployed, among high-status, well-paid occupations and low-status, poorly paid ones. From this perspective, inter-class variations are secondary to inter-ethnic variations.

If the 20 per cent of the population living below the poverty level are all in one ethnic group, an issue of discrimination and social policy is posed. If the poor represent each of the country's ethnic groups in proportion to their population, it is an issue of economic policy. Thus a rearrangement of ethnic groups among the poor does not in itself reduce the misery within a population.

Ethnic Versus Class Inequalities

There are at least two reasons for considering ethnic inequality more offensive than class inequality. One is that differences among ethnic groups are seen as an indication of differences in opportunities, proof that society has allocated *access* to education and employment unfairly and that dominant groups are using their position to restrict others in moving upward. In contrast, class differences are not necessarily an indication of inequality of opportunity. They may, in fact, result from equality of opportunity. A society that provides equal opportunity is one in which the results are uneven and in which unequal results are considered legitimate. Winners believe that they deserve more, losers that they deserve less, in a competitive race in which all have an equal opportunity to move up. If one has succeeded and another has failed, presumably, differences in ability, skill, hard work and ambition are reflected. If the outcome is stratified by ethnic group, however, the presumption is made that the results may have been fixed, that is, that some groups were discriminated against while others were favoured. Thus, in both India and the United States, the low status and the low income of ex-untouchables and blacks is widely viewed as the result of discrimination by dominant ethnic groups, whereas poverty among Brahmins and Protestant whites is ordinarily not seen as a result of prejudice.

The second reason why ethnic inequality is often of greater concern than class differences is, when ethnic differences lead to ethnic conflict, the result sometimes is more disruptive to the social order than class conflicts. Ethnic conflicts are often more violent than class conflicts. On a global basis, more people have been killed in this century because of the ethnic group to which they belong than to their class. Forceful expulsion of populations, genocide, civil wars, and a variety of internal upheavals linked to ethnic conflicts have marked social and political life in the advanced industrial countries no less than in the newly independent states of Asia and Africa. Ties of blood (real or a social invention) have driven mankind to commit acts that exceed the brutalities committed on behalf of class.

It is this concern for both distributive justice and minimising ethnic conflict that leads governments to turn their attention to reducing inequalities among ethnic groups. What are the possible responses of a political system to the demand for greater ethnic equality? Under what circumstances are preferential policies an attractive option?

Policy Options

The options available to governments are determined partly by the ethnic divisions that exist in a society. One must first distinguish between ethnic divisions that are along *horizontal* lines and those along *vertical* lines. *Horizontal division* refers to a hierarchical, ethnically stratified social system, whereas *vertical division* refers to a society in which each ethnic group occupies its own territory. The divisions in pre-1971 Pakistan between the less developed Bengali region in the east and the more developed Punjabi-majority region in the west is an example of a vertically divided nation. India's caste system and America's racial divisions are both forms of a hierarchically stratified social system. Vertical divisions become horizontal when the people of one cultural or linguistic region migrate to another and take their place within a stratified social order.

A second distinction is whether the subordinate ethnic group is a minority or a majority. The majority may be subordinate in all respects, as in the case of blacks in South Africa, or it may be subordinate economically but dominant politically, as in the case of Malays in Malaysia or Assamese in the Indian state of Assam.

What policy options are available for a government committed to reducing ethnic inequalities depends upon whether ethnic divisions are horizontal or vertical, whether the subordinate group is a minority or a majority and whether the group's subordination is economic, social or political.

Various policies are available to governments, aimed at increasing the income and occupational equality of ethnic groups; preferential treatment is only one of several such alternatives. Among the others are regional and urban development programmes when disadvantaged ethnic groups are geographically concentrated; government aid for selected sectors of the economy when disadvantaged ethnic groups are concentrated in agriculture, fishing, forestry or particular industries; social service programmes for improving the health, education and housing of low-income groups; wealth- and income-distribution policies, such as land reform, tenancy reform, and minimum wages, which differentially benefit one ethnic group in relation to another; and a variety of policies that increase the political power of selected ethnic groups, such as the devolution of authority, redrawing administrative boundaries, and electoral reform. Most such policies, though intended to benefit particular ethnic groups, do not use ethnic *criteria* as their basis. Preferential policies do. Under preferential policies, individuals are given special benefits, not because they live in poor regions, work in lagging sectors of the economy, or are educationally and economically disadvantaged, but because they belong to a particular ethnic category—a caste, tribe, religion, linguistic or cultural group which, on the average, is less educated, earns less, and has lower-status employment than other ethnic groups.

Which policy for reducing ethnic inequalities works best depends, among other things, upon the reasons for the ethnic inequalities, what kind of stratification exists, whether the inequalities are economic, social or political and on how effective the administrative system is in implementing policies. A growing but still small number of social scientists have given their attention to assessing the efficacy of alternative policies. The controversy over preferential policies, however, is not only over their efficacy but the deeper philosophical question of the justice of employing *ethnic* criteria as the basis for the redistribution of benefits—that is, whether the characteristics of the group, rather than of the individual who belongs to the group, should be the basis for the receipt of entitlements and preferences.

At the heart of this controversy is the question of individual versus group rights. The form this controversy has taken, and how the outcome of the debate affects the subsequent development of preferential policies can be seen by comparing and contrasting the American and Indian experiences, two countries that have approached the issue of preferential policies from different philosophical traditions.

II

The United States

In the United States, advocates of ethnic equality initially directed their attention to eliminating discrimination in education, employment, housing and civil rights. A series of US Supreme Court decisions—particularly *Brown* v *Board of Education* (1954) and legislative decisions, especially the 1964 Civil Rights Act—attempted to break the barriers to equality of opportunity and equality of treatment. A prime target of reform was school segregation. American civil rights supporters argued that the integration of whites and blacks in the schools, combined with elimination of discrimination in employment and housing, would enable disadvantaged blacks to compete with whites, and that in time most of the disparities would disappear. Others argued that, since the effects of past discrimination were reflected in current individual capabilities, equal opportunity would result in unequal outcomes. They argued that the assumption that the removal of discrimination in education would equalise opportunity and bring about more equal results was false. Holders of this view rejected the classic liberal view that the educational system could even out class barriers and that subsequent differences in income or productivity could then be explained by examining the personal deficiencies of workers. Even if cultural differences affected the ability of groups to compete, under conditions of perfect competition, some ethnic groups would win a disproportionate share of the higher occupations and incomes.

Affirmative action programmes were proposed as a way to equalise the races; but there was division between those who saw such programmes as a goal and those who saw them as a system of quotas or preference. For some, *affirmative action* meant programmes of training and recruitment in support of a national commitment to equal *opportunity* in education and employment. Others stressed reserving a certain percentage of positions for exclusive use by blacks, Hispanics and other targeted groups. The line between goals and actual quotas is difficult to draw in practice; to many non-Americans, it probably is an arcane distinction with no significant difference of outcomes. None the less, the issue calls attention to the widespread American belief in equality of opportunity (but not necessarily equality of results) and, more fundamentally, to the American preference for individual rights as opposed to group rights.

These issues were drawn in the Bakke case, a case involving a white male who argued that he was denied admission to the Davis (California)

Medical School because sixteen out of one hundred places in the entering class had been reserved for minorities. Supporters of affirmative action argued that the unequal distribution of benefits among races with respect to the number of doctors reflected discrimination against minorities, that group performance was a way to determine whether equal opportunities existed. Most supporters of the Davis Medical School also subscribed to the notion that it was individual performance that counted; they argued that affirmative action in education would lead to equal opportunity in employment, which ultimately would bring equal results. This classic liberal position was articulated by Archibald Cox, professor of law at Harvard and the lawyer for Davis. In fact, Cox said, if the Davis programme were to 'give rise to some notion of group entitlement regardless either of the ability of . . . [individuals] or of their potential contribution to society . . . I would first, as a faculty member, criticize and oppose it; as a constitutional lawyer, the further it went, the more doubts I would have.' (O'Neill, 1981, p. 627.)

Some observers interpreted the Bakke case as a classic clash between the principle of meritocracy and the goal of racial equality; defenders of meritocracy argued that merit was the only way to guarantee equal opportunity. Some saw the case as a test of the theory of compensatory justice, while others argued that nothing was more unfair than to measure individuals by their race. Also arguments were advanced about the need for role models, analogies between proportionality in politics and proportionality in education and a controversy over whether there had to be prior discrimination on the part of the Davis Medical School to justify a compensatory admissions policy. At the heart of the debate, however, lay the question: Are constitutional rights for individuals or for groups? To supporters of the doctrine of individual rights, the meaning of the Fourteenth Amendment was clear and decisive: 'No state shall . . . deny to any *person* within its jurisdiction the equal protection of the laws.'

According to public opinion polls, most Americans object to the notion of group rights and quotas but support other measures to advance greater ethnic equality. Congress—and with some important exceptions, the courts—have held to the individual-rights position while in effect sanctioning goals and timetables designed to achieve equality for disadvantaged groups. Civil rights organisations and many government agencies charged with implementing affirmative action programmes tend to operate on the basis of group rights and goals. As with many political debates, code words became a shorthand way of expressing deeper philosophical positions. *Quotas* has come to mean a group-rights position, while for many liberals *goals* is a device for preserving the commitment to individual rights while advocating steps to reduce inequalities among ethnic groups.

India

The Indian position is more explicitly in support of group than individual rights, though both positions have a place in the country's constitution. Indeed, embedded in the Indian constitution are two conflicting notions of equality, each derived from an opposing philosophical tradition. Article 15 of the Indian constitution states: 'The state shall not discriminate against any citizens on grounds only of religion, race, caste, sex or place of birth'. Similarly, Article 16(2) states that no citizen 'shall on grounds only of religion, race, caste, sex, descent, place of birth, residence or any [combination] of them be ineligible for or discriminated against in state employment'. This is the standard liberal position on individual rights.

Article 15(4), an amendment adopted in 1951, modifies Article 15 with a clause that states: 'Nothing in this article . . . shall prevent the state from making any special provision for the advancement of any socially and educationally backward classes of citizens or for the scheduled castes and the scheduled tribes.' Similarly, Article 16(4) modifies Article 16: 'Nothing in this article shall prevent the state from making any provision for the reservation of appointments or posts in favour of any backward class of citizens'. This is the standard group-rights principle.

Thus, after boldly reconfirming the nineteenth-century liberal conception of the rights of citizens, the Indian constitution asserts the principle of collective rights of 'classes of citizens based upon religion, race, caste, sex, descent, place of birth or residence' when the claims are made on behalf of classes 'socially and educationally backward'. Other provisions of the Constitution go beyond enabling the government to give preference to specified classes of citizens by *requiring* the government to do so. Article 335 provides for reservations of appointments of scheduled castes and scheduled tribes to the administrative services, and other provisions provide for reservations in Parliament and the state assemblies.

Thus the Indian government—in its constitution and in subsequent legislative and administrative decisions, and confirmed in court rulings—established the policy that the government can and should allocate seats in legislative bodies, admit students to educational institutions, grant scholarships, provide employment in government services and make available various other entitlements to individuals on the basis of membership in a group. Once this principle was established, the political controversies centred on two ancillary questions: What groups should be entitled to preferences? and What preferences should be provided?

An earlier legislative history largely settled the identity of the scheduled castes and scheduled tribes. These groups are widely known and locally accepted and are often specified in the census, as well as various other administrative and legislative acts. The only significant controversy concerned whether ex-untouchables who had opted out of Hinduism by converting to Christianity or Buddhism qualified as members of scheduled castes, since the latter were initially defined as castes within the Hindu religious framework. The controversy was ultimately settled by broadening rather than narrowing the definition of 'scheduled castes'. Similarly, a legislative effort to exclude Christian tribals from the reservations provided scheduled tribes was rejected by India's Parliament.

The issue of giving other 'backward' castes benefits, and how the castes should be chosen, was more controversial. The 'backward-caste category' is an especially elastic one, since the criteria for inclusion are left to the political arena. As Ambedkar, India's law minister at the time when the constitutional provision for backward castes was written, said: 'A backward community is a community which is backward in the opinion of the government'. And T. T. Krishnamachari, another member of the Constituent Assembly, described Article 16(4) as a 'paradise for lawyers'. (Galanter, 1978, p. 1,814.)

The debate over the choice of criteria for including particular communities has been indecisive. Some government commissions urge that objective measures of 'backwardness' be employed, for example, average education or income levels. Other commissions emphasise position in the social hierarchy: a caste should be included as 'backward' on the basis of its low status or the inferior treatment of its members by other communities. Whether the test for inclusion is an economic or a caste one, the consensus is that the criteria should be applied to groups, not individuals.

Some states were highly selective, but others chose to define as 'backward' virtually any non-Brahmin caste. Efforts by the central government to develop a uniform set of criteria, if not a uniform list, were rejected by Parliament and the courts, with the result that each state government has its own criteria and its own list. One consequence is that, while members of scheduled castes and scheduled tribes are given reservations in the central services and in centrally run educational institutions as well as at the state level, reservations for the backward castes are confined to state and locally run institutions and administrative services.

Although virtually all states provide benefits to some backward classes, several states have aggressively incorporated a substantial number of castes with large populations in their list. It is not unusual for 20 to 25 per cent of the population of a state to appear on lists of backward classes, in addition to the 15 per cent of the Indian population classified as scheduled caste and another 7 per cent as scheduled tribe.

In addition, most states have extended preferences to *residents* of the state, particularly in educational admissions and employment for the state government. Although the laws and administrative rulings are usually explicit in specifying a time period as a definition of residence, it is not uncommon for residence to be used as a surrogate for ethnicity. The widely used term is 'sons of the soil', referring to populations indigenous to a particular area, as distinct from migrants. Thus, in Assam, 'sons of the soil' rules specify residence; both private and public employers, however, understand that the intent of these policies is to give employment preference to Assamese over Bengalis. Similar policies in Bombay are intended to benefit those who speak the Maharashtrian language over Tamils and other migrant communities, irrespective of the duration of their residence.

The main argument for extending reservations to sons of the soil is that they, too, are 'socially and educationally backward' in relation to some migrant communities. In many regions of India, an ethnic division of labour has developed, involving migrants and natives, with migrants holding positions in the state and central administrative services, the professions, the colleges and universities and business and trade. The demand for preferential policies to protect the native middle classes over the migrant middle classes is an old one; in the 1920s, preference was given in Hyderabad to residents of the state, and in Bihar in the 1930s. In the 1960s and early 1970s, similar policies were adopted in Assam (against Bengalis), in Maharashtra (against Tamils) and within the Telengana region of Andhra (against people from the delta).

An interesting feature of Andhra's policies that may foreshadow developments elsewhere is that 'local' was defined not in terms of residence in the state but as residence in regions and districts of the state. Demands for the 'regionalisation' of preferences have already been made in other states.

There was thus a progression in the application of the principle of reservations: from scheduled-caste and scheduled-tribe minorities that were lowest on the social scale, to the more numerous and somewhat better-off backward castes, to autochthonous populations, a majority diverse in its social and economic characteristics yet backward in relation to its migrant competitors.

These extensions have not been without controversy, however. In some states both scheduled castes and forward castes have opposed extension of preferences to backward castes, most notably in Bihar, where a recommendation by the state government was accompanied by massive demonstrations in the colleges. Sons-of-the-soil preferences were opposed not only by migrant communities but often by the state governments migrants came from, along with warnings of reprisals if state governments became too restrictive.

Some critics of reservations for backward castes and for sons of the soil urged the state governments to put aside all benefits for castes and linguistic groups, proposing instead that benefits go only to individuals from families that lacked education or adequate income. The proposal (for replacing group characteristics with individual characteristics), however, was uniformly rejected by policymakers.

Many objections notwithstanding, the extension of preferences to communities previously not receiving preferences has, over the past three decades, moved forward inexorably. The only limitation imposed by the courts is that, with respect to scheduled castes, scheduled tribes and backward castes, the total number of reservations for admission to colleges and for positions in the administrative services must be below 50 per cent. No such numerical restriction, however, was placed on preferences for sons of the soil.

There has also been a progression in types of reservations provided. Initially, reservations were provided for admission to schools and colleges, including engineering and medical schools. They were provided for appointments to the state administrative services and, in the case of scheduled castes and tribes, to the central administrative services. Reservations were then extended to the entire public sector, though not to private employment. Private employers, however, are under pressure from state and central governments to provide reservations for scheduled castes and tribes and for sons of the soil.

The system of reservations originally was intended for admission to educational institutions and for government employment. In some instances, preferences were also extended to promotions. More recently, there have been demands that preferences in educational admissions to medical schools be 'held over'; that is, seats not filled one year must be added to reservations for the next.

The Indian policy, then, is to create a new kind of labour market in which each ethnic group is given a share commensurate with its population. Shares are first apportioned in educational institutions, then in various categories of employment in the public sector and ultimately in private employment. From this perspective, the model society is not a socialist one in which all individuals have if not equal levels of education at least equal incomes and wealth. Nor is it the liberal model of a society based upon equal opportunity in which individuals compete for higher education and higher incomes. Rather, it is a society in which each of the upper levels of education, income and occupation are proportionately made up of persons from all the country's ethnic groups. This objective is to be achieved not by an open competitive market but by a government-regulated educational and labour market that ensures an appropriate place for each group. Social justice thus requires a public policy that guarantees individual mobility by means of group allocation.

III

To view policy options, policy choices and programme implementation simply in rational cost–benefit terms based upon an assessment of policy outcomes, its gainers and losers, is to ignore the political dimension of the policy process. On the other hand, to reduce the system of reservations to a struggle by various groups for economic position, or by one group for mastery over another, is to miss the deeper conceptual issues underlying political struggles. Neither approach provides a satisfactory answer to the question of why two countries—the United States and India, both committed to ethnic equality, both employing similar policy instruments—none the less continue to deal with the question of ethnic equality in different ways. Behind such words as *ethnicity*, *equality*, *integration*, and even *preferences* lie fundamentally different beliefs.

At another level, there is a convergence of countries that chose to follow the path of preferential policies, a convergence dictated by the *political logic* of preferential policies. This logic is especially clear in the Indian case precisely because India has so explicitly made a policy commitment to ethnic-group preferences. By 'political logic', I mean a policy decision that creates a political space, shaping the terms of subsequent policy debates and substantially influencing political responses and new policy choices. In the Indian case, the political logic of preferential policies worked as follows:

1. *Group preferences.* Here, there has been a progression in the allocation of preferences from one group to another. As we have seen, a policy initially intended to benefit scheduled castes and tribes was extended to backward castes and to autochthonous populations. There were pressures to expand the list of backward castes and to define *autochthonous* in an increasingly localised manner, as well as demands that reservations be extended to Muslims, to the families and children of immigrants overseas and to various other groups.

2. *Kinds of preference.* The Indian constitution asserts that government can make provisions for the 'reservations of appointments or posts', but leaves to the legislature the determination of what precise reservations should be provided. The result has been a debate over whether reservations should be provided in engineering and medical schools as well as in colleges in public-sector companies and government services, and for both privately owned and publicly owned firms. Controversy has arisen over what categories of employment to impose quotas on, and whether promotions *and* initial appointments should be by quota.

Determining the limits of group preference has become an issue for some national leaders and for the courts. At what point should other values outweigh ethnic-group equality? The principle that preferences should be given to *local* people conflicts, for example, with the principle of *national* citizenship. Mrs Gandhi said:

This is a matter in which one has to have a certain balance. While we stand for the principle that any Indian should be able to work in any part of India, at the same time it is true that if a large number of people came from outside to seek employment ... that is bound to create tension in that area. Therefore, while I do not like the idea of having such a rule, one [must] have some balance and see that the local people are not deprived of employment. [Weiner and Katzenstein, 1981, p. 25.]

But at what point do ethnic claims conflict with meritocratic principles? When is the efficiency of an institution reduced if appointments are made on the basis of ethnic membership rather than on individual merit? Heads of public-sector firms have pressed for exclusion of certain categories of employment (by skill level or rank) from reservations, but what is an acceptable 'balance' to the manager is often not an acceptable balance to ethnic communities.

What preferences and for whom thus are political matters, resolved not by legal doctrines or general principles but in the political arena, with struggles in the streets, at the polls, within the government bureaucracy and in state legislatures. Concessions granted to one group then become the basis of demands by another.

3. *Mobilisation.* Because the question of what groups are to be given preferences is constitutionally and politically open, the demand for preferences becomes a device for political mobilisation. Politicians can mobilise members of their caste, religious, or linguistic community around the demand for inclusion on the list of those to be given preferences. Leaders of ethnic groups and their supporters have demanded preferences either on the grounds that they are economically backward or that they have suffered from discrimination as a result of their low status in the caste hierarchy, or both.

As an issue around which to organise ethnic groups, the demand for reservations has been highly effective. This is particularly true in the case of the backward castes—a variety of groups diverse in their occupations, income, education and size who have banded together politically (especially in northern India) around the claim for preferential treatment. Similarly, it has been a unifying demand for autochthonous groups (of many castes and religious affiliations) united in their opposition to 'outsiders'.

4. *Backlash.* As preferences were extended to backward castes, and as more benefits were given to scheduled castes and scheduled tribes, the 'forward' castes have mobilised in opposition. In the state of Gujarat, for example, upper-caste students launched a movement to end preferences for the scheduled castes; meanwhile, in Bihar, the upper castes won the support of the scheduled castes to oppose reservations for the backward castes. Increasingly, political groups are organising either to resist the further expansion of preferences or to oppose those in place.

One reason for the backlash is an awareness that some individuals receiving preferences are not themselves from educationally backward or economically deprived families. The more successful reservations are in producing a middle class within the backward community, the more such cases increase and the more resentful are members of communities denied reservations.

5. *Supernumerary positions.* As the number of reservations increase, categories are expanded and a backlash emerges, governments seek to reduce ethnic conflict by creating supernumerary positions, both in education and in employment. In Andhra, for example, when the state government agreed to reserve admissions to Osmania University in proportion to the number of people residing in each district of the state (a policy intended to increase the proportion of students from the backward western districts and reduce the number from the more advanced eastern districts), the government mollified the losers by creating another university, one that would be open to everyone in the state without regard to place of birth or residence. Similarly, when the state government agreed to establish regional representation in appointments to the administrative services, it created supernumerary positions in order not to fire those who came from 'overrepresented' districts. In Gujarat, when the forward castes agitated against reservations for scheduled castes and tribes in the medical schools, the state government agreed to expand admissions in proportion to the number of reservations, so the forward castes would not feel deprived by the admission of scheduled castes and tribes.

6. *Institutional opposition.* The need by institutions—private and public firms, government departments, hospitals, universities and research organisations—for individuals of particular skills and motivation are sometimes at variance with the requirement that appointments and promotions be based on membership in an ethnic group. Institutions may fight for the exclusion of certain categories from the system of reservations or resist the allocation of a particular position to a less qualified member of a scheduled caste, tribe or backward caste. Alternatively, heads of institutions may take the supernumerary route, make more appointments than are needed so that double appointments can be made, one for the reserved candidate and the second for a more skilled person who can do the work and exercise genuine authority. The result is often bitterness on the part of those holding the reserved slot that they have been given rank without actual responsibility, and resentfulness on the part of others that they have been given responsibility without commensurate rank and salary.

7. *Intra-group conflict.* Preferences may lead to conflicts within ethnic groups as to whether reservations are allocated fairly. Since the ethnic category to which preferences have been given is often a composite of numerous ethnic groups, tension develops when an ethnic group receives

more benefits than another. If the winners in the competition for reserved positions come predominantly from one identifiable ethnic group (say, Christian tribals as against non-Christian, or the Oraon tribe as against the Mundas, or the Mahar caste of ex-untouchables as against the Chamars), demands may be made for subdividing preferences or for dropping one or more groups from the list. As we have noted, some Hindu tribals want to exclude Christian tribals, and some scheduled castes want to exclude those converted to Christianity or Buddhism or to Islam. Some critics have called for the application of socio-economic criteria to individuals so as to exclude from benefits the children of prosperous members of the community. Understandably, the advanced sections of the targeted community resist proposals that deprive them of benefits, by emphasising the demands that unite their ethnic group. For this reason, it is not uncommon for the advanced sections to be among the most militant in their espousal of ethnic-group rights.

8. *Social marking.* The policies strengthen ethnic-group membership by establishing a new form of social marking: individuals are labelled in the occupational structure in terms of the community from which they come. This marking may ensure greater access to education, employment and, in some instances, promotion, but it makes social mobility contingent upon membership in an ethnic group. Individuals are what they are because of the group they belong to—a statement that once described an individual's subordinate status but which now explains (and even facilitates) mobility. There is a kind of justice; the same principle that prevented mobility has become an instrument for mobility.

An Oraon tribesman, for example, a college graduate now employed in a government department, told me that he is looked down upon because the community to which he belongs is regarded by caste Hindus as primitive. He concluded that he could only raise his social status when the social status of his entire tribe was raised. A hierarchical system based upon caste ranking does not easily permit individuals to escape their status. Individuals are treated with condescension or deference, as impure or pure, because of their native community. This powerful linkage of individual status to community status is an element that makes the system of preferences based upon group membership as acceptable as it is. For lower castes, reservations facilitate educational and occupational mobility, but they do not remove the stigma of social rank. An ex-untouchable remains an ex-untouchable although he and 3.5 per cent of his colleagues in the senior administrative services are ex-untouchables. The preferential system thus helps preserve caste membership. Individuals are members of scheduled castes or scheduled tribes or backward castes no matter what level of education they possess, what income they earn, what occupation they practise or what authority they exercise.

Supporters of the system argue that in a hierarchical society based upon inequality, the introduction of the merit principle would worsen inequalities, that equality among ethnic groups can take place only when individuals are accorded education and employment on the basis of the ascriptive group they belong to. Preferential policies may deepen ethnic attachments, but they can also be viewed as an adaptation to the demand for equality in a society which has a tradition of hierarchy, where status and benefits historically have been allocated on the basis of group membership and group relationships.

IV

Once the principle of preferences along ethnic lines is a feature of public policy, the Indian experience suggests that it further facilitates the mobilisation of groups to demand preferences or their extension, as well as creating political struggles over how the state should allocate benefits to ethnic groups, generating a backlash on the part of those ethnic groups excluded from benefits, intensifying the militancy of the beneficiaries and reinforcing the importance of ascription as the principle of choice for allocating social benefits and facilitating mobility. A major consequence of preferential policies, therefore, is that they create a political process, influencing the ways in which groups organise, the demands they make, the issues over which policies are debated and the coalitions formed. From a political perspective, it is the impact of preferences on ethnic group cohesion, group status and political mobilisation that are significant. Preferential policies are not intended to destroy the system of caste or other kinds of ethnic hierarchy but to improve the position of groups within the hierarchy. The purpose of such policies is not only to facilitate the movement of some individuals upward but to move an entire group within the hierarchy. Positional change, not individual mobility, is the aim.

Integration thus has a quite different meaning in a hierarchical social order than it does in a society concerned with equality of opportunity and treatment. The mixing of children in schools and of families in neighbourhoods, so central to the American concept of integration, is not a goal in India, where it is assumed that linguistic and caste groups may attend their own schools and live in their own quarters. The proponents of 'integration' in India envisage a social order in which each group has a proportional share of benefits and statutes, not that they necessarily mix together socially.

By now it should be clear that the political process set in motion by adoption of preferential policies in India is not confined to India. Even though American courts have abjured quotas, in practice, policy skirts close to the principle of group rights, and many of the same questions raised in India have been raised in the United States as well.

To what groups should preferences be given—blacks, native Indians, Hispanics, Orientals, women?

What ethnic groups should be classified under each category? Are Portuguese and Brazilians to be classified as Hispanics? Should well-educated Chilean and Argentinian refugees be included, along with less educated Chicanos and Puerto Ricans? Should African students who recently settled in the United States be included in 'blacks'? Should recent migrants from Taiwan, Vietnam, South Korea or India be included in 'Orientals'?

What constitutes group membership? What degree of consanguinity makes one an Indian or a black or an Oriental? What *is* a Hispanic? A surname? Can one become Hispanic through marriage?

What preferences should be granted? Promotions as well as hiring? Membership on the law school journal as well as admission to the law school?

Should individuals be given preferences even when they do not come from disadvantaged families and have themselves never personally been disadvantaged?

How far should an institution modify its admissions, employment or promotion criteria to meet group quotas?

With respect to the kinds of positions, might reservations undermine efficiency by the appointment of less qualified individuals?

At what point do appointments based upon affirmative action goals or quotas become discriminatory against others?

The issues raised by preferential policies are not only for the courts, legislatures and administrative agencies but among and within ethnic groups and within each institution engaged in the process of recruitment, hiring and promotion. Thus, both 'mini-political processes' and a national political process are created around these issues.

The many similarities between the Indian and the American experience suggest that there is a political logic to preferential policies. However great the differences between the social systems of the two countries, and however different the effects of preferential policies on group equality, there is a convergence with respect to the kind of political process produced by preferential policies. It is this convergence that leads to the positing of three questions for those who argue for the use of preferential policies, ethnic group rights and equality of results:

1. Is the kind of society produced by a system of ethnic-group preferences more just than the society that might be produced by other kinds of policies intended to reduce ethnic differences?
2. If a policy of ethnic-group preferences is put in place, is it politically possible to place limits on who receives preferences, and what kind?
3. If preferential policies are adopted, how, if at all, can they ever be terminated?

Supporters of preferential policies may well reply that what ultimately matters is whether the policies work. Are these policies better able than other policies to reduce the gap separating the well-being of one ethnic group from another? Opponents of preferential policies must, in turn, demonstrate that alternative policies are available—within their framework of individual rights and a commitment to the goal of equal opportunity—that will bring about a more equitable distribution of social benefits.

The position one takes in this debate may ultimately depend upon whether one believes it is possible to create a social order in which the significance of ethnic-group membership in gaining equal access to education and employment can be substantially reduced, or even eliminated. Those who think it can be reduced or eliminated will prefer ethnic-blind social policies and oppose preferences as a policy that will merely reinforce ethnic differences. Those who believe that an ethnic-blind society is not possible, and that people can be educated, hired and promoted on the basis of their group membership will advocate preferences as the most feasible way of reducing ethnic inequalities. They will see the policy issues and political controversies discussed in this chapter as an acceptable cost.

On one point at least, both sides agree: no democratic political system can long tolerate a social order in which the major educational, income and occupational divisions are along ethnic lines. The question is not whether but how these divisions can be bridged.

References

Timothy J. O'Neil, 'The Language of Equality in a Constitutional Order', *American Political Science Review*, vol. 75, no. 3 (September 1981), 626–35.

Marc Galanter, 'Who Are the Other Backward Classes? An Introduction to a Constitutional Puzzle', *Economic and Political Weekly*, vol. 13, nos. 43 and 44 (28 October 1978).

Myron Weiner and Mary Fainsod Katzenstein, *India's Preferential Policies: Migrants, the Middle Classes, and Ethnic Equality*, Chicago, Univ. of Chicago Press, 1981.

6 UNEQUAL GEOGRAPHICAL DISTRIBUTION OF ECONOMIC OPPORTUNITIES IN TANZANIA AND AFFIRMATIVE POLICY EFFORTS TOWARDS EQUALISATION

B. J. Ndulu

Introduction

Unequal distribution of income and the well-being of various groups of citizens within an economy is one of the most important and volatile issues in any polity. It is the basis of currently silent but potentially explosive conflict. Even at the global level, the current North–South dialogues are a manifestation, in broader terms, of the recognition of this potential conflict. It is thus important to understand the characteristics and roots of these differences and of the policies adopted to correct them through the equalisation of opportunities.

Statistically recorded differences in incomes and in standards of living are most often present in terms of class groupings that cut across ethnic and geographical lines. Progressive taxation is the most widely used instrument for dealing with this type of vertical inequality. The other type—horizontal inequality, which cuts across vertical groupings—is just as important. Politically, horizontal inequality is thought to undermine national cohesion (from the nationalists' point of view), and ideologically it is seen as numbing class consciousness and solidarity (from the point of view of radical political analysts). Horizontal inequality and its impact have received little attention, because of the political or ideological tendency to shy away from it. Slowly, it is becoming clearer that horizontal differentiation must be faced. Geographical differences tend to parallel ethnic (tribal, in Tanzania) demarcations, making the subject politically even more undesirable.

Nevertheless, this paper concentrates on horizontal inequality and Tanzania's attempts to correct it. This in no way is meant to say that we play down vertical inequality (since, ideologically, it is the key issue in Tanzania), but rather that the other inequality has long been in the shadow (though it is currently gaining prominence). Specifically, this chapter looks at the following issues in Tanzania:

(a) the extent of regional inequality prior to the affirmative policy era (post-1969);
(b) the bases of unequal regional distribution of economic opportunities;
(c) general affirmative policies adopted, and their impact;
(d) specific affirmative policies, their impact and problems.

The Extent of Regional Inequality Prior to the Affirmative Policy Era

Affirmative policies to reduce regional inequality were introduced in the post-Arusha Declaration era and, more explicitly, starting with the Second Five-Year Plan (SFYP 1969–74). Before that time, Tanzania maintained the colonial legacy of concentrating development efforts in areas already more developed than others, while neglecting areas that had not attracted colonial interests.

The extent of regional inequality will be shown in terms of four main social-economic indicators: gross domestic product (GDP) per capita; employment per adult member of the population; primary school enrolment as a percentage of children up to age 15; and health services relative to size of population in each region.

In 1966, the regional disparities in the distribution of GDP per capita were large. The poorest region registered a GDP per capita of 290 shs., whereas the region with the highest GDP per capita showed a level of 3,625 shs. (more than twelve times the lowest). The mean regional GDP per capita was 664 shs. The standard deviation was 733.50 shs., whereas the coefficient of variation (the standard deviation relative to the mean) was 110.4 per cent. The Pearsonian measure of skewness showed a positive skewness of 0.744. In terms of total GDP shares, the top one-third of the regions (based on per capita GDP) generated 50.2 per cent of GDP, the middle one-third 31.3 per cent, and the poorest one-third only 18.5 per cent. The top one-third of the regions included Dar es Salaam (with maximum GDP per capita), Arusha, Tanga, Kilimanjaro, Tabora and Shinyanga; the lowest one-third included Mtwara, Ruvuma, Singida, Kigoma, Dodoma and Iringa.

In terms of employment as a proportion of the labour force in each region (1967), the range was from 40.4 per cent for Dar es Salaam to 1.6 per cent for Singida (twenty-five times less). The average employment ratio was 7.3 per cent, whereas the standard deviation was 8.96 per cent. The coefficient of variation was 123 per cent and the Pearsonian measure of skewness 1.071, showing a very high positive skewness. Dar es Salaam is the main cause for this skewness. If one considers the five main industrial and estate agricultural regions Dar es Salaam, Arusha, Tanga, Kilimanjaro and Morogoro, the share of this group's total employment rises to 60.4 per cent.

The inequality in education was much less significant. School enrolment of pupils up to age 15 ranged from 17.7 per cent for the lowest to 50.7 for the highest region. The mean ratio was 32.6, whereas the standard deviation was 9.15 per cent. An extremely low coefficient of variation (28 per cent) was the result; the Pearsonian measure of skewness showed a low positive value of 0.109. Here, the regions with the highest ratios were Dar es Salaam/Coast, Kilimanjaro, West Lake, Ruvuma and Tanga. Those with the lowest ratio (of less than 30 per cent) were Shinyanga, Dodoma, Kigoma, Mbeya, Arusha, Tabora and Mwanza. Missionary schools played a significant role in reducing inequality, while size of population seemed to be a key factor in explaining low ratios in such regions as Mwanza, Mbeya, Shinyanga and Tabora. Disparities in secondary education opportunities were much more severe.

In the area of health (1969), population per doctor ranged from a low of 14,725 (Tanga) to a high of 111,450 (Coast, excluding Dar es Salaam, which also functions as a referral hospital). The mean ratio was 22,988. The regions with the lowest ratios (that is, the best served) were Tanga, Kilimanjaro, Tabora, Arusha and Morogoro. In terms of population per dispensary, the range (excluding Dar es Salaam) was 5,066 for Coast to 12,063 for Mtwara. The regions best served by dispensaries were Coast, Kigoma, Ruvuma and Morogoro. Generally, dispensaries were more frequent where there were few hospitals or where hospitals were scattered over great distances within the same region.

From these data, two conclusions emerge: first, economic well-being and opportunities were more unequally distributed than social services. Second, in general, the top one-third of the regions, in terms of per capita GDP and employment, also fared above average in terms of social services, whereas, for the bottom one-third, the statistics are reversed.

The Bases of Unequal Regional Distribution of Economic Opportunities

Three main factors can be distinguished that determined differences in economic opportunities and, indeed, in development across the various administrative regions of Tanzania:

(1) differential distribution of natural-resource endowment (land, climate and minerals) whose occurrence is determined by nature;
(2) differential economic and social infrastructural development in various regions over the historical period;
(3) government policies with respect to regional development.

Differential distribution of natural resources across regions is by far the most independent factor identified. Tanzania's most important natural resource is land. Agriculture accounts for the income of about 88 per cent of the population, and agricultural production for 50 per cent of the national income. The pattern of land distribution is a major determinant for differential development *potential* of various regions.

In 1967, J. E. Moore made a study of the relationship of land to population in terms of the capacity of available land to support, or 'carry', people. Using this study, three groups of regions can be identified. Kigoma, Mbeya, Rukwa, Lindi, Ruvuma and Tabora constitute the first group; members of the group have population-carrying capacity ratios above 2.5. These regions have the highest potential for expanding agricultural production. The second group, with ratios between 1.5 and 2.5, consists of Coast, Morogoro, Mtwara, West Lake, Singida, Shinyanga and Iringa—regions that have not yet reached critical levels of land-based population pressure. In fact, in some districts, such as Kilombero (Morogoro region) and Rufiji (Coast region), the potential for expanding agriculture is as high, or higher, than that of the first group. In the third group are Arusha, Kilimanjaro, Mara, Mwanza, Tanga and Dodoma—regions that are either near the critical levels of population pressure or that are already experiencing the pressure (e.g., Kilimanjaro and Mwanza). An interesting observation here is that the regions with high population-carrying capacity also tend to be those least developed in terms of per capita income; while those with critical population pressures often are regions with high per capita income levels. Thus, there seems to be no direct relationship between availability of land per inhabitant in a given region and the rate of its current utilisation. Therefore, as far as agricultural production is concerned, we must look elsewhere for an explanation of systematic differentiation of economic development.

In the case of land, a factor in addition to size is the land's climatic suitability for production. Here again, regions with stable, adequate rainfall appear in all three groups of regions in terms of per capita income. Kilimanjaro—part of Arusha, Tanga and West Lake—are in the higher GDP per capita group, whereas Ruvuma, Rukwa, Mbeya, and Iringa are in the lower group.

The major factor responsible for different levels of rural development seems to be accessibility to major export and food-consumption centres. The colonial governments (both German and British) had as their basic objective the development of the export sector, with growth of other sectors to support export production. The first regions to receive direct railway service were Tanga, Coast, Morogoro, Kilimanjaro, Arusha, Tabora, Kigoma, Dodoma, Singida and Mwanza; connected by steamer service to railway lines were West Lake and Mara. Within this group, proximity to export points, and the quality of land, further limited immediate, intensive agricultural exploitation to Tanga, Kilimanjaro, Coast, Morogoro and Arusha. Estate agriculture (sisal and coffee), and food production to support non-subsistent populations in the estates and major towns in these regions set the pace of development and were major factors in leaving other regions behind. Peasant agriculture was encouraged and developed in regions along the railway lines, especially the Lake Zone. Regions not served by the railway system could not be developed. It is only with the later development of a road network and the more recent railway development that they began to develop despite their high natural potential. Today, some regions of high potential in southern Tanzania are still hampered by the inadequate transport infrastructure.

The second important factor behind the inequality was industrial location pattern and policy. Most industries were located according to 'economic' considerations (Rweyemamu, 1973), taking into account transport costs associated with proximity to either markets or raw materials. Again, concentration of industrial activity was in the five regions. By 1968, Dar es Salaam, together with the Coast region, had 58 per cent of total net industrial output; Morogoro had 9.6; Tanga had 9 per cent; Kilimanjaro, together with Arusha, 13.7; Mwanza, 4.5; and the rest of the country, 5.2 per cent. In addition, industrial employment and related employment in such supporting sectors as water power, finance and commercial services were concentrated in these regions.

The third factor behind regional inequality was the local government-financing system. This is especially the case with respect to differing provisions for social and economic infrastructure. District councils had to raise their own revenue for maintenance and development of primary schools, dispensaries and feeder roads. A district with a low revenue base thus was incapable of undertaking adequate maintenance and expansion of facilities. Districts with a good revenue base could undertake a more rapid expansion of the facilities and of their development potential. The differences in the growth of services in different regions created disparities and regional polarisation.

In short, growth in the richer regions basically resulted from agricultural expansion, which in turn acted as a stimulus to other development. Regional development may be seen as a cumulative process: once development is initiated at a high rate, additional investment opportunities are spontaneously developed. In the neglected areas, the opposite process operates. Because of a lack of potential traffic, infrastructural development is not justified. Lack of infrastructure hinders attraction of investment and increased production, and the region stagnates at a poor level of development. Left unchecked, these processes result in polarisation of development in the country.

Affirmative Policies Adopted and Their General Impact

With the advent of the Arusha Declaration and adoption of a socialist ideology, equity became a main objective of Tanzanian socio-economic policy. Regional inequality became a key problem to be tackled. The Second Five-Year Plan (1969–74) contained the first major, comprehensive statement affirming action to reduce all kinds of inequality, including regional inequality.

Tanzania is a big country with diverse natural resources. For various historical reasons, the development of economic potential has been very regionally imbalanced. During the Second Plan the government will strive to redress the regional imbalance by promoting an economically effective regional division of labour which incorporates a much more positive role for regions neglected in the past and by so doing tap unutilized human and natural resources. [SFYP, p.9]

Although this statement captures the general direction of affirmative policy as far as regional inequality is concerned, more specific statements were also made on ways to achieve the objective.

In the case of industrialisation, the decision was to decentralise by shifting industrial development away from Dar es Salaam and concentrating on the creation of other urban growth points. In selecting industries, industrial location and promotion, the attainment of greater regional balance was considered critical. Decentralisation of industries would be achieved through cost reduction in several regional centres by improving transportation, decentralisation of construction materials, expanding technical education and training programmes to serve the entire country and developing markets for manufacturers located outside Dar es Salaam. Newly built-up market areas, each with an agricultural and industrial base, would provide the strongest dynamic for continued decentralised development.

In agriculture, production was to be encouraged in the underdeveloped regions through development of the infrastructure. The need to open new areas through construction of transport facilities was recognised, to provide development opportunities to areas where in the past the absence of facilities themselves prevented development. Pan-territorial pricing was later introduced to equalise earnings from unit production, irrespective of the disadvantages of poorly accessible regions.

Concerning social services, affirmative policies were enacted designed to remove regional inequalities. Primary education for all was targeted. The need to make limited hospital facilities accessible to people in all districts was recognised. To achieve this, an increase in public expenditure was required, especially in the poorer districts; but, given the local government, public finance system (where expenditure on primary education, health and feeder roads was financed by the district council revenues), the districts with poorer revenue bases were to be assisted by the central government. After 1972, with the abolition of district councils, maintenance and development expenditures for social services were disbursed centrally, allowing for shifting of resources from richer to poorer regions.

To move towards equality of purchasing power a National Price Control Advisory Board (later, the National Price Commission) would secure just, uniform price levels for basic consumer goods. A primary objective of the board is to prevent discriminatory pricing among individuals. The currently enforced pan-territorial pricing of basic consumer goods has resulted from establishment of this body.

The impact of these affirmative policies on behalf of less developed regions will be assessed through use of three major indicators before and after implementation of the policies. These indicators are GDP per capita, ratio of wage employment to labour force in each region and public consumption of services per inhabitant.

Table 6.1 compares regional distribution characteristics of GDP per capita in 1966 (before the enactment of the policy) and 1976 (after enactment), with 1976 being the latest figures on a regional basis. Although the standard deviation increased from 733 shs. in 1966 to 980 shs. in 1976, relative to the respective means, the relative dispersion of GDP

Table 6.1. Comparative Regional GDP Per Capita Summary
         (1966 and 1976 factor cost at current prices)*

Measurement	1966	1976
(a) Mean regional GDP per capita (shs.)	664	139
(b) Range: Minimum	290	749
(shs.) Maximum	3625	5545
(c) Standard deviation (shs.)	733.5	980
(d) Coefficient of variation (relative dispersion)	110.4 per cent	70.45 per cent
(e) Pearsonian measure of skewness	0.744	0.58
Percentage share of total GDP of		
Top third of regions	50.8	43.8
Middle third of regions	31.3	36.7
Lower third of regions	18.5	19.5

* Classification by size of GNP per capita.
Source: computed on the basis of data from Central Statistical Bureau, Regional GDP figures, unpublished.

per capita (measured by coefficient of variation) fell from 110.4 to 70.45 per cent. This shows a substantial decrease in the disparities of distribution of GDP per capita in different regions. Using the Pearsonian measure of skewness, the same result is obtained: the measure falls from 0.744 in 1977 to 0.58 in 1976.

The reduction in inequality of distribution is further shown through regional contribution to national GDP. The top third of regions (based on GDP per capita) contributed 50.2 per cent of total GDP in 1966, but its share declined to 43.8 per cent in 1976. The middle third's share increased from 18.5 per cent in 1966 to 36.7 per cent in 1976, while the lower third's share increased slightly, from 18.5 per cent to 19.5 per cent. The changes in relative shares suggest that the reduction in inequality in terms of GDP was due more to an increase in the contribution to GDP by the middle one-third of the regions than by the poorest one-third. It also suggests that GDP growth has been highest in middle-level regions, followed by the poorest, and the slowest in more well-off regions. A World Bank study in 1977 indicates increased inequality of income of small land-holders in all regions, but in regional terms, this is not borne out by the data presented here.

In terms of the relationship of employment to total labour force, the trend is also positive. As Table 6.2 shows, the coefficient of variation fell

Table 6.2. Comparative Regional Wage Employment
(as a percentage of the labour force)

Measurement	1967	1978
(a) Standard deviation	8.96	6.4
(b) Coefficient of variation	1.23	1.05
(c) Pearsonian measure of skewness	1.077	1.051

Source: computed on the basis of data from Central Bureau of Statistics: Survey of Employment and Earnings, 1967 and 1978 (unpub.); Population census, 1967 and 1978.

from 1.23 per cent in 1967 to 1.05 per cent in 1978—a smaller decline than the one of GDP per capita, but the dispersion is still quite high. The Pearsonian measure of skewness fell slightly, from 1.071 to 1.051, indicating persistent highly positive skewness.

The slower reduction of inequality of wages is due mostly to the continuing trend to locate new manufacturing plants in the more developed regions. Looking at Table 6.3, we see that the shares of manufacturing-sector employment located in the six major industrial centres (Dar es Salaam, Arusha, Moshi, Morogoro, Tanga and Mwanza) declined slightly, from 88.5 to 86.6 per cent. The increase in the manufacturing sector's employment share in the rest of the country was slight, from 11.5 to 13.4 per cent. The relatively faster expansion of wage employment in the poorer regions was more a result of an increase in the number of government and administrative jobs, due to regional decentralisation of governments.

Table 6.3. Manufacturing Sector Employment: Distribution

	1967	Share of total %	1978	Share of total %
Dar es Salaam	15,231	53.3	50.346	50.3
Arusha	2,439		6,169	
Kilimanjaro	908		5,264	
Morogoro	656		9,566	
Tanga	3,152		8,630	
Mwanza	2,995		6,640	
Subtotal	25,311	88.5	86,615	86.6
Rest of the country	3,275	11.5	13,457	13.4
Within subgroup 1, share of DSM (per cent)		60.2		58.7

Source: Central Bureau of Statistics: Survey of Employment and Earnings, 1967 and 1978 (unpub).

Educational opportunities, significantly unequal in 1969, were expanded most rapidly in poor regions, before universal primary education was introduced in 1976. Health services, on the other hand (especially in terms of population per doctor) were expanded most rapidly in the wealthier regions (World Bank, 1977, p. 21). In, aggregate, however the increase in public expenditure was an equalising force. Table 6.4 shows that the increase in public consumption between 1969 and 1975 was highest in low-income regions (73 per cent), followed by middle-income regions (64 per cent) and in high-income regions (44 per cent).

Table 6.4. Regional Distribution of Public Consumption (1969 = 100)

Regional group	1975
High income	144
Middle income	164
Low income	173

Source: World Bank, Tanzania Basic Economic Report—Annex III, Table 17, p. 23.

In general, looking at the trends of the various indicators, one gets a picture of the general effectiveness of the affirmative policies over the first decade of their implementation; regional inequality seems to have been on the decline in Tanzania. Looking, however, at the individual policies and their impact, and at some problems of implementation, adds insights that are important in any evaluation of these efforts.

Specific Affirmative Policies: Impacts and Problems

Industrial Decentralisation

A primary, clearly stated policy aimed at reducing inequalities in regional development lay in the adoption of a growth policy designed to spread location of industries throughout the country. As we have shown, earlier, before the Second Five-Year Plan, location of industries was concentrated in the five major towns of the coastal zones—Dar es Salaam, Tanga, Moshi, Arusha and Morogoro, as well as Mwanza on Lake Victoria.

Ten major regional centres were identified for the purpose of implementing the policy. Newly identified public industrial projects were to be located with a view to decentralising industries from existing centres, especially Dar es Salaam. Average income per inhabitant was calculated, and industries were to be located preferably in areas with the lowest average income per inhabitant, to achieve the goal of spreading and stimulating development in the less developed regions.

Yet this objective immediately raises major problems of implementation. The first problem is whether the infrastructure is adequate for efficient industrial operation. The traditional industrial centres had a well-developed infrastructure (a power, water and transport network) that had proved attractive for various industries.

Inadequate infrastructure raises production costs, interrupts production, or delays its start; and, of course, it leads to underutilisation and loss of capacity, the cost of which must be borne by the nation, either through forgone benefits from tied-up capital or through subsidisation of inefficient production.

The second problem is related to the location of raw materials and the market for the goods produced. Because of clear cost advantages, these two forces may predetermine potential locations for certain industrial projects. Large weight loss in production processes or high perishability of raw material limits a location to sources of raw material. Large weight gain in the production processes or high perishability of the product ties down locational possibilities to major market centres, for example, Dar es Salaam, Tanga, Arusha, Moshi, Morogoro, Mwanza and Mbeya. Ignoring the presence of these two forces subjects the economy to major economic costs.

Thus, right from the start, one faces the problem of a delicate balance between the economic costs of spreading industries to reduce income inequality and achieve regional balance. In Tanzania's case, a major problem seems to be lack of an evenly distributed infrastructure. Two alternative strategies present themselves as a way to solve the problem. One is to locate industries regardless of the current inadequacy of the infrastructure in less-developed regions and let pressure from idle capacity attract infrastructure investment in the areas. The cost to the economy is the forgone output of tied-up capital before completion of the infra-structure investment. The second approach is to undertake the necessary infrastructure investment first, then make the necessary industrial invest-ments. The cost of this strategy seems to be longer delay in achieving the equalisation objective, since there is less pressure for infrastructure invest-ment in the poor regions. Recently, the first strategy has predominated in Tanzania. New industrial projects in Mbeya and Musoma, for example, were started before development of adequate infrastructure.

Clearly, these problems have hindered implementation of the policy. If one compares the pre-1969 picture with that of 1978, a picture of negligible decentralisation of industrial activities emerges that is pre-dominantly away from Dar es Salaam to the other five main industrial centres—that is, Tanga, Arusha, Moshi, Morogoro and Mwanza. The other regions, due to the problems discussed above, seem to have experienced many more small-scale industrial developments than medium- or large-scale investments. Dar es Salaam's share of total manufacturing-sector wage employment has declined only slightly relative to the other five centres and the rest of the country (see Table 6.4).

Agricultural Pan-Territorial Produce-Pricing

In the agricultural sector, the government of Tanzania introduced uniform product-pricing across the country in 1973/74. Until now, only cotton had uniform pan-territorial producer prices. The main goal was to equalise income-earning opportunities for all farmers producing the same crop, regardless of their location. The policy was to subsidise those producers in regions of high transport costs relative to the local market or export point, and tax producers in lower transport cost regions, thus sharing the total transport bill between all the producers of the crops. Producers shared the transport cost bill and other marketing costs equally, regardless of their location; hence, they received the same price per unit weight of a given crop. Previously, distant disadvantaged regions receiving lower prices had their prices raised substantially, whereas locationally advantaged regions were forced to sell at lower prices than they would have sold at in the absence of the policy. (See Ndulu (1980) for a simulation model for studying the impact of the policy in the case of food grains in Tanzania).

The impact of this policy, especially in food grains, was to increase substantially the share of marketed production in the less-developed distant regions (see Table 6.5). Overall marketed production, though, did not increase for a considerable period after introduction of the policy. Among other reasons, crop-switching in the distant regions from cash crops to food grains (bulky and receiving higher transport cost subsidy per unit value) and relatively lower incentive for production in the taxed regions (since the increase in their producer prices of food crops were less than in the distant regions) accounted for the poorer overall performance.

The main cost of the policy, despite its achievement in stimulating production of the relevant crop in less-developed distant regions, was an increase in transport cost, which raised the consumer price. Since a larger share of domestic food supplies came from regions of higher transport cost, overall unit costs to consumers were raised. Although most food grains have subsidised consumer prices, the subsidy must be raised through taxation; therefore, the higher the subsidy, the heavier the tax burden. Clearly, if subsidies had been removed, the impact of the policy would have been higher consumer prices.

The second major problem with the policy concerns the general achievement of equalisation of earned incomes. The policy ignores ecological differences. As it happens, some poorer regions, such as Dodoma and Singida, while not distant from the main food-consuming and food-exporting centres, are poor in terms of ecology (semi-arid): yet regions with the highest per capita incomes, such as West Lake, are distant but ecologically well endowed. Because of this policy, however, West Lake is subsidised and Dodoma is taxed, though, to be in line with the objective of income equalisation, it should be the other way round.

The existence of these problems argues against continued, broad road implementation of the policy. Ways are being sought to minimise the distances various food crops must be moved by rationalising the distribution system and strategically locating processing centres in relation to consumption points. Some level of price differentiation is increasingly becoming acceptable to reduce the cost of such broad implementation.

Pan-Territorial Pricing of Basic Consumer Goods

To reduce differences of real incomes across regions, Tanzania has adopted the policy of pan-territorial pricing of such basic necessities as food grains, manufactured consumer necessities (sugar, kerosene, soap, etc.) and basic construction materials and hardware. The purpose is the same as in the case of uniform agricultural pricing: advantaged regions subsidise disadvantaged regions, since the total transport bill must be met equally by the consumers of the commodity, regardless of their location.

A lack of reliable statistics precludes quantitative assessment of the impact of this policy. Nevertheless, a qualitative assessment supported by empirical estimates may shed some light. First, let me present the major problems encountered in the effective implementation of the policy. The first, and by far most serious, problem is a general shortage of the commodities in question. Under conditions of excess demand, it benefits the distributor to limit his sales area near to the supply centre, since he would receive the same price regardless of where he sells. In so doing, he reaps greater profits, because the uniform price assumes an average transport cost in distributing the commodity to the country at large. Thus, unless a regional quota system is enforced, distant regions may receive only limited, or no, supplies.

The second problem is inadequate institutional structures for implementing the policy. Due to excess demand, shortages in distant regions put intense upward pressure on prices, a situation private retailers can easily take advantage of even though they buy supplies from regional trading companies (public institutions) at official wholesale prices. For the system to be effective, public distribution systems would have to be set up all the way down to the retailing level, or to the wholesale level, with intensive policing at the retail level, using consumers as watchdogs. As it turns out, this would not suffice at the retail level, for a new secondary retailing level by consumer-hawkers has emerged. A consumer who receives commodities from a public retailer (a cooperative shop, where not every citizen is a member) in quantities larger than necessary for his 'immediate' consumption re-sells the commodity to non-members at a higher price, and we end up with the same problem. Thus policing is required at this level as well. The more efficient and less costly way to implement the policy is to have adequate supplies, a condition difficult to achieve given the current economic situation.

In general, it appears that the more remote regions—those to benefit from the policy—have had more severe shortages, ending up with consumers paying higher prices than normal. In fact, in such situations, black market prices predominate. Of course, a minority of consumers manage to purchase commodities at the official uniform prices. The situation is not uniform across all regions. Where there is more policing and where public retail outlets are more numerous, the situation is less severe. Where consumers are nearer supplies, the official market predominates. In general, however, the effectiveness of the policy falls far short of its objective. The key to the policy's success, as mentioned above, lies in having adequate supplies or, failing that, more public retail outlets and better policing.

Public Finance Affirmative Policy

Before 1972, recurrent and capital expenditures for dispensaries, primary schools and feeder roads were financed by locally generated revenue. District and town councils were responsible for collecting and disbursing revenue. Hence, the ability of a district to maintain and develop its economic and social infrastructure was dependent upon its tax base. Higher-income districts were better equipped to maintain and develop their infrastructure, giving them a stronger base for economic and social development. The public finance system thus had a built-in reinforcing mechanism for polarising development.

With the adoption of regional decentralisation in 1972, but with all regional governments under the office of the prime minister, local governments were abolished and expenditures disbursed centrally from a national revenue pool. This philosophy of financial allocation moved from one of 'each according to ability' to 'each according to need'. A regional budget (incorporating district budgets) is compiled, then based on the overall needs of the region. Allocations are made from central national revenues. This system allows budgeting to take into account the objective of balanced development by allowing implicitly an interregional flow of funds. Under the local government system, such policies as 'universal primary education' and 'clean water to the whole population by 1990' would not be possible in poorer districts, given the districts' low tax bases.

The change in policy has impaired the growth rate of higher-income areas while raising that of poorer regions as expected. The narrowing of the GDP per capita gap is an indirect indicator of this effect, while the further narrowing of the gap in providing health and education is a direct indicator. The problem with the new financial system is the implied budgetary burden on the revenues of the central government, given a reduced direct incentive for the regions to increase generation of their own recurrent revenues. In view of the proliferation of new, centrally financed infrastructural development projects (mostly externally financed), without corresponding increases in recurrent revenues to cover recurrent expenditures, the maintenance capacity of the national infrastructure will be reduced. Recently, this problem has manifested itself through re-institution of town councils. But unless re-institution of the councils is undertaken with the provision that only part of total expenditures will be financed locally, with the rest being centrally financed, the entire basis of using finance as a tool for spreading development evenly will disappear.

Concluding Remarks

Regional inequality as an issue has been seriously taken up by the government of Tanzania in the post-Arusha Declaration period. Recognition of the problem was clearly articulated in the Second Five-Year Plan document, and policies were adopted for distributing economic opportunities and public consumption so as to reduce development gaps between regions. Some methods used in the equalisation effort were the establishment of several regional growth bases for decentralising development, uniform pricing (agricultural on the earnings side and basic consumer goods to minimise differentiation of the purchasing power of a shilling) and public finance. These methods have had some degree of success, but they have also given rise to new problems centering on the trade-off between efficiency and equality. In some cases (such as pan-territorial pricing) the problems are more serious, in that the policy is counter-productive because of either blanket application (agricultural) or ineffective implementation (consumer goods).

Viewing the record in the decade 1969–79, we can see that regional inequality was reduced through the deliberate use of affirmative policies. The successes in this period look remarkable. The main worry is whether the movement's momentum can be maintained, given the country's resource gaps (made wider by implications of inefficiencies in equalisation policies and implementation). One thing is clear, however: the inability to finance expansion of new capacity in the short run may arrest decentralisation. Nevertheless, in the long run, the expectation is for continued implementation of decentralisation of economic development.

7 UNIVERSITY ADMISSIONS AND ETHNIC TENSION IN SRI LANKA, 1977-82

*K. M. de Silva**

Few issues have contributed more substantially and dramatically to the sharp deterioration of ethnic relations in Sri Lanka in the last decade, or to radicalising the politics of the Tamil areas in the north and east of the island, than the question of university admissions. C. R. de Silva, who has pioneered research in the complexities of this problem and its political implications in the Sri Lankan context, has provided a cogently argued paper on its origins. This author's task is the much simpler one of explaining how the present government coped with this poisoned chalice which it inherited when it came to power in 1977. The background needs briefly sketching in, however, and the published papers of C. R. de Silva will provide that. To begin with a brief extract from one of his papers:

Education, especially university education, is a key channel of social mobility in most developing countries and hence the distribution of opportunities for higher education is often regarded as the distribution of future wealth, status and power. In countries like Sri Lanka where university education is available only to a small minority, the competition . . . becomes . . . intense. Further problems arise, when in the context of a plural society each ethnic and religious group tends to evaluate the ratio of university admissions obtained by its members as an index of equality of opportunity or of discrimination. University admissions thus cease to be the exclusive preserve of academics and become the concern of politicians and leaders of various groups and interests.[1]

I

Sri Lanka's politicians have long regarded university admissions as too important to be left to university teachers alone. Since the mid-1960s, university places (that is, the number of students to be admitted to the universities) and the basis of admission have been settled at the highest political level—the cabinet no less. So it was in the 1970s, and so it is today.

* The author is at the University of Peradeniya and is a member of Sri Lanka's University Grants Commission, the body that at present handles admission to Sri Lanka's universities. The views expressed in this chapter are his own and do not necessarily reflect those of the University Grants Commission.

Dr de Silva reminds us that in the 1960s Sinhalese and Tamil replaced English as the medium of instruction in the higher classes of the secondary schools and political and sectional (ethnic) pressures on university education began to build up.[2] The rapid growth of secondary education has resulted in intense competition for entry into the universities, especially to the prestigious University of Ceylon at Peradeniya. Such political pressure as there was in the 1960s was for expanding the universities to accommodate an ever-increasing number of students. There was as yet no questioning of the procedure for admission to the universities: that came with the victory of the United Front coalition in 1970, and when it came it was quickly recognised as part of the wider problem of Sinhalese–Tamil rivalry in language, employment, and education. The crux of the problem was that the indigenous Tamils, who constitute no more than a tenth of the island's total population, had for years enjoyed a dominant position in the science-based faculties. This position was facilitated by the Tamils' higher rate of literacy in English and by the excellent facilities for science education in the schools of Jaffna District, from which many of them entered the universities. In 1970, for instance, the Tamils gained just over 35 per cent of the admissions to the science-based faculties; in engineering and medicine it was about 40 per cent.

With the change in the medium of instruction from English to the indigenous languages, there were, in effect, two distinct streams of students seeking admission to the university: one educated in Sinhalese and the other in Tamil. (There was also a much smaller 'English stream', consisting of students of almost all ethnic groups.) Because examiners marked in one or another of these streams and not both, it was only a matter of time before the superior performance record of the Tamils was attributed to deliberate over-marking by Tamil examiners. In fact, this was what had happened when, in 1970, a rumour that the Tamils had obtained almost 60 per cent of the admissions to the engineering faculty of the University of Ceylon at Peradeniya triggered a major change of policy on university admissions.

The allegation of favouritism among Tamil examiners was investigated but although no evidence was found to substantiate such a charge, the government decided to change the existing basis of admission. The change took the form of a lower qualifying mark for Sinhalese medium students, so that a 'politically acceptable' proportion of Tamil students could be admitted to the university.[3] The significance of this policy change was that 'at long last the principle of choice of candidates for university education on the basis of their academic performance, as reflected in the raw marks, had been successfully challenged.'[4]

Although Tamil leaders protested strongly against the 'iniquitous nature of differential "qualifying marks" for Sinhalese and Tamil candidates, the immediate effect of the change in terms of the number of Tamil students admitted to science-based faculties was marginal—a drop from 35.3 to 33.6 per cent and an actual increase in the aggregate from 337 to 339'.[5]

As Dr de Silva points out:

the real significance of the change in 1971 does not lie in these figures. It marked the ascendancy of a group of Sinhalese [officials and advisers] in the Ministry of Education, a group which firmly believed that some adjusting mechanism was necessary to give Sinhalese students a chance in competing for the coveted places in science-based courses at the university. (During the period 1972–8 all existing universities on the island were merged into one monolithic university, the University of Sri Lanka.) This group came up with the suggestion for 'media-wise' standardisation for the 1973 admissions.[6]

Under media-wise standardisation, all marks are reduced to a uniform scale so that in the end the number qualifying in each language is proportionate to the number sitting for the examination in that medium. It was a device to neutralise the superior performance of Tamil medium students in science subjects, as depicted by 'raw marks'. The proponents of the measure argued that the difference in performance between Sinhalese and Tamil students must be attributed to differences in facilities, teaching, or marking that standardisation was merely a device to check imbalances. The fact that differences in the facilities and teaching available to students in a particular language were often as great or greater than any overall difference between the two languages was glossed over.

Once again, the immediate effect on the number of Tamils entering the university was marginal and far less damaging to Tamil interests than the acrimony caused by the change would appear to suggest. To quote Dr de Silva again:

The Sri Lankan Tamils, though they constituted just 11.1 per cent of the population, provided about 30 per cent of the science students in the secondary schools and the scheme of [media-wise] standardization ensured that this proportion of places in the university accrued to them.[7]

In 1972, the 'district quota system' was introduced, to satisfy, it would seem, two interest groups, the Kandyans among the Sinhalese and the Moor/Malay group. Each group regarded itself as educationally backward, and neither was content with the changes in admissions policy effected since 1970. So far as the Moor/Malay group was concerned, since most of them were educated in Tamil, standardisation pitted them against Tamils in the competition for places in that medium of instruction. Thus, they saw the contest as unequal. (Badiuddin Mahmud, leader of the Islamic Socialist Front and Minister of Education, was not unmindful of this group's interests.)

The district quota system was designed to allocate university places in proportion to the total population of each district. The scheme benefited the Kandyan regions and the rural areas generally, as well as the Moor/Malays. One little-known refinement of the district quota system devised to benefit this last group was as follows: the criterion used in determining a student's district for purposes of this quota, in the case of Sinhalese and Tamil students, was the location of the school in which they sat for the examination. In the case of the Moor/Malays, it was the district of their birth. Thus, a Sinhalese or Tamil from a backward district who won a scholarship to a Colombo school and sat the examination from Colombo would form part of the Colombo quota. A Moor/Malay in the same circumstances would qualify for admission through his home district, where the qualifying mark was substantially lower than that for Colombo schools. For the Tamils, the district quota system was a heavy blow; the percentage of university places in science that they held fell from 35.3 in 1970 to 20.9 in 1974, and 19 in 1975. In 1974 there was, for the first time, a substantial fall in the absolute number of Tamils entering science-based courses, despite a continued expansion in total intake into those courses.

The Sinhalese, however, profited enormously from this quota system, even though those resident in Colombo (and, to a lesser extent, in other urban areas) suffered a drop in the number of admissions. In science-based courses in 1974 they constituted 75.4 per cent, a figure that rose even higher in 1975, to 78.0 per cent. Because the Sinhalese held more than 86 per cent of the places in the humanities and social sciences, Sinhalese students were now in the same privileged position in the university as their leaders were in the national legislature. The Moor/Malays saw their number of admissions to science-based courses double between 1970 and 1975, even though they were still well below the magic level of 6 to 7 per cent— the ethnic quota which some of their political leaders advocated as their due.

Writing in 1975, Dr de Silva spelled out the political consequences of the district quota system:

The political impact of the district quota system has been little short of disastrous. It has convinced many Sri Lankan Tamils that it was futile to expect equality of treatment with the Sinhalese majority. It has immensely strengthened separatist forces within the Tamil United Front and contributed to the acceptance of a policy campaigning for a separate state in early 1975.[8]

The district quota base for admissions thus proved a double-edged weapon. Not only did it bring a sharp deterioration in relations between Sinhalese and Tamils, but it proved to be 'communally' divisive among the Sinhalese themselves. Firstly, it distorted the pattern of entry between urban and rural populations, between heavily populated low-country Sinhalese regions, where competition for places was acutely felt, and thinly populated Kandyan areas, where the minimum marks for admission to the universities were so much lower than elsewhere. Secondly, it resulted in resentment against the Muslims in both Tamil and Sinhalese areas and contributed greatly to the series of clashes between Sinhalese and Muslims throughout the island in the mid-1970s, culminating in a fearful anti-Muslim riot in Puttalam in 1975. And thirdly:

The quotas allotted to many Kandyan districts were swollen by large numbers of resident plantation Tamils whose estate schools gave them but a fractional chance of a secondary education, much less of entering the university. Thus . . . Sinhalese living in the Kandyan areas . . . obtained relatively easy access to the universities in 1975 by the operation of a weighted quota system. The high drop-out rate in the Kandyan provinces . . . [ensured] that these places [were] reserved for a relatively small group of . . . students, many of them from the affluent classes.[9]

Opposition to the changes was swift, vocal, and strong. Inevitably, it came from the Tamils; their views had not been considered or, if considered, had been given little weight. But opposition—more effective in terms of its potential impact on government policy—also came from the Sinhalese in low-country urban areas. The matter came up for discussion before the Sectoral Committee on Social Overheads, Mass Media and Transport of the National Planning Council, a cabinet sub-committee. The sub-committee submitted its report early in October 1975, recommending abolition of media-wise standardisation, and commented adversely on the district quota system and the rationale behind it, so far as this could be discerned in the reports and arguments of the officials who advocated it. The sub-committee did not take its criticisms to their logical conclusion, however, recommending merely the abandonment of the district quota system; quite clearly, the political forces favouring the district quota system were too strong for that. Eventually it recommended a complicated modification of the admissions system: 70 per cent on 'raw marks' and 30 per cent on a district basis, of which half, or 15 per cent was to be reserved for 'educationally backward areas'. When these proposals were submitted to the cabinet, only a modified district quota system was adopted; district quota places were granted to Jaffna and Colombo along with other districts, but media-wise standardisation was retained.[10]

However, even these modest changes were too much for a small, influential group of Sinhalese activists, the Sinhala Tharuna Sanvidhanaya (Sinhalese Youth Organisation), who strongly opposed the changes and who had the support of a powerful group of *bhikkhus* (Buddhist monks, members of the Buddhist Order). Their campaign failed, however, because the government stood firm against them. More significantly, for the future,

J. R. Jayawardene, as leader of the United National Party, pledged the UNP to the abolition of standardisation if the party was returned to power in the next general election. Modification of the university admissions policy, introduced in 1975, brought distinct advantages to Tamils, and their share of admissions to the science-based faculties rose by 35 per cent in 1975-6, with the total percentage rising to 25. To the Tamils, however, these gains seemed minor and intrinsically illusory. Too much had happened between 1970 and 1975 for them to feel that no further change would be hastily introduced to deprive them of their new gains. In brief, there was no guarantee that the advantage would be secure over the next few years.

II

The university admissions problem assumed such importance in the years 1970-7 in regard to ethnic relations in the island that the abolition of standardisation became an election pledge of the United National Party, then seeking to win power at the 1977 general elections. Indeed, abolition of standardisation was one of the first policy decisions taken (and announced) soon after the party's victory. Given all that had happened with regard to the controversy over university admissions in 1970-7, it was a bold political decision even for a government that had inflicted a stunning defeat on its opponents and now commanded an overwhelming majority in parliament.

To announce the abolition of standardisation was one thing; to evolve a new and viable university admissions system both politically and academically was quite another. Before it could set about this complicated business, a time-consuming, complex process at the best of times, the government had to cope with the communal riots that erupted unexpectedly in August 1977, the worst such riots since those of 1956-8.

Sri Lanka had hardly recovered from the riots when the university admissions question for the academic year 1978-9 once more became a major political issue. Ever since the abolition of standardisation had been announced, Sinhalese nationalist groups had been awaiting the release of the examination results, to scrutinise them for their ethnic composition. In the absence of a new policy on university admissions, the only one available was the policy in force before 1970, when the sole criterion was the aggregate of marks scored by a candidate. In a period of acute ethnic rivalry and incipient conflict, rumour-mongers found fertile soil. Rumours were afloat that the pendulum had swung decisively in favour of the Tamils and that the Sinhalese had been reduced to a minority in terms of admissions to the prestigious science-based faculties. One rumour held that few, or indeed no, Sinhalese students in some major state schools in

Colombo, which normally sent numerous students to the university each year, had qualified for admission in 1978-9. This rumour formed the basis of a concerted attempt to organise a strike in secondary schools in opposition to the abolition of standardisation. Organised for mid-February, the strike might have occurred had not an unscheduled school holiday been declared for that date. The closure of the schools averted a strike, and the arrest of the alleged organisers of the strike prevented the revival of plans for a strike in the immediate future. Among those arrested were some leading figures of the Sinhala Tharuna Sanvidhanaya who the previous year had helped organise opposition to the decision by the United Front government to move away from the rigid district quota system that had prevailed since 1975.

While the government stood firm on its decision to abandon standardisation, significant concessions were made to the critics of its policy of reverting to the pre-1970 system. First, in a move that could be described only as one of those rare, successful attempts to pursue two diametrically opposed policies at the same time without damaging its own interests, the government decided that, though standardisation had been abandoned, all students who would have gained admission to the university had there been standardisation should be admitted. Secondly, special consideration was given to students from districts which were 'under-privileged in terms of educational facilities'. The 3,700 students originally admitted on the basis of raw marks were now joined by nearly 900 others, many of them Sinhalese.[11] Subsequently, more than 250 students were admitted on a 'district' basis.

This classic exercise in pragmatism brought advantages to everyone. As we have seen, the government refused to give way on the issue of standardisation. Tamil leaders tacitly accepted the compromise, largely for the reason that the number of Tamil entrants to the medical and engineering faculties rose by 250 per cent compared with the previous year. Indeed, on the basis of the change, the proportion of Tamil students entering science-based courses equalled or exceeded the 35 per cent they had obtained under the system of open competition in 1969-70 and 1970-1. Third, those who had been agitating for an increase in the total intake to the university had reason to be satisfied; admissions were up 25 per cent. Fourth, there was also an increase in the number of Sinhalese entering the universities, especially from the rural areas.

The changes, however, were not regarded as permanent or even long-term; by mid-1978, the entire question of university admissions had once more become an acute political controversy, because many 'Sinhalese nationalists' were distinctly unhappy with the 1978 compromise. These dissidents argued that the Sri Lankan Tamil minority of 11 per cent could only have consistently obtained such good results by unfair means. It was alleged that at the 1977 examination many Tamil examiners gave excessively high marks to students of their ethnic group. Cyril Mathew, a member of the cabinet and the minister of Industries and Scientific Affairs, alleged in parliament that some Tamil examiners were deliberately and consistently giving Tamil students higher marks than they were entitled to. To substantiate his charge, Mathew produced six answer scripts in Sinhalese and Tamil from the 1977 GCE (General Certificate of Education) examination.

Shortly afterwards the minister was associated at a press conference on the issues with the vice-chancellor of the University of Sri Lanka. Mathew and the vice-chancellor urged that the only reasonable solution to the problem was to impose quotas based on numbers in relation to the total population for the various ethnic groups in Sri Lanka. Although there was no official support for the policy from the government, it is significant that it has been taken up enthusiastically by the Moor-Malay groups who will benefit most if quotas are introduced.

Once more, the university admissions policy was sent back to the drawing board. Once more, a committee was appointed (significantly, and unfortunately, the committee contained no Tamils), and with effect from the October admissions in 1979–80 a new formula was devised. There was no return to standardisation, nor to ethnic quotas; but the district quotas returned in a different form from those of the mid-1970s. The new admissions formula was: 30 per cent on an 'all-island' basis, 55 per cent on a district basis computed on the total population of each district, and 15 per cent for twelve specified, educationally underprivileged areas. In each instance, selection was by merit, determined solely by aggregate marks scored by candidates at the examination; that is, merit was the criterion in each of the three categories. In the case of the 55 per cent groups, aggregates for admission varied from one district to another. This formula, first applied in 1979–80, caused no serious hardship to the Tamils, whose proportion of places in the medicine, engineering, and science-based faculties remained about 35 per cent. The formula was used again in 1980–1 and 1981–2.[12]

It was soon evident that the formula had one serious flaw: in the special allocation of 15 per cent of places to the so-called educationally disadvantaged districts, twelve were from half of the island's twenty-four administrative districts, the number was subsequently raised to thirteen during 1980.[13] The minimum mark for admission in some of these districts was lower than that for the Colombo and Jaffna districts, where the competition was keenest, by as much as 100 out of a total of 400. In a situation where a single mark could make the difference between admission to a medical faculty rather than an agriculture faculty or a science faculty, this differential was seen to be grossly unfair. There were other disadvantages as well, especially the growing clamour from politicians in other rural districts to partake of the largesse distributed to the fortunate thirteen districts, an agitation based on the argument that by any standard of assessment their districts were only slightly better off in terms of schools, equipment, and teachers than the thirteen that benefited from the current quota on university admissions.

In late 1981 a new formula was announced for 1982–3. The merit quota had increased to 40 per cent; the district quota had increased to 60 per cent; and the 15 per cent special allocation was eliminated. The abolition of the 15 per cent allocation was received with a sigh of relief by those convinced that the pendulum had swung too far toward 'underprivileged districts'. Representatives from the latter group of districts put up a spirited defence of the 15 per cent special allocation but eventually yielded to the inevitable, with a plea that for 1982–3 at least, some slight adjustment be made to ensure that there was no drastic reduction in the number of students entering the universities from their districts. What these adjustments are to be is still not known.[14]

III

Few issues in recent years have caused more anguish or put greater strain on ethnic relations in Sri Lanka than the issue of university admissions and the examination procedure associated with it. It is an issue whose public debate seems to create the worst conflict, as became evident when this complex issue was discussed, acrimoniously and at great length, in 1978 before the Sansoni Commission, appointed to investigate the communal riots of 1977.

The two parties to this ill-informed public debate on a highly sensitive issue had very different motivation. The Tamils were clearly on the defensive, whereas the Sinhalese, who had raised these issues, hoped to embarrass both the Tamils and the new government—the latter for initiating the abandonment of standardisation and the former for alleged manipulation of examination procedure to the benefit of students in the Tamil medium. Confidence in this examination procedure was further undermined when some highly-placed Sinhalese officials associated themselves with these charges. The gains that accrued to the Tamils by way of a higher percentage of places in science-based faculties after 1977 appear all the more significant when set against this sombre background. But that is of no comfort to the Tamils; they cannot hope, by the very nature of conditions in such a sensitive area of ethnic competition, to retain this advantage for long. Their percentage of places can only go down, not up; and that has little or nothing to do with policies of discrimination. As education facilities improve in Sinhalese areas of Sri Lanka—

and the process is an inevitable one, even if it is somewhat slow and uneven—the Tamils' advantages will diminish rapidly in the face of the fierce competition they will meet. Nor are the Sinhalese the only rivals of the indigenous Tamils. Within the Tamil-medium itself, they face increasing pressure from the Moor/Malay group, who, firstly, have less than 2 per cent of the places in the universities though they form 7 per cent of the population; and second, over the next decade they will be challenged for places by the Indian Tamils who conceivably could also be the beneficiaries of a Sri Lankan version of affirmative action. Among the indigenous Tamils themselves, those in the Jaffna peninsula and Colombo face the competitive zeal of their fellow Tamils in such educationally backward areas as Mannar, Mullaitivu, and Vavuniya in the Northern Province and Batticaloa and Trincomalee in the Eastern Province.

Nor is there any guarantee that the present system for admissions or the examination procedure will remain unchanged. Changes are likely in both system and examination even if there is no return to standardisation. District quotas introduced originally as an avowedly temporary device have survived into the 1980s. Indeed, in Sri Lanka seemingly temporary devices often enjoy a longevity denied measures and institutions designed to last a long time. The anguish of the Tamils over the issue of university admissions stems mainly from a sense of deprivation, the sense—indeed, the knowledge—that the halcyon days of the late 1960s when Tamils dominated the science-based faculties of the universities are not likely to return and that present gains are temporary. Even if standardisation and the district quota system had not been adopted in the early 1970s, a reduction in the percentage of places gained by the Tamils in the science-based faculties would have come, gradually at first, but with increasing speed by the end of the decade; and in the 1980s, as the Sinhalese areas caught up with the Jaffna peninsula in terms of well-equipped schools, and would eventually have overtaken it. By stepping in to force the pace of this inevitable development, and by doing so in an obviously discriminatory manner, the United Front government of the 1970s caused enormous harm to ethnic relations while converting the university admissions issue from a controversial educational problem to a complex, emotionally-charged political issue, the consequences of which will likely persist throughout most of this decade.

Notes

1. C. R. de Silva, 'The Politics of University Admissions: A Review of Some Aspects of the Admissions Policy in Sri Lanka, 1971–78,' *Sri Lanka Journal of Social Sciences,* **1** (2) 85–123. The quotation is from p. 85.

2. Ibid., pp. 85ff.
3. The qualifying mark for admission to the medical faculties was 250 (out of 400) for Tamil students, whereas it was only 229 for the Sinhalese. Worse still, this same pattern of a lower qualifying mark applied even when Sinhalese and Tamil students sat for the examination in English. In short, students sitting for examinations in the same language, but belonging to two ethnic groups, had different qualifying marks.
4. C. R. de Silva, 'The Politics of University Admissions', p. 87.
5. Ibid.
6. C. R. de Silva, op. cit pp. 89–90.
7. Ibid., p. 90.
8. C. R. de Silva, 'Weightage in University Admissions: Standardisation and District Quotas in Sri Lanka', *Modern Ceylon Studies*, V (2) p. 166.
9. Ibid.
10. C. R. de Silva, 'The Politics of University Admissions,' pp. 93–7.
11. Each district was given a minimum number of places, nine each for medicine and engineering, six each for physical science and biological science. In the case of new admissions to the humanities and social science courses, it was provided that each parliamentary *electorate* would be offered a minimum of eight places.
12. See the Appendix for a statistical breakdown of university admissions for the period 1978–81 analysed on the basis of administrative districts and ethnic groups.
13. The districts were Anuradhapura, Badulla, Batticaloa, Hambantota, Monaragala, Mullaitivu, Nuwara-Eliya, Polonnaruva, Mannar, Vavuniya, Amparai, and Trincomalee and subsequently, Puttalam.
14. It now seems that, as of 19 January 1982, the change will not come into effect just yet. Political pressure from the thirteen 'educationally backward' districts has been too great.

Appendix 1. Summary of Admissions—1979-80 (Academic Year 1979-80)
(According to Districts, Courses of Study, and Ethnic Groups)

District	Arts (inc. law)				Commerce (inc. management studies)				Medicine and dental surgery				Engineering and applied science				Biological science				Physical science (inc. architecture)			
	S	T	Mu	O	S	T	Mu	O	S	T	Mu	O	S	T	Mu	O	S	T	Mu	O	S	T	Mu	O
1. Kegalle	80	—	11	—	31	01	—	—	12	—	—	—	16	—	—	—	18	—	—	—	21	—	—	—
2. Ratnapura	77	01	01	—	04	22	—	—	14	—	—	—	12	—	—	—	15	—	—	—	10	—	—	—
3. Anuradhapura	91	02	02	—	26	01	01	—	05	—	—	—	01	—	—	—	05	—	—	—	05	—	—	—
4. Polonnaruwa	37	—	01	—	15	01	—	—	04	—	—	—	03	—	—	—	02	—	—	—	02	—	—	—
5. Galle	112	—	—	—	43	—	—	—	18	—	—	—	19	—	—	—	19	—	—	—	37	—	—	—
6. Matara	90	—	03	—	29	—	01	—	12	—	—	—	16	—	—	—	15	—	—	—	21	—	—	—
7. Hambantota	93	—	01	—	28	—	—	—	19	—	—	—	09	—	—	—	16	—	—	—	13	—	—	—
8. Badulla	127	05	03	—	42	02	—	—	14	06	01	—	12	01	01	—	15	01	—	—	13	03	—	—
9. Monaragala	48	—	—	—	15	—	—	—	01	—	—	—	01	—	—	—	—	—	—	—	02	—	—	—
10. Kurunegala	175	—	06	—	46	01	—	—	22	—	—	—	22	—	—	—	24	—	—	—	37	—	—	—
11. Puttalam	44	—	—	—	18	—	—	—	07	—	—	—	09	—	—	—	09	—	—	—	15	—	—	—
12. Matale	31	06	07	—	11	—	—	—	07	—	01	—	06	—	01	—	05	—	—	—	10	—	—	—
13. Nuwara-Eliya	71	13	15	01	29	—	—	—	—	—	—	—	—	—	—	—	03	—	—	—	03	—	—	—
14. Kandy	124	12	15	01	46	—	01	—	18	07	03	—	20	04	02	—	22	04	01	—	31	03	10	—
15. Jaffna	—	128	—	—	—	41	—	—	—	74	—	—	—	67	—	—	—	100	—	—	—	124	—	—
16. Mannar	—	14	10	—	—	03	02	—	—	02	04	01	—	03	—	—	—	08	02	—	—	02	03	—
17. Vavuniya	06	10	—	—	04	04	—	—	—	02	—	—	—	02	—	—	—	02	01	—	—	03	—	—
18. Mullaitivu	—	09	—	—	—	03	—	—	—	03	—	—	—	02	—	—	—	09	01	—	—	01	—	—
19. Trincomalee	11	28	08	—	04	08	02	—	02	06	02	—	—	09	02	01	01	03	03	—	—	05	—	—
20. Batticaloa	—	58	23	—	01	15	06	—	—	33	—	—	—	19	02	—	—	51	05	—	01	16	05	—
21. Amparai	17	27	19	—	07	07	07	—	—	05	01	—	—	01	—	—	—	03	01	—	—	04	01	—
22. Kalutara	127	01	03	—	45	03	03	—	17	—	—	—	20	—	—	—	17	01	01	—	25	—	—	—
23. Colombo	183	18	12	04	77	03	03	—	60	18	01	—	66	07	05	03	81	19	01	02	103	06	02	01
24. Gampaha	150	02	—	—	86	—	—	—	24	—	—	—	25	—	—	—	28	—	—	—	40	—	—	—
Total	1,694	334	125	05	607	112	23	—	256	156	13	01	257	115	13	04	296	200	14	05	389	168	22	01

S—Sinhalese
T—Tamils
Mu—Muslims
O—Others
Source: University Grants Commission.

Appendix II. Summary of Admissions—1980–1 (Academic Year 1980–1)
(According to Districts, Courses of Study, and Ethnic Groups)

District	Arts (inc. law)				Commerce (inc. management studies)				Medicine and dental surgery				Engineering and applied science				Biological science				Physical science (inc. architecture)			
	S	T	Mu	O	S	T	Mu	O	S	T	Mu	O	S	T	Mu	O	S	T	Mu	O	S	T	Mu	O
1. Kegalle	89	—	02	—	38	01	—	—	14	—	—	—	13	02	01	—	20	01	—	—	13	—	01	—
2. Ratnapura	98	—	—	—	22	—	—	—	12	—	—	—	15	—	01	—	19	01	—	—	12	—	—	—
3. Anuradhapura	94	03	02	—	30	—	—	—	15	02	—	—	17	01	—	—	08	01	—	—	12	—	—	—
4. Polonnaruwa	42	—	01	—	12	—	—	—	04	—	—	—	03	—	—	—	06	—	—	—	03	—	—	—
5. Galle	117	—	01	—	29	—	—	—	21	—	—	—	24	—	—	—	27	—	—	—	23	—	—	—
6. Matara	108	—	—	—	40	—	—	—	16	—	—	—	22	—	—	—	12	—	—	—	23	—	—	—
7. Hambantota	89	—	—	—	28	—	—	—	15	—	—	—	16	—	—	—	24	—	—	—	18	—	—	—
8. Badulla	134	02	01	—	41	02	01	—	24	01	—	—	22	03	—	—	23	—	—	01	14	—	02	—
9. Monaragala	54	—	—	—	13	—	—	—	02	—	—	—	—	—	—	—	—	—	—	—	—	—	—	—
10. Kurunegala	190	02	12	—	42	—	01	—	22	—	—	—	23	—	01	—	22	—	—	—	15	—	03	—
11. Puttalam	86	02	01	—	27	01	01	—	18	01	—	—	19	02	—	—	20	—	—	—	29	01	02	—
12. Matale	48	02	01	—	10	01	—	—	09	—	—	—	09	—	—	—	08	—	—	—	04	02	—	—
13. Nuwara-Eliya	80	03	03	—	24	02	—	—	01	01	—	—	04	01	—	—	05	01	01	—	—	—	—	—
14. Kandy	132	10	09	—	39	—	01	—	23	04	—	—	20	04	04	—	30	—	—	—	24	—	01	—
15. Jaffna	—	122	01	—	02	40	—	—	—	53	—	—	—	73	—	—	—	55	03	—	—	75	—	—
16. Mannar	—	16	01	—	—	01	04	—	—	01	—	—	—	—	—	—	—	02	—	—	—	04	01	—
17. Vavuniya	03	10	—	—	01	03	02	—	—	02	—	—	—	02	02	—	01	—	—	—	—	04	—	—
18. Trincomalee	06	23	09	—	02	03	02	—	02	05	01	—	01	08	—	—	—	12	—	—	03	08	—	—
19. Batticaloa	02	71	04	—	—	07	02	—	—	09	02	—	—	10	01	—	—	08	01	—	—	08	05	—
20. Amparai	19	12	28	01	10	02	09	—	01	04	08	—	03	04	07	—	02	07	07	—	03	06	—	—
21. Kalutara	127	02	02	—	30	—	01	—	18	—	—	—	19	—	—	—	18	01	—	—	15	—	—	—
22. Colombo	200	12	08	01	88	03	03	—	93	15	—	—	72	16	—	01	102	12	01	—	109	13	01	—
23. Gampaha	150	01	03	—	83	—	—	—	24	—	—	—	32	—	—	—	32	—	—	—	25	—	—	—
24. Mullaitivu	—	17	—	—	—	02	—	—	—	03	—	—	—	02	—	—	—	03	—	—	—	01	—	—
Total	1,868	308	79	02	611	67	25	02	334	101	11	—	334	128	16	01	379	103	13	01	335	122	16	—

S – Sinhalese
T – Tamils
Mu – Muslims
O – Others
Source: University Grants Commission.

Appendix III. Summary of Admissions—1981-2 (Academic Year 1981-2)
(According to Districts, Courses of Study, and Ethnic Groups)

District	Arts (inc. law)				Commerce (inc. management studies)				Medicine and dental surgery				Engineering and applied science				Biological science				Physical science (inc. architecture)			
	S	T	Mu	O	S	T	Mu	O	S	T	Mu	O	S	T	Mu	O	S	T	Mu	O	S	T	Mu	O
1. Kegalle	103	01	02	—	32	—	01	—	15	—	01	—	14	—	—	—	18	—	01	—	18	—	—	—
2. Ratnapura	92	01	01	—	25	—	01	—	15	—	—	—	14	—	—	—	16	—	01	—	18	—	—	—
3. Anuradhapura	86	03	03	—	24	—	—	—	16	02	—	—	10	02	01	—	17	02	01	—	02	—	—	—
4. Polonnaruwa	38	—	—	—	12	—	—	—	05	—	—	—	05	—	—	—	07	—	—	—	01	—	—	—
5. Galle	98	—	04	—	36	—	01	—	20	—	—	—	19	—	—	—	23	—	—	—	21	—	—	—
6. Matara	92	—	02	—	29	—	01	—	13	—	—	—	16	—	—	—	20	—	—	—	14	—	01	—
7. Hambantota	105	—	01	01	22	—	—	—	13	—	—	—	19	—	—	—	22	—	—	—	11	—	01	—
8. Badulla	120	04	03	—	35	03	—	—	22	01	01	—	22	05	01	—	21	03	—	—	20	02	03	—
9. Monaragala	49	—	—	—	13	—	—	—	05	—	—	—	—	—	—	—	06	—	—	—	—	—	—	—
10. Kurunegala	180	—	05	—	38	—	01	01	21	—	—	—	22	—	01	—	28	01	—	—	33	—	01	—
11. Puttalam	87	01	02	—	26	01	02	—	19	—	—	—	21	—	—	—	23	02	—	—	30	01	01	—
12. Matale	31	04	06	01	08	03	—	—	06	—	—	—	05	01	—	—	07	02	—	—	14	01	—	—
13. Nuwara-Eliya	66	09	01	01	21	03	03	—	16	01	—	—	03	—	—	—	12	01	01	—	—	—	—	—
14. Kandy	156	09	09	01	40	03	03	—	25	—	02	—	22	01	03	01	28	02	01	01	29	—	03	—
15. Jaffna	01	120	02	—	—	42	—	—	—	54	02	—	—	69	—	—	—	77	01	—	—	126	01	—
16. Mannar	—	18	03	—	—	04	02	—	—	01	01	—	—	04	01	—	—	02	02	—	—	04	02	—
17. Vavuniya	01	13	10	—	02	02	—	—	—	02	—	—	—	05	—	—	—	03	—	—	—	05	—	—
18. Trincomalee	13	20	10	—	04	08	01	—	—	08	02	—	01	07	01	—	01	11	01	—	01	11	02	01
19. Batticaloa	03	56	05	01	—	14	08	02	—	10	06	—	—	18	—	—	—	15	01	—	—	20	01	01
20. Amparai	30	09	23	—	06	02	10	02	02	06	06	—	—	07	09	—	01	08	06	—	01	13	09	—
21. Kalutara	108	—	02	—	33	—	—	—	16	—	—	—	16	01	01	—	20	—	—	—	21	01	—	—
22. Colombo	194	16	05	05	82	01	02	01	70	24	02	02	79	06	01	02	107	20	03	—	103	19	01	03
23. Gampaha	148	—	05	—	76	03	01	02	23	01	—	—	24	03	—	—	29	—	—	—	28	02	—	—
24. Mullaitivu	—	11	—	—	—	05	—	—	—	02	—	—	—	03	—	—	—	02	—	—	—	03	—	—
Total	1,801	295	94	09	364	94	33	07	322	112	17	02	312	132	19	03	405	150	18	01	375	208	26	05

S—Sinhalese
T—Tamils
Mu—Muslims
O—Others
Source: University Grants Commission.

8   SINHALA-TAMIL ETHNIC RIVALRY:
THE BACKGROUND

Chandra Richard de Silva

Sri Lanka, widely known as an example of a plural society, consists of several ethnic groups—the Sinhalese who comprise 71.0 per cent of the population, the Tamils (Indians and Sri Lankans) who make up 20.4 per cent, and the Moors who total 6.7 per cent.[1] Other minor ethnic groups are the Malays, Burghers, Eurasians, Europeans, and Veddahs.[2] The two major groups, the Sinhalese and the Tamils, are subdivided along caste and regional lines. There is also considerable religious diversity, with Buddhists (Sinhalese) making up 69.3 per cent of the population, Hindus 17.6 per cent, Christians of all denominations 7.5 per cent and Muslims 7.1 per cent. As might be predicted, conflicts and tensions have occurred between these groups over the past century.[3] In recent times, however, caste conflict and religious conflict have subsided and tension and conflict have come to be concentrated along ethnic lines—particularly between the majority Sinhalese and the Tamils.[4]

Some historical background is needed to comprehend the factors that led to conflict and tension between these two groups. The Sinhalese speak an Aryan language called Sinhala. The first Sinhalese migrants arrived in Sri Lanka some two thousand five hundred years ago. Since then, they have eliminated or assimilated most of the original Veddah inhabitants of the island. They have also intermixed considerably with later Dravidian migrants from south India. Nevertheless, the Sinhalese have maintained a distinct identity, not only through their language but because virtually all of them were converted to Buddhism by about the third century BC. In time, a strong belief grew that Sri Lanka was the land of the Sinhalese (*Sihadipa*) and of Buddhism (*Dhammadipa*).[5] This belief was fostered by a considerable written and oral tradition. In actual fact, until about the eleventh century AD the theory was generally in accord with fact, and modern Sinhalese nationalists often refer nostalgically to that early period.

Some Tamils might have come to Sri Lanka as early as, or even before, the Sinhalese, though the available evidence suggests that substantial

Tamil settlement occurred some centuries later. In the early period ethnic conflict does not appear to have been an important factor. Sinhalese princes often fled to south India and returned with Dravidian mercenary troops to fight their rivals.[6] In fact, historians have suggested that the perception of the Sinhalese ethnic identity came later.[7] The situation changed somewhat after the rise of powerful south Indian Hindu states, beginning in the fifth century. From time to time, these states invaded Sri Lanka, and the conflict that resulted apparently aroused ethnic consciousness among both Tamils and Sinhalese. The Hindu Tamil population in the north gradually grew; when the Sinhalese kingdom on the northern plains collapsed in the thirteenth century, the Sinhalese moved south and an independent Tamil kingdom based on the northern Jaffna peninsula came into existence. This kingdom lasted from the mid-thirteenth to the early seventeenth century. Conflict between the Sinhalese and the Tamils during this period was sporadic, due partly to a long tradition of mutual tolerance and co-operation, partly because neither group had the resources to subjugate the other, and partly because of an extensive no man's land between the two groups—an area consisting of the largely abandoned centres of the old Sinhalese kingdom. There was considerable trade between the two areas, and Tamil officials rose to high positions in the Sinhalese court.

Finally, to the political developments of the twentieth century: the Legislative Council, which with various changes lasted from 1833 to 1931, never truly reflected the numerical proportions of the various ethnic groups in the population. Minority groups generally obtained more than their proportionate share of representation, a position that was radically changed with the introduction of universal franchise in 1931. Of the fifty elective seats in the new legislature, out of a total of sixty-one, thirty-eight were won by Sinhalese. This caused fears of Sinhalese domination, and the minorities devised a scheme whereby the Sinhalese would be restricted to half the seats in the legislature—a scheme bitterly opposed by Sinhalese leaders.[8]

Historically, the nationalism of Sinhalese Buddhists has been a powerful force, kept alive by their leaders through the centuries of foreign rule. Under British rule, and thereafter, it ran into conflict with the other elements of the island's multi-ethnic society; at the same time, it was the only factor that kindled the spirit of protest and resistance. The rural masses understood best the language of religion, race and culture; Western style nationalism was to them an alien concept. On the other hand, an all-inclusive nationalist movement, such as the one that emerged in Ceylon during the latter half of the nineteenth century, was both artificial and ephemeral. It was not broad-based; instead it was confined to a narrow class of Western-educated gentry. It was a weak, ineffective movement, for its constituent elements had at most times to consciously avoid drawing any kind of inspiration from the past. The past, it should be noted, was largely a record of internecine struggle. The Tamil invasions have long been a grim reminder to the Sinhalese of the danger they face of being overwhelmed by neighbouring Dravidian mainlanders. The two movements, therefore, seldom interacted.

That Sinhalese Buddhism bore the stamp of an all-Sinhala nationalism was evident in the very terms of the Kandyan Convention of 1815, when the chiefs of the Kingdom of Kandy in central Sri Lanka agreed to hand over the kingdom to the British Crown, which in turn, gave an undertaking that the Buddhist religion 'professed by the Chiefs and inhabitants of those Provinces is declared inviolable, and its Rites, Ministers and Places of worship are to be maintained and protected'. But two years after the signing of the Convention, however, dissatisfaction with British rule, especially among the chiefs—became endemic, and open rebellion broke out in many of the Kandyan provinces.

It was against the Sinhalese Buddhists that colonial foreign policy was directed—by the Portuguese, the Dutch and the British. (Christian converts of course received preferential treatment.) The British had no quarrel with the other groups—Sinhalese Christians, Indian and Ceylon Tamils, and Muslims or Burghers. Within a few years of the suppression of the Great Rebellion of 1817–18, Buddhist opposition began to be directed against Christian missionaries who were accused of proselytising.

Overt opposition to British rule broke out in 1848, again mainly in the Kandyan Sinhalese provinces. By 1848, the chiefs and *bhikkus* had been alienated, and even the lower classes were affected. The rebellion that broke out in 1848 was put down with the usual force and violence of a superior military power but, as the British governor Torrington himself sensed, it was the spirit of Kandyan nationalism that inspired the rebels.

Meanwhile, the work of the Christian missionaries proceeded apace, and by mid-century its success seemed assured. In succeeding decades, however, Buddhist leaders came to the fore in revitalising their religion by providing it with an intellectual, aggressive content. The Sinhalese-Buddhist militants preached a coherent, complete nationalism which expressed itself unequivocally in cultural, economic, and political matters. They tended, however, to place greater emphasis on the cultural goal and it was left to the leaders of the movement for constitutional reform to urge the cause of greater self-government.

Towards the latter part of the nineteenth century, members of the emerging English-educated Sinhalese and Tamil middle class began to take an interest in the problem of constitutional reform. They were more reformist, eager to obtain a progressively greater share in the country's political and administrative life. These urban, English-educated Sinhalese

and Tamils who were the mainstay of the Sri Lankan nationalist movement appeared to unite in sole pursuit of these narrow objectives. When
the two groups later parted company, it was because the Sinhalese leaders
felt the demands of the Tamils to be extravagant.

There were significant nationalist developments in the years that
followed. Temperance workers, led by the patriotic Buddhist leader
Anagarika Dharmapala, organised a campaign against the excise ordinance
of 1912. This movement, which had a mass following among Sinhalese
Buddhists, was directed against both the colonial government and the
Christians. That same year, a strike by railway workers received the
support of Anagarika Dharmapala and his followers. Sri Lankan reformers,
however, were lukewarm.

With the outbreak of World War I the question of further reforms
was postponed. There was a lull until May 1915, when deep-rooted
antagonism between Sinhalese Buddhists and Coast Moors broke out
in riots. Meanwhile, a militant strain of political nationalism emerged
under the leadership of a group of young intellectuals. A prominent
member of this group was A. E. Goonesinha, a radical who later became
the foremost labour leader of the 1920s. The objective of the group was
swaraj (self-government) and the league affiliated itself to the Ceylon
National Congress after the latter was inaugurated in December 1919.
Although Goonesinha pressed for self-government based on universal
suffrage, he made little progress in Congress. Despite formation of the
Congress and the consequent organisation of dissent on a firmer footing,
the two constitutional changes made by Britain in 1920 and 1923
remained a niggardly concession. The Congress opposed the communal
principle in representation, (which would allow a seat to the Tamils)
claiming it would 'result in keeping the different communities perpetually
apart'.

In the working of the Constitution of 1924, unofficial Sri Lankan
members, particularly the Sinhalese showed anger and contempt in their
dealings with European officials. As a result, a special commission of
inquiry, headed by the Earl of Donoughmore, came to Ceylon in 1927 to
investigate implementation of the Constitution. In its representations to
the Donoughmore Commission, the Ceylon National Congress had asked
for full responsible government; when this was not forthcoming, the
Congress merely expressed its 'grave disappointment', adding that it was
prepared to implement the new scheme, subject to certain modifications
which it would suggest. The new scheme had some attractive features,
among them the decision to abolish communal representation, and the
provision of ministers and their executive committees (the legislature,
called the 'State Council', was to divide itself into seven executive committees which would elect ministers), to be in charge of various govern-

mental departments. The minorities, however—especially the Sri Lankan Tamils—did not approve of the reforms.

The 1930s saw a decline in relations between the Sinhalese and the Sri Lankan Tamils. The latter felt that despite its safeguards for minority communities, the new constitution would expose them to the communalism of the majority Sinhalese. Therefore they pressed their demand for what came to be called 'balanced representation' that is, that 50 per cent of the seats in the legislature should be reserved for the country's minority communities. In 1943, Sri Lankan Tamils formed their own political organisation—the All Ceylon Tamil Congress—for the purpose of advancing their claims.

This tug of war between the Sinhalese and the minority communities eventually led to the formation by the Sinhalese themselves of a communal organisation. In 1937, under the leadership of S. W. R. D. Bandaranaike, the Sinhala Maha Sabha (the Great Council of the Sinhalese) was founded. It was the Sinhalese and the minority parties that carried Bandaranaike's Sri Lanka Freedom Party successor to the Sinhala Maha Sabha and its allies to electoral victory in 1956.

In the early 1930s an aggressive anti-colonial nationalism appeared from an unexpected quarter. A group of Sinhalese intellectuals and professionals, having imbibed Marxist teachings while studying abroad, returned and began voicing strong protest against the inequities of British imperialism. Through trade union action they organised a struggle against what they regarded as the exploitation of workers, especially by the British. Next, on 18 December 1935, they launched the Lanka Sama Samaja Party (the Ceylon Equal Society Party). The party opposed Ceylon's participation in World War I, and shortly after the outbreak of war, its leaders were placed under detention. Subsequently, the party's press was sealed, and in 1942 the party was suppressed. At war's end, the party, which had by now separated from the pro-Moscow communists and become Trotskyist in its orientation, resumed its activities, both on the trade union front and in opposition to the imperial policies of Britain.

However, the effects of colonial rule were not all unfavourable to the Tamils. For instance, the success of the highland Sinhalese in maintaining their independence up to 1815 resulted in distinction between the Kandyan (or Up-Country) Sinhalese and the Low-Country Sinhalese. The latter, being a more Westernised group due to their long tutelage under the Europeans, were better placed to seize the economic opportunities available in the highlands after plantations were developed there in the nineteenth century. They moved to the highlands as traders, contractors and entrepreneurs and often encountered the hostility of the more traditional Kandyan Sinhalese who found themselves outstripped in the changing political and social environment.[9] This enabled the Tamil community in the north to lay claim to being one of the country's three major ethnic groups.

Such claims were fostered by the influx of Tamil labour from south India to work on the plantations and to undertake some of the ill-paid and unpleasant work in the urban sector. By 1931 Indian Tamil immigrants outnumbered the descendants of the original Tamil settlers, and together the two groups made up 25 per cent of the country's population. The new immigrants were settled far from the areas where the original Tamil settlers (generally called Sri Lankan or Ceylon Tamils) predomin-ated and the caste composition of the immigrant group precluded close links between the two groups. Meanwhile, the settlement of a large number of Tamils in the highlands roused considerable anti-Tamil feeling among the conservative Kandyan Sinhalese.

By the early twentieth century education in English had become a key factor in access to the higher posts in government service and to the pro-fessions. The establishment of a number of Christian missionary schools in the north enabled the Ceylon Tamils to gain an early lead here. The growth of state schools in Sinhalese areas, especially after 1920, narrowed the lead but even in 1946, 33 per cent of the personnel in the elite Ceylon Civil Service and 40 per cent of those in the Judicial Service were Tamils. Together with this development occurred a sharpening sense of identity among both Sinhalese and Tamils. The religious movements that emerged in the late nineteenth century among the two groups were partly responsible for this development, while the growth of newspapers and literature in both Sinhala and Tamil languages re-enforced the trend.

The colonial impact brought many changes. Despite European aware-ness of the ethnic and cultural identity of the Tamils, administrative unification tended to integrate the Tamil areas into a united Sri Lanka. The development of road and rail transport had the same effect. On the other hand, local government institutions were slow to develop. Thus, at independence, Sri Lanka's new rulers had a workable machinery for governing the country.

Thus, even at the attainment of independence in 1948 some ingredients of a possible Sinhalese–Tamil conflict were present. A majority com-munity which had access to political power felt that it had not obtained its fair share of economic opportunity. In contrast, there was a minority community with a strong sense of identity, which feared that the eco-nomic advantages it had gained through the efforts of its members would be eroded by the use of political power by the majority Sinhalese.

Unlike the neighbouring subcontinent of India, or even Burma, inde-pendence in Sri Lanka was not accompanied by internecine struggles and armed conflict due largely to a political compromise among both Sinhalese and Tamil leaders. The compromise was based on certain implicit premises: the concept of a secular state in which all religious groups enjoyed equal rights, and the gradual replacement of English as the official language by Sinhalese and Tamil. Equal opportunities for both communities would thus be provided. Moreover, Section 29(2) of the *1948 (Independence) Constitution* laid down that no disability or advantage should be conferred on persons of any community or religion which were not conferred on persons of other communities or religions. Finally, there was a retreat from the 'equal electorates' formula which had prevailed from 1931-47. From 1947 twenty-five of the seats in parliament were distributed according to area. The formula was intended to benefit the minority groups who lived in more sparsely populated areas. Thus, for instance the Northern and Eastern Provinces, largely peopled by Tamils and Moors and containing some 13 per cent of the population received eight seats out of the twenty-five distributed for area, thus giving some weight in representation to the minority communities living there. Provision was also made in the constitution for the representation of 'unrepresented interests' in parliament by the nomination of six additional members.[10]

These arrangements did not satisfy most of the Tamil leadership at independence as the results of the general election of 1947 indicated, especially in the Northern Province. The leader of the largest Tamil political organisation, G. G. Ponnambalam, rather than sit in sterile opposition, joined the first government of independent Sri Lanka led by D. S. Senanayake. Ponnambalam's decision split his Tamil Congress. It saw the birth of the Tamil Federal Party which was to dominate Tamil politics after 1956.

However, there were two snags. Firstly, the political compromise was a considerable deviation from the idea prevalent among the Sinhalese that Sri Lanka was essentially the land of the Sinhalese and of Buddhism. The efforts of the leadership of the day to promote a Ceylonese or Sri Lankan nationalism as against Sinhalese and Tamil nationalisms did not succeed. The settlement thus did not have grass-roots support among the Sinhalese.

Secondly, the Sinhalese leadership refused to include the Indian Tamils in Sri Lanka in the political compromise. The Indian group included some Moors and others from all parts of India who had come to Sri Lanka as traders and money-lenders. There were also numbers of Tamil urban labourers. Most of them, however, were workers on the plantations. Senanayake and the party he founded, the United National Party (UNP), determinedly regarded the majority of the Indians as mere temporary residents. This was partly because Senanayake understood the fears of the Kandyan Sinhalese who feared becoming a minority in parts of the highlands. He was also alienated by the Indian leaders' opposition, first to the Independence Constitution, and then to his party in the general elections of 1947. Thus, by a series of laws in 1948–9, the majority of the Indians were removed from the electoral register.[11]

The disfranchisement of the Indians led to three important results. In the first place it upset part of the political compromise that ethnic harmony had been built on in Sri Lanka. Because seats in parliament were also distributed on the basis of one seat per 75,000 people, the exclusion of the Indians from the electoral process resulted in no decrease in the number of seats allotted to the plantation areas. What happened was that the seats went to the Sinhalese who lived in the area; Sinhalese representation in parliament after 1952 rose to about 80 per cent of the total membership. Weighting in favour of the minorities was transformed into weighting in favour of the majority community.

Secondly, part of the Tamil leadership broke away as a result of this legislation and formed the Tamil Federal Party under S. J. V. Chelvanayakam. The Federal Party provided an organisation for the more uncompromising Tamils. When ethnic tensions and conflict worsened in the mid-1950s, the Federal Party was the one the Tamils turned to.

Thirdly, the Indian Tamils felt that most of the Sri Lankan Tamil leaders had failed them. For them the key demand of the Federal Party—autonomous rule for the Tamils in the north and the east—had little relevance. They were unionised, but their lack of financial resources and poor educational background prevented them from mounting an effective campaign against the government. Eventually their leadership accepted, in consultation with the Tamil Federal Party, agreements negotiated by the governments of India and Sri Lanka between 1964 and 1974, according to which the Sri Lankan government agreed to award citizenship to approximately 46.2 per cent of Indians (and their descendants) living in Sri Lanka in 1948. The government of India agreed to accept the others, and by 1980 there were approximately 400,000 'Indian Tamils' who had gained Sri Lankan citizenship.[12]

The Indian Tamils on the plantations have been the most oppressed minority in Sri Lanka. Health and education standards are distinctly lower in the plantations than in the rest of the country. In the mid-1970s the Indian Tamils were harassed, evicted from plantations, and even starved. They were consistently discriminated against in land grants under the land-reform legislation of the 1970s. In many areas they were attacked by the Sinhalese in the riots of August 1977. Their leaders, however, have acted with great patience and moderation, partly because of the low economic status of the community and the low level of education among the people. Their leaders were also conscious of the community's immigrant status in an area dominated by Sinhalese. Whatever the cause, the result has been that while a rift between Indian Tamils and Sinhalese has existed in general, actual confrontations occurred more often between Sri Lankan Tamils and Sinhalese.

The four basic issues that fuel conflict between the Sinhalese and the Sri Lankan Tamils are (1) language and employment; (2) regional autonomy; (3) land settlement; and (4) access to higher education. The language issue arose in the 1950s. Up to that time the Sinhalese elite accepted that both Sinhalese and Tamil would jointly replace English as the official language. In the early fifties however, a movement originating outside the established political elite campaigned for the establishment of Sinhala alone as the official language. Fears were raised that with equal status, Tamil, as the language spoken in a large part of south India, would eventually swamp the less developed Sinhala language. The 'Sinhala only' movement was connected with a Buddhist revival triggered by the impending commemoration of the 2,500th anniversary of the decease of the Buddha, scheduled for 1956. Sinhala Buddhist activists looked round for a leader and in 1955 found one in S. W. R. D. Bandaranaike, a former UNP minister who had formed the populist Sri Lanka Freedom Party in 1951. The campaign gathered momentum, and by early 1956 even the governing UNP felt it politic to espouse the cause and announced some-what belatedly its conversion to the new policy.

The language question was perhaps the pivotal factor in the Tamils' loss of faith in Sinhalese leaders. Those who had advocated co-operation with the Sinhalese found their position drastically undermined in 1956, and in the elections that year, the more uncompromising Tamil Federal Party leaders swept the polls in the Tamil-dominated north and east. The Sinhalese nationalists, who gained a majority in parliament under Mr Bandaranaike, promptly passed the Official Languages Act, which declared that 'the Sinhala language shall be the one official language of Sri Lanka'. The Tamils feared they would be shut out of state employment and the professions and that their language and culture would gradually be strangled. Open fighting between Sinhalese and Tamils broke out in a settlement scheme in the Eastern Province, and Tamil demonstrators in Colombo were attacked by a Sinhalese mob.

Alarmed by the increase in violence, Prime Minister Bandaranaike and the leader of the Federal Party (S. J. V. Chelvanayakam), on 20 July 1957 negotiated an agreement that came to be called the 'Bandaranaike-Chelvanayakam Pact.' The pact provided for the 'recognition of Tamil as the language of a national minority' and that the 'language of adminis-tration in the Northern and Eastern provinces shall be Tamil.' The agree-ment also provided for a measure of regional autonomy through regional councils with directly elected councillors having power in agriculture, education, and the settlement of colonists. The Federal Party preferred to refer to the agreement as an 'interim adjustment'; for it still believed that a lasting solution to the problems of the Tamil-speaking peoples could only be provided for within the rigid framework of a federal constitution. The 'interim adjustment', however, took into account the main grievances of the party in the areas of preservation of the language and culture of the Tamil-speaking peoples and in regard to the protection of their 'territories' from Sinhala colonisation. The principle agreed on here was that even though there might be Sinhala people settled in the 'Tamil territories', the government would not disturb the demographic composition of the two communities as they stood, at the time of the signing of the agreement.

The agreement met with a storm of protest among the Sinhalese, and Bandaranaike was forced to repudiate it in May 1958. Widespread rioting led to hundreds of deaths, while thousands were rendered homeless. The gulf between the two communities grew wider. Bandaranaike made one last attempt to unilaterally carry out part of the pact. The Tamil Language (Special Provisions) Act of 1958 provided that specific regulations could be made to protect the use of Tamil in education, public examinations, official correspondence with the Tamil-speaking public, and in the administration of the Northern and Eastern Provinces, but for years, no such regulations were framed.[13]

In the early 1960s the Federal Party strove unsuccessfully to obtain a settlement. The SLFP, under Mrs Sirimavo Bandaranaike, proved reluctant to concede ground. The Official Languages Act was implemented on 1 January 1961, and public servants recruited after 1956 were required to become proficient in Sinhala to retain their posts. The Languages of the Courts Act of 1961 provided for the progressive replacement of English by Sinhala. Thus the Federal Party turned to the UNP, which promised to introduce regulations for the use of Tamil and to establish district councils in return for support in the elections of 1965. After the UNP victory of 1965, the first of the two pledges was redeemed despite strong opposition, not only from the SLFP but also from the Trotskyist Lanka Samasamaj Party (LSSP) and the Communist Party (CP), parties that had supported Tamil as one of the two official languages even as late as 1964. The government, however, eventually had to abandon its plan to establish district councils, although the councils were envisaged as possessing limited functions and working under the direction of the central government.

Meanwhile, there was the issue of land settlement. All governments since the 1930s have tried to ease population pressure in the south-west by developing irrigation projects to settle colonists in the sparsely populated northern plains. Since most colonists were Sinhalese, the Tamils tended to view such schemes as devices to convert Tamil-majority areas to Sinhalese-majority areas. The Tamil leadership claimed that the people of the area should have preferential treatment in land settlement. The Sinhalese opposed this proposal, viewing it as an attempt to secure large tracts of sparsely populated land solely for the purpose of settling Tamils. The increasing settlement of the 'frontier' region led to heightened tension in this area, and ethnic antipathy appears to have been greater in such areas than in Tamil Jaffna or the Sinhalese south-west.[14]

In 1970 the UNP, which had enjoyed broad support among Sri Lankan Tamils, was defeated at a general election by a united front of SLFP, LSSP, and CP. The united front, which obtained a three-fourths majority in parliament, proceeded to introduce a new constitution. To the dismay of the Tamils the new constitution not only reiterated that Sinhalese would be the sole official language but specified that the regulations passed under the Tamil Language (Special Provisions) Act would be regarded as subordinate legislation. Then again, the new constitution did not incorporate section 29 (2) of the 1946/48 constitution, which, despite its shortcomings, had come to be regarded as an important instrument protecting minority rights. The much vaunted section on fundamental rights, substituted instead, proved of no value as it was not justiciable. Then again, the judiciary was specifically declared subordinate to the legislature—once again causing concern among the minorities. Finally, Sinhalese Buddhist elements succeeded in enacting a special clause which declared: 'Buddhism shall have the foremost place', a clause strongly resented by the Tamil leadership of the north. By the end of June 1971 the Federal Party had decided to boycott the Constituent Assembly, taking the position that the new constitution of 1972 lacked the approval of the Tamil people.[15]

Around this time the university admissions crisis arose. Up to 1969, admission to universities in Sri Lanka was based on the final examination at the senior secondary school level (grade XII). In 1971, however, the new government, having reviewed the exceptional performance of Tamil students in science subjects, took the position that it was difficult to compare standards between the Sinhalese-medium and the Tamil-medium students and decided to set arbitrary cut-off points to regulate the quota of admissions from each ethnic group. In effect, this meant that Tamil students had to obtain higher marks to enter the science faculties. Because of the protests aroused by the scheme, the government changed its policy in 1973 to one of 'standardising' marks. It had various schemes of standardisation and district quotas from 1974 onwards, but the final result of all these schemes was to progressively restrict the admission of Sri Lankan Tamil students to the desirable medical and engineering faculties. Thus, for example, the percentage of Tamil students admitted to engineering courses fell from 48.3 per cent of the total in 1969 to 24.4 per cent in 1973, and 14.2 per cent in 1975. This led to considerable frustration and disappointment among Tamil youth in Jaffna, who pressed Tamil leaders to declare for a separate state.[16]

Sri Lankan Tamil leaders had by now begun to despair. Negotiations with the UNP and the SLFP over nearly twenty years had brought them few tangible results, and the new government used the insurrection of 1971 (which did not affect the Tamil areas) as an excuse to maintain emergency rule well after all danger to security had passed, largely to suppress the government's political opponents. At this time, the Indian Tamil leadership was also alienated by the government policy of distributing estate lands only to citizens of the country, thus leaving the Indian estate workers with no land or employment. In 1974, for the first time since independence, the Sri Lankan Tamil leadership joined with the Indian Tamil leadership (the Ceylon Workers Congress led by Mr Thondaman) to form the Tamil United Front. In 1975 the new organisation openly espoused the cause of a separate state and renamed itself the Tamil United Liberation Front (TULF). Although the TULF leaders pledged themselves to a policy of non-violence, sporadic attacks on police personnel occurred from time to time and acts of sabotage, including the destruction of a civil airplane, were attributed to a group of Tamil 'fighters' called the 'Liberation Tigers of Eelam'. Mr Thondaman was never reconciled to the separatist solution, for that would have involved a mass migration of his followers from the highlands to the north and the east. In the elections of 1977 he made an informal agreement with the UNP and swung much of the Indian Tamil vote to that party.

The victory of the UNP, now led by J. R. Jayewardene, marked the beginning of an effort to reconcile the two ethnic groups, but early on, there was a serious setback: the riots of August 1977. The origins of the riots are as yet obscure, but they were fuelled at least partly by Sinhalese frustration over repeated reports of successful armed attacks on the police by 'Liberation Tigers'. Inflammatory speeches by some Tamil politicians who campaigned (and won a sweeping mandate in the north) on a platform of a separate state for the Tamils aroused passions still further. Stories of attacks on Sinhalese in Jaffna, reminiscent of the rumours that spread in 1958, swept Sinhalese areas, resulting in attacks on Tamil residents in the south; attacks on Sinhalese on the north-east coast followed. The death toll was over one hundred, and thousands were made homeless. It was also alleged by government sources that SLFP infiltrators in the police and armed forces encouraged the looting, arson and murders. It was in the context of this particular conflict that a determined effort was made to effect structural changes to ease ethnic tensions. The changes were embodied in the Constitution of the Democratic Socialist Republic of Sri Lanka (1978).[17]

The constitutional changes mentioned above have enabled the UNP to seek support among Tamils on a large scale for the first time since 1956. Mr Thondaman, leader of the Indian Tamils, and Mr C. Rajadurai, a former vice-president of the TULF, have joined the government as ministers.

The UNP emerged as a political force in all Tamil-majority areas except the Jaffna district in the Development Council elections of 1981. The opposition parties have recognised the value of minority support under the new constitutional structure and have begun to woo the Tamils.

Nevertheless, a substantial segment of Sri Lankan Tamil opinion remains unreconciled, partly because Sri Lankan Tamils are convinced that structural change has not gone far enough. Article 2 of Sri Lanka's constitution specifically states that it is a unitary state, thus standing firm against federalism. Article 9 states that Buddhism shall have 'the foremost place'. Some constitutional guarantees, such as the requirement that all official publications shall be in Sinhala *and* Tamil, are not always complied with. It is also felt that numerous fundamental rights are inadequately protected by the constitution.

President Jayewardene made strong efforts to stem the Tamil United Liberation Front's demand for a separate state by having parliament enact legislation for district development councils in August 1980. The legislation is a modified version of the Bandaranaike–Chelvanayakam pact of July 1957. The two parties concerned in the Sinhala–Tamil dispute (the governing United National Party and the TULF) continue to wrangle since the legislation has yet to be fully implemented. Consequently important sections of Tamil opinion fear that the district development councils will never be able to exercise any degree of autonomy. Disturbances and clashes continue to the present day between the security services and Tamil militants in the Tamil majority Northern Province. The Tamils of the north and east have specific grievances relating to education, employment, and land settlement. They deeply resent the use of the largely Sinhalese police and army to maintain order in Tamil areas. There is as yet no indication that support for a separate state among the Tamils has declined. It is gradually being realised that structural arrangements are only a necessary, not a sufficient, condition for the easing of ethnic tensions.

Notes

1. The figures are from the census of 1981.
2. The Burghers are descendants of Dutch settlers; the Veddahs are the aboriginal inhabitants of the island.
3. For details, see *University of Ceylon History of Ceylon*, vol. **III**, K. M. de Silva (ed.) Colombo, University of Ceylon Press Board, 1972; Francois Houtart, *Religion and Ideology in Sri Lanka*, Colombo, Hansa Publishers, 1974; Robert Kearney, *Communalism and Language in the Politics of Ceylon*, Durham, North Carolina, Duke University Press, 1967; and *Collective Identities, Nationalisms and Protest in*

Modern Sri Lanka, Michael Roberts (ed.) Colombo, Marga Institute, 1979.

4. See a pioneering though controversial study by Janice Jiggins, *Family and Caste in the Politics of Sinhalese, 1947-1976*, Cambridge, Cambridge University Press, 1979, and Francois Houtart, *Religion and Ideology*.

5. Malalgoda, Kitsiri, *Millennialism in Relation to Buddhism; Comparative Studies in Society and History*, **XII** (4), October 1970, pp. 424–41.

6. Indrapala, K., 'Dravidian Settlements in Ceylon and the Rise of the Kingdom of Jaffna,' Ph.D thesis, University of London, 1966.

7. Gunawardana, R. A. L. H., 'The People of the Lion: The Sinhala Identity and Ideology in History and Historiography,' *Sri Lanka Journal of the Humanities*, **V**, (1 & 2), 1979, pp. 1–36.

8. See, for example, V. Samaraweera, 'Land, Labour and Sectional Interests in the National Politics of Sri Lanka', *Modern Asian Studies*, **XV**, (1) 1981, pp. 140–1; note: 50 elected, 8 nominated, 3 officials.

9. *University of Ceylon History of Ceylon*, especially pp. 249–61 and 389–407.

10. de Silva, K. M., *History of Sri Lanka*, New Delhi, Oxford University Press, 1981.

11. de Silva, K. M., 'Minorities and Universal Suffrage, 1931–1946', in *Universal Franchise: The Sri Lankan Experience*, K. M. de Silva, (ed.), Colombo, Government Press, 1981, pp. 75–92.

12. On the agreements relating to Indians in Sri Lanka, see S. U. Kodikara, *Indo-Ceylon Relations since Independence*, Colombo, Ceylon Institute of World Affairs, 1965, pp. 79ff.; and K. M. de Silva, 'Discrimination in Sri Lanka,' *Case Studies in Human Rights and Fundamental Freedoms: A World Survey*, W. A. Veenhovon (ed.), The Hague, Martinus Nijhoff, 1976, Vol. **III**, pp. 80–2.

13. For a perceptive account of the ethnic conflict and the language crisis of the 1950s, see W. Howard Wriggins, *Ceylon: Dilemmas of a New Nation*, Princeton, N J, Princeton University Press, 1960, pp. 169–269.

14. For further details, see A. Jeyaratnam Wilson, *Politics in Sri Lanka, 1947-1979*, London, Macmillan, 1980.

15. de Silva, K. M., 'The Constitution and Constitutional Reform since 1948,' in *Sri Lanka: A Survey*, K. M. de Silva, (ed.), London, C. Hurst, 1977, pp. 317–27.

16. de Silva, C. R., 'The Politics of University Admissions: A review of Some Aspects of the Admissions Policy in Sri Lanka, 1970–1978,' *Sri Lanka Journal of the Social Sciences*, **I**, (2), 1978, pp. 85–123.

17. Colombo, Department of Government Printing, 1978.

9 SINHALA-TAMIL RELATIONS AND EDUCATION IN SRI LANKA: THE UNIVERSITY ADMISSIONS ISSUE— THE FIRST PHASE, 1971–7

Chandra Richard de Silva

University education has long been a scarce commodity in Sri Lanka. The socio-economic survey of 1969/70 estimated that less than 1 per cent of the population had qualified beyond the grade 10 examination in secondary schools.[1] This pattern has changed since then, but very gradually. Even in 1970, only 1 per cent of young people in the relevant age category secured admission to universities in Sri Lanka, only a tiny minority of the population could afford to send their children to universities abroad. Thus a high premium was placed on university education. Social prestige could be gained by securing a university degree, particularly one in medicine or engineering.[2] There were tangible economic advantages, too. For example, in 1979, in the United States, differences in the mean earnings of people with an elementary education and those with a college degree in the age group 25–34 was only 84 per cent. In Sri Lanka, the difference was much higher: 164 per cent. In relation to the age group 55–64, the difference, at 396 per cent, was even wider in Sri Lanka, compared to 194 per cent in the United States.[3] University education in Sri Lanka, as in many developing countries, has provided upward mobility. The distribution of opportunities for higher education was regarded—as it is in many other countries, in Africa and in Asia—as the distribution of future wealth, status, and power.[4] Thus there is a tendency in a pluralistic society for each ethnic group to evaluate the ratio of university admissions obtained by its members as an index either of equal opportunity or of discrimination.

The problem is complicated by the regional imbalance in providing educational opportunities.[5] Secondary schools have tended to be concentrated along the south-west coast (largely inhabited by Low-Country Sinhalese) and in the Jaffna Peninsula (peopled by Sri Lankan Tamils). In contrast, the Kandyan Sinhalese, who live chiefly in the interior of the country, and the Moors, many of whom live on the east coast and in scattered groups in other parts of the island, have poorer access to secondary education. However, the question of university admissions did not have a significant impact on ethnic relations until the 1970s, for two major reasons. Firstly, until 1960, all university admission examinations were conducted in English, and the number of applicants was low. Thus, every year up to 1960, at least 30 per cent of those who sought entry in a given year could be admitted to the universities.[6] Furthermore, the existence of a neutral language in which the examination was held lessened the likelihood of favouritism in the assessment of answer scripts, because examiners had no certain way of determining the ethnic identity of candidates.

Secondly, the universities responded to political pressure for more admissions in the decade following 1958. The pressure was related to a change in the medium of instruction in secondary schools from English to the national languages, Sinhalese and Tamil; further, there was a progressive widening of the network of secondary schools. The enrolment of students in secondary schools in grades 9 to 12 rose from 65,000 in 1950 to 225,000 in 1960, and 351,000 in 1970. This led to the creation in 1958 of two new universities—Vidyodaya University of Ceylon and Vidyalankara University of Ceylon—to supplement the intake of students to the existing University of Ceylon (founded in 1942). The University of Ceylon itself was persuaded to duplicate its arts, science, and medical faculties in the early 1960s. Thus, between 1959 and 1967, total fulltime enrolment in universities in Sri Lanka rose from 3,196 to 14,287.[7]

Certain factors, however, have aggravated the problem since the early 1970s. In the first place, funds available for educational expansion were limited. The cost of education to the state rose from Rs.105.6 million in 1950 to Rs.472.4 million in 1969/70. In 1969/70, state expenditure on education accounted for 16.2 per cent of government expenditure and 4.47 per cent of the gross national product. Much of this money was spent on primary and secondary education. In the context of slow growth rates in the economy in the 1960s and early 1970s, there was little prospect of significant extra funding for university expansion after 1965. In fact, total university admissions were virtually at a standstill from 1964 to 1974; thus, competition for places in universities became intense. By 1965, only 20 per cent of the applicants could be offered university admission, and by 1969/70, the proportion was down to 11.3 per cent.[8] Then again, expansion in the universities was confined largely to the humanities and social sciences; the number of students admitted rose from 436, or 49 per cent, of total admissions in 1958, to a peak of 5,345, or 84.1 per cent, of all admissions in 1965. Such a rapid expansion eventually led to a surplus of graduates and a backlog of unemployed graduates qualified in the humanities and social sciences began to build up.

Naturally, in this context, admission to science-based courses, rather than the humanities and social sciences, became highly competitive.

This, however, was the field in which educational opportunity was distributed most unequally. As late as 1958, there were only fifty schools in the entire country that prepared students up to the grade 12 examination, and most of them were in the Colombo and Jaffna districts. The government made a determined effort to spread science education at the higher secondary level to other areas, and by 1967 the number of schools teaching science up to grade 12 had risen to 146, and by 1972 to 209. Progress in building good schools was much slower though, partly because equipment was expensive and partly because it was difficult to find science teachers capable of teaching in the national languages, particularly Sinhalese. In any case, even in the 1970s over 70 per cent of the schools in Sri Lanka that prepared students for the grade 12 (and university admission) examination had no science classes up to that level.

The inequalities in facilities in Tamil areas were as great as those in Sinhalese areas but, for a variety of reasons, Sri Lankan Tamils as a group performed better in science subjects on university admission tests. This is partly explained by higher literacy in English and more extensive facilities for science teaching in Jaffna district. Another reason was motivation—particularly strong in Jaffna—where employment opportunities in other fields were limited. The concentration of Sri Lankan Tamil students in professional courses had been identified as early as 1950. The adoption in 1956 of Sinhalese as the sole official language strengthened this trend since it was felt that administrative posts in the public sector, for which many students graduating in the social sciences and humanities competed, were becoming increasingly difficult to obtain for those who had studied in Tamil. Thus, by 1964, though 85 per cent of the students studying social sciences, law, and the humanities in universities were Sinhalese, the percentage in the other faculties was much lower: 59 in science and engineering, 45.5 in medicine and dentistry, 54.7 in agriculture and the veterinary sciences. In contrast, Sri Lankan Tamils, with only 12.0 per cent of the students in arts-based subjects, had 37.2 per cent of the places in science and engineering, 40.5 per cent in medicine and dentistry and 41.9 per cent in agriculture and veterinary science. Even in 1970, the Tamils (almost all of them Sri Lankan Tamils) gained 35.3 per cent of admissions to science-based courses, including 40.8 per cent of the places in engineering and 40.9 per cent of the places in medicine.[9]

It was in this context that changing the medium of instruction in the secondary schools became critical. In the case of social studies and the humanities, by 1961, the bulk of the students entering the university sat for the admission test in Sinhalese or Tamil. The changeover, however, was slower for the sciences; until the late 1960s, many students were studying in English; but by 1970 the majority of those taking science courses in secondary schools had switched to the national languages. With Sinhalese-Tamil rivalry increasing in the 1950s and 60s in language, politics, and employment, the changeover became a key issue. Certain groups of Sinhalese had long argued that the advantages conferred on certain areas and communities by virtue of their history should be corrected by state policy. In a pre-emptive effort, the Department of Education (whose bureaucracy was from 1960 dominated by a Sinhalese-Buddhist group) had in the previous two decades expended great effort in improving school facilities in outlying areas. Other steps were to follow. In 1972 the practical examinations for science for the GCE examination (grade 12) were abolished, largely to reduce the advantages enjoyed by students from a minority of schools with superior laboratory facilities. In addition, curricular reforms in the lower secondary schools implemented in 1972 were aimed partly at spreading science education to all schools, especially those in rural areas. By 1970, however, some Sinhalese 'nationalist' factions were manifesting increasing impatience. That year, before the admissions were officially announced, it was rumoured that 60 per cent of admissions to the faculty of engineering would be Tamil students. It was alleged that this high figure was due largely to favouritism and 'over-marking'. The allegation was investigated, but no evidence was uncovered to substantiate it. Nevertheless, the ruling United Front government made an adjustment in university admissions; different minimum marks were set for students sitting for the examination in Sinhalese and Tamil, so that a politically acceptable number of Sinhalese students would be recruited to the science-based faculties.[10]

This measure was strongly criticised by a number of university academics from the various ethnic groups, but the criticism had little political impact. The Tamils, too, were heavily critical, but at this time the position of the Tamil political leadership was weak. The Indian Tamils had not elected a representative to Parliament since 1952, and their percentage of the population had fallen from 13.5 per cent in 1951 to 9.4 per cent in 1971.[11] The Sri Lankan Tamils, unlike the Moors and the Malays, had by and large not joined one of the two major parties, and since 1956 they had been represented primarily by the Tamil Federal Party and to some extent by the Tamil Congress. The parties had co-operated with the government of Dudley Senanayake (1965–70); with its defeat in 1970, the successful United Front government obtained a two-thirds majority in Parliament without support from any substantial faction of Tamils. The political situation was one factor which enabled the government to be openly discriminatory, the consequence of which was that education was added to areas such as employment and language in which the Tamils felt strongly discriminated against.[12]

In fact the losses suffered by the Tamils as a group were marginal. Even with the new formula, they gained 34.7 per cent of the places in engineering and 39.3 per cent of those in medicine in 1971, as opposed to 40.8 and 40.9 per cent respectively, in 1970. The proportion of Tamils entering science-based courses fell slightly, from 35.3 to 33.6 per cent, and the total number of places gained by Tamils actually rose from 337 to 359. More important was the alienation caused by the realisation that political power was being used to discriminate against people of a particular ethno-linguistic group.[13] It caused Tamil leaders to call for a return to university admission on the basis of merit as determined by examination scores.

There were no admissions in 1972, and by the time admissions for 1973 were being processed, the Ministry of Education had devised a standard-isation scheme as a mechanism for adjusting the ethnic balance in university admissions. Standardisation was of course justified by ministry officials on various grounds as a measure for correcting disparities in marking standards between different subjects and different media and as a way to compensate for the unequal provision of facilities to different groups. It was clear to all concerned, however, that the primary purpose of standardisation was to neutralise the superior performance of Tamil-language students in science subjects.[14] This was done by reducing the sets of marks from all three media—English, Sinhalese, and Tamil—to a uniform scale so that eventually the number qualifying in each language would be proportionate to the number sitting for the examination in each language.[15]

Once again the scheme was vehemently opposed. The Tamils in particular resented it. As far as university admissions were concerned, though, the actual result was less than what might have been expected. Admission of Tamils to engineering courses fell precipitately to 24.4 per cent, and the overall percentage of Tamil students entering science-based courses dropped below 30 per cent, probably for the first time in the history of university education in Sri Lanka. On the other hand, the total number of places obtained by Tamils in science-based courses was 347—only 12 less than the 1971 figures and 10 more than in 1969/70. Sri Lankan Tamils, although they constituted only 11.1 per cent of the population, provided about 30 per cent of the science students in secondary schools in the early 1970s. At least the standardisation plan ensured that this proportion of university places accrued to them.

At this stage, however, two other factors emerged: the Kandyan lobby and the Moor/Malay interest group. The Kandyan Sinhalese constituted only 28.1 per cent of the total population, but the disfranchisement of the plantation Tamils had increased their share of representation in the legislature to nearly 40 per cent. They were particularly strong in the 1970

United Front government, with the prime minister herself sensitive to their interests (she had aristocratic Kandyan origins). The Kandyans had long been underpriviledged in terms of secondary education facilities. The five provinces where they predominated contained 47 per cent of the country's total population, but students from these provinces gained only 19 per cent of university places in science-oriented courses even after standardisation in 1973. Dr Premadasa Udagama, the secretary to the ministry of education, belonged to one of the Kandyan communities within the ministry. Soon after his appointment, the minister proposed to reserve 25 per cent of the intake to the University of Peradeniya to those living within twenty miles of the campus.[16] Nor was the Moor/Malay group content with standardisation; they too had long been educationally backward. Since most of them were educated in Tamil, standardisation affected them adversely. The number of Moor/Malay students entering the university (107 in 1969 and the same number in 1970) fell to 72 in 1971 and to 70 in 1973. The minister of education, Al-Haj Badi-ud-din Mahmud, leader of the Islamic Socialist Front, was not unmindful of their interests.

It was at this stage that several senior officers of the ministry of education suggested a 'district quota' system. This system was designed to allocate university places in proportion to the total population of each district. Separate quotas were to be granted for medicine (including dental surgery), engineering, physical science, biological science, and the arts. It is reported that the original proposal by the officials was to restrict the district quota to a proportion of the vacant places and to leave the others to be filled according to standardised test scores. However, it was quickly seen as greatly aiding the Kandyan areas, the Moors in the Batticaloa district, and rural areas in general. Thus, the quota system generated sufficient support to be implemented for all admissions. Little importance was attached to the adverse reaction of Sri Lankan Tamils. Indeed, the district quota system placed Sri Lankan Tamil students in a parlous position. Most of them were concentrated in Jaffna district, a district that for years had provided 25 per cent or more of the entrants to science-based courses. If strictly applied, the district quota would restrict students from Jaffna to 5.54 per cent of the places. In 1974, however, the district quota system was modified and put into operation. Only those who attained a minimum standard (of three passes plus 25 per cent in the fourth subject) were admitted to the university, and some of the places left vacant in less developed districts were redistributed among the other districts. By this means, 52 students from Jaffna and 133 from Colombo qualified to enter science-based courses. Of these, 47 from Jaffna and 58 from Colombo had their admissions deferred to 1975; therefore, this factor softened the figures relating to university admissions in both 1974 and 1975.

Nevertheless, the restriction on Tamil admissions was drastic. The total share of Tamil admissions for science-based courses in 1974 fell to 20.9 per cent (from 25.9 per cent in 1973 and 35.3 per cent in 1970). Tamil share of admission to engineering courses fell to 16.3 per cent and that for medicine to 25.9 per cent. For the first time there was a substantial drop in the absolute number of Tamils entering science-based courses (from 337 in 1973 to 294 in 1974), despite a continued expansion in the total intake to such courses (from 1,177 in 1973 to 1,403 in 1974). Their position in 1975 was even worse; the percentage of Tamils entering all science-based courses fell to 14.2 per cent and for those to medicine to 17.4 per cent. The only compensation available to them was a rise in the intake of arts students from the 1970 (open competition) figure of 7.6 per cent (187 students) and the 1973 (standardised marks) figure of 6.1 per cent (136 students) to the 1974 percentage of 10 per cent (226 students) and the 1975 percentage of 10.1 per cent (211 students). Between 1970 and 1975, however, the total number of Tamil students entering the university fell both in terms of percentages and in absolute numbers. Inevitably, the major benefits accrued to the Sinhalese. Although they were only 71.9 per cent of the total population, in 1974 they gained 75.4 per cent of the places in science-based courses, 78.8 per cent of the places in engineering, and 70 per cent of the places in medicine. In 1975 their position was even better, the figures being 78.0, 83.4, and 78.9 per cent, respectively. Because they also gained more than 85 per cent of the places in arts-oriented subjects, Sinhalese students had now gained a predominant position in the university, one comparable to that of their political leaders in the legislature. The Moor/Malays also benefited from the new system; from 1971 to 1975, their share of places in science-based courses increased significantly as their total science admissions doubled (from 21 to 41). True, they were still grossly under-represented in terms of total population.

By late 1974, however, opposition to both the district quota system and standardisation was gaining momentum. University dons continued to criticise the system in national newspapers.[17] The presentation of an official report on standardisation in the National State Assembly stimulated further discussion. Of even greater significance, however, several educated, influential Sinhalese were convinced that the scheme was iniquitous. Although the differences in performance among candidates entering the university from different districts was not officially revealed, it was known that the differences were substantial. Many were alienated by the spectacle of students with inferior performance entering the university while those with higher grades in the same school were left out simply because the more fortunate students had received their early education in 'undeveloped districts'.[18]

Then again, although the district quota system helped students in certain districts, it brought little or no benefit to areas where educational facilities in science had not been developed. For example, in 1974, Polonnaruwa, Moneragala, and Vavuniya together had eight places reserved in the faculty of medicine; but these areas failed to produce a single qualified candidate to fill the places. In 1975, one student from Polonnaruwa entered the medical faculty, but the five places alloted to Amparai, the four given to Moneragala, and the two reserved for Vavuniya were unfilled. It was becoming apparent that without better schooling facilities a district quota would not benefit the really undeveloped districts.

Two other factors were significant. Firstly, the government, anticipating early elections, became more sensitive to Tamil opinion. Indeed, disillusion among Tamils had grown apace. Tamil youth, radicalised by what they saw as open discrimination against them in university admissions, had pushed Tamil leaders to declare for a separate state. The formation of the Tamil United Front to achieve this aim alarmed the United Front government. Mr Kumarasuriar, minister of posts and the only Tamil in the cabinet was given some leeway in correcting the situation. He secured a university campus for Jaffna and lent his influence to the modification of the district quota system.

More ominous was the disillusion of the Sinhalese of Colombo district. The district quota system, while it benefited the Sinhalese as a whole, was a disaster for Sinhalese students in Colombo. Had selection been made in 1975 according to standardised test scores, without district quotas, the number selected from Colombo district for engineering and the applied sciences would have risen from 71 to 129. (The corresponding figures for Jaffna were 18 to 56.) The government thus faced considerable pressure from articulate parents in Colombo.

The problem was submitted to the Sectoral Committee on Social Overheads, Mass Media and Transport of the National Planning Council. The committee included Pieter Keuneman, minister of housing and member for the Colombo Central seat in Parliament, K. Kumarasuriar, and K. B. Ratnayake, minister of sports and member for Anuradnapura. It received memoranda from a number of associations and from members of the public. The committee eventually submitted its report in October 1975. The report recommended abolition of standardisation, arguing that 'its contribution both to deepening and indeed institutionalising suspicions between communities and promoting distrust in the fairness and impartiality of examinations' was great, while its benefit in correcting examiner variability was limited. In relation to district quotas the Sectoral Committee felt: that it had been made operational without sufficient notice and without a sufficiently deep study of its educational consequences and anticipated social repercussions; that the system did not take into consideration the disparity of facilities within the districts; that it would have been fairer to base quotas on student population (in grade 12) rather than on the total population; that most educationally backward districts appeared to have benefited only marginally; and that the main beneficiaries appeared to be students from the more affluent families, who also received their primary education in less developed districts and were thus allowed to claim places for those districts. Nevertheless, the committee did not recommend total abolition of the district quota system; the political forces supporting it were too strong for that. The committee recommended that 70 per cent of admissions be made solely on marks achieved in examinations and the other 30 per cent according to district. Of this 30 per cent, however, half, of 15 per cent, would be reserved for the backward districts of Amparai, Anuradhapura, Badulla, Hambantota, Mannar, Moneragala, Nuwara Eliya, Polonnaruwa, Trincomalee, and Vavuniya. Colombo and Jaffna districts would get no places on district quotas, since they were considered educationally developed districts well able to compete with others.

The proposals were eventually submitted to the cabinet, which accepted the district quota scheme as modified; but Sinhalese interests were strong enough to retain standardisation on the basis of language. Also, in implementation, district places were granted to Colombo and Jaffna along with the other districts. The new system as it operated in 1976 brought distinct gains for the Tamils. Their share of total admissions to the science-oriented faculties rose by 35 per cent, from 268 in 1975 to 362 in 1976, although total admission of students to the science faculties fell slightly, from 1,411 in 1975 to 1,395 in 1976. This gave them a proportion of 25.9 per cent of places in science-based courses, well above the 19 per cent in 1975 or the 20.9 per cent of 1974 but still well below the 1973 (standardisation only) percentage of 29.5 or the 1970 (open competition) of 35.3. The percentage of Tamils entering the university to study medicine rose to 30.4 per cent and that of Tamils who entered for engineering came up to 22.4 per cent of total students' enrolment. On the other hand, the Sinhalese lost little; they still had 71.3 per cent of overall university admissions for science-based courses, including 65.8 per cent for medicine and 76.4 per cent for engineering.

In 1977 the proportion of Tamil entrants to science-based courses fell slightly to a total of 350, or 23.6 per cent. Their share of admissions for medicine was only 27.8 per cent, and for engineering, 19.1 per cent. The admission figure for the Sinhalese rose correspondingly; the figures being 73.3, 68.0 and 79.5 per cent. By 1977 the issue of university admissions had become a focal point of the conflict between the government and Tamil leaders. Tamil youth, embittered by what they considered discrimination against them, formed the radical wing of the Tamil United Liberation Front. Many advocated the use of violence to establish a separate Tamil state of Ealam. It was an object lesson in how inept policy measures and insensitivity to minority interests can exacerbate ethnic tensions.

Notes

1. Ceylon, Department of Census and Statistics, *Preliminary Report of the Socio-Economic Survey of Ceylon, 1969–70*, Colombo, Ceylon Government Press, 1971; Statistical appendix, in *Sri Lanka: A survey*, K. M. de Silva (ed.), London, C. Hurst, 1977, p. 274.
2. For statistics on university admissions up to 1977, see D. L. Jayasuriya, 'Developments in University Education: The Growth of the University of Ceylon, 1942–1965,' *University of Ceylon Review*, **XXIII**, 1 and 2, (April and December 1965), pp. 146–50; C. R. de Silva, 'Education' in K. M. de Silva (ed.), *Sri Lanka: A Survey*, London, C. Hurst and Co., 1977, p. 426, and 'The Politics of University Admissions: A Review of Some Aspects of the Admissions Policy in Sri Lanka, 1971–1978,' *Sri Lanka Journal of Social Sciences*, vol.I, 2, 1978, pp. 85–123. For instance, P. T. M. Fernando, 'Factors Affecting Marital Selection: Matrimonial Advertisements by Middle-Class Sinhalese,' *Ceylon Journal of Historical & Social Studies*. vol.7, 2 (July–December 1964), pp. 171–188.
3. P. Richards and M. Leonov, *Education and Income Distribution in Asia*, London, Croom Helm, 1981, p. 26.
4. See, for example, David Court, 'The Education System as a Response to Inequality in Tanzania and Kenya,' *Journal of Modern African Studies*, vol. 14, 4, pp. 664–5.
5. See C. S. V. Jayaweera, 'Regional Imbalances in Education in Ceylon,' *Journal of the National Education Society of Ceylon*, **vol. 20** (1971), pp. 29–51.
6. de Silva, C. R., *Education in Sri Lanka*, p. 423; Bogoda Premaratne, *Examination Reforms in Sri Lanka*, Paris, UNESCO Press, 1976, pp. 41–6.
7. de Silva, C. R., *Education in Sri Lanka*, pp. 412–25.
8. de Silva, C. R., 'Weightage in University Admissions: Standardization and District Quotas in Sri Lanka, 1970–1975,' *Modern Ceylon Studies*, vol. 5, 2 (1974), pp. 154–5; C. R. de Silva, *Education in Sri Lanka*, p. 423.
9. de Silva, C. R., 'The Politics of University Admissions,' 86–7; D. L. Jayasuriya, 'Developments in University Education,' pp. 86–93, C. R. de Silva, 'Weightage in University Admissions,' op cit. p. 154
10. Ibid., pp. 155–7 and the sources cited there.
11. On the question of political rights for Indian Tamils see A. Jeyaratnam Wilson, *Electoral Politics in an Emergent State: The Ceylon General Election of May 1970*, Cambridge University Press,

1975; and K. M. de Silva (ed.), *Universal Franchise 1931-1981: The Sri Lankan Experience*, Colombo, Department of Information, 1981, pp. 83–9, 114–17.

12. *A Memorandum on Discrimination Submitted to the International Commission of Jurists by the Tamil United Front of Ceylon*, Colombo, 1973, pp. 29–30.

13. Included in those who studied in the Tamil language were numerous Moors, as well as all the Tamils.

14. For a summary of the debate see C. R. de Silva, 'Weightage in University Admissions,' pp. 158–162.

15. The formula adopted was: $x^1 = SD^1/SD \ (X-M) + M^1$, X^1 any standardised mark, SD^1. Standard deviation obtained, S deviation required, X any mark obtained, M– Mean obtained, M^1 required. The mean required was fixed at 50 and the standard required was fixed at 12.

16. *Report of the National Council of Higher Education for the year 1969-70*, November 1971, p. 114.

17. *Ceylon Daily News*, 3 October 1974.

18. *Ceylon Daily News*, 10 February 1975.

Table 9.1. Population of ethnic groups (in 000s)

	1946 No.	1946 %	1953 No.	1953 %	1963 No.	1963 %	1971 No.	1971 %	1981 No.	1981 %
Low-Country Sinhalese	2,903	43.6	3,470	42.9	4,470	42.2	5,446	42.8	10,985	74.0
Kandyan Sinhalese										
Sri Lanka Tamils	1,718	26.0	2,147	26.5	3,043	28.8	3,701	29.1	1,872	12.6
Indian Tamils	734	11.0	885	10.9	1,165	11.0	1,416	11.0	825	5.6
Sri Lanka Moors	781	11.7	974	12.0	1,123	10.6	1,195	9.4	1,087	7.3
Indian Moors	374	5.6	464	5.7	627	5.9	824	6.5		
Burghers and Eurasians	36	0.5	47	0.6	55	0.5	29	0.2		
Malays	42	0.6	46	0.6	46	0.5	44	0.3	38	0.3
Others	23	0.4	25	0.3	33	0.3	42	0.3	43	0.3
	49	0.6	40	0.5	20	0.2	14	0.1	24	0.2
Total	6,660	100	8,098	100	10,582	100	12,711	100	14,874	100

Sources: Statistical appendix, in *Sri Lanka: A Survey*, p. 277; *Preliminary Report of the Census of 1981.*

Table 9.2. Schools having classes up to grade 12, by district and province in 1972 (schools teaching science up to grade 12 given in parentheses)

Colombo	192 (42)		
Kalutara	63 (17)	Western Province	255 (59)
Kandy	108 (15)		
Matale	27 (3)		
Nuwara Eliya	35 (8)	Central Province	170 (26)
Jaffna	49 (34)		
Mannar	2 (1)		
Vavuniya	9 (4)	Northern Province	60 (39)
Anuradhapura	48 (3)		
Polonnaruwa	10 (1)	North-Central Province	58 (4)
Galle	93 (11)		
Matara	64 (10)		
Hambantota	30 (2)	Southern Province	187 (23)
Batticaloa	26 (11)		
Trincomalee	7 (1)	Eastern Province	33 (12)
Kegalle	77 (15)		
Ratnapura	49 (5)	Sabaragamuwa Province	126 (20)
Bandarawela (Badulla)	30 (6)		
Moneragala	18 (1)	Uva Province	48 (7)
Kurunegala	101 (12)		
Chilaw	48 (7)	North-Western Province	149 (19)
TOTAL	1,086(209)		

Source: Statistical Branch, Department of Education, Colombo, 1973.

Table 9.3. University admissions to science-based courses, 1971

		Number admitted	Minimum total mark for admission
Engineering – Peradeniya	Sinhalese	86	227
	Tamil	60	250
Engineering – Katubedda	Sinhalese	60	212
	Tamil	53	232
Medicine and dentistry – Peradeniya and Colombo	Sinhalese	154	229
	Tamil	127	250
Biological sciences – all four universities	Sinhalese	151	175
	Tamil	63	181
Agriculture – Peradeniya Veterinary science – Peradeniya	Sinhalese	178	183
Physical science – all four universities	Tamil	92	204
Architecture – Katubedda	Sinhalese	16	180
	Tamil	28	194

Source: Hansard, vol. 83, book 5, col. 15, 514-578 (6–1-1971).

Table 9.4. University Admissions (1969–77) by ethnic origin and course of study

1969–70 Course of Study	Sinhalese No.	%	Tamil No.	%	Moor-Malay No.	%	Others No.	%	TOTAL
Phy. Sc., Bio-Sc. &									
Architecture	235	69.7	93	27.6	7	2.1	2	0.6	337
Engineering	77	51.7	72	48.3	–	–	–	–	149
Medicine	112	48.9	112	48.9	2	0.9	3	1.3	229
Dental surgery	11	52.4	8	38.1	2	9.5	–	–	21
Agriculture	17	44.7	18	47.4	2	5.3	1	2.6	38
Vet. science	5	27.7	12	66.7	–	–	1	5.6	18
TOTAL Science	457	57.7	315	39.8	13	1.6	7	0.9	792
Arts oriented studies									
(excluding law)	2035	89.1	158	6.9	91	4.0	1	0.0	2285
Law	30	57.7	18	34.6	3	5.8	1	1.9	52
TOTAL Arts	2522	88.4	176	7.5	94	4.0	2	0.1	2337
GRAND TOTAL	2979	80.6	491	15.7	107	3.4	9	0.3	3129
1970–71									
Phy. Sc. Bio-Sc. &									
Architecture	307	68.0	129	28.6	8	1.8	7	1.6	451
Engineering	85	55.9	62	40.8	3	2.0	2	1.3	152
Medicine	132	53.5	101	40.9	6	2.4	8	3.2	247
Dental surgery	17	41.5	23	56.1	1	2.4	–	–	41
Agriculture	23	53.5	17	39.5	2	4.7	1	2.3	43
Vet. science	15	71.4	5	23.8	1	4.8	–	–	21
TOTAL Science	579	60.6	337	35.3	21	2.2	18	1.9	955
Arts oriented studies									
(excluding law)	2200	89.7	171	7.0	81	3.3	2	0.0	2454
Law	26	54.2	16	33.3	5	10.4	1	2.1	48
TOTAL Arts	2226	88.9	187	7.6	86	3.4	3	0.1	2502
GRAND TOTAL	2805	81.1	524	15.2	107	3.1	21	0.6	3457
1971–2									
Phy. Sc., Bio-Sc. &									
Architecture	299	67.0	139	31.2	5	1.1	3	0.7	446
Engineering	171	62.4	95	34.7	5	1.8	3	1.1	274
Medicine	124	56.1	87	39.3	5	2.3	5	2.3	221

Table 9.4. continued

1969–70 Course of Study	Sinhalese No.	%	Tamil No.	%	Moor-Malay No.	%	Others No.	%	TOTAL
Dental surgery	21	42.8	26	53.0	1	2.1	1	2.1	49
Agriculture	48	58.6	32	39.0	2	2.4	–	–	82
Vet. science	17	63.0	10	37.0	–	–	–	–	27
TOTAL Science	680	63.6	389	33.6	18	1.7	12	1.1	1069
Art oriented studies (excluding law)	2031	92.7	102	4.7	53	2.4	4	0.2	2190
Law	42	85.8	5	10.2	1	2.0	1	2.0	49
TOTAL Arts	2073	92.6	107	4.8	54	2.4	5	0.2	2239
GRAND TOTAL	2753	83.2	466	14.1	72	2.2	17	0.5	3308
1973 Phy. Sc., Bio-Sc. & Architecture	356	73.1	115	23.6	10	2.1	6	1.2	487
Engineering	201	73.1	67	24.4	5	1.8	2	0.7	275
Medicine	150	58.8	94	36.9	6	2.3	5	2.0	255
Dental surgery	25	51.0	23	46.9	1	2.1	–	–	49
Agriculture	41	46.6	45	51.1	2	2.3	–	–	88
Vet. science	20	87.0	3	13.0	–	–	–	–	23
TOTAL Science	793	67.4	347	29.5	24	2.0	13	1.1	1177
Art oriented studies (excluding law)	2019	91.8	128	5.9	45	2.0	7	0.3	2199
Law	34	77.3	8	18.1	1	2.3	1	2.3	44
TOTAL Arts	2053	91.5	136	6.1	46	2.0	8	0.4	2243
GRAND TOTAL	2846	83.2	483	14.1	70	2.1	21	0.6	3420
1974 Phy. Sc., Bio-Sc. & Architecture	511	75.5	146	21.6	18	2.6	2	0.3	677
Engineering	223	78.8	46	16.3	14	4.9	–	–	283
Medicine	184	70.0	68	25.9	8	3.0	3	1.1	263
Dental surgery	34	69.4	14	28.6	1	2.0	–	–	49
Agriculture	83	83.8	11	11.1	5	5.1	–	–	99
Vet. science	23	71.9	9	28.1	–	–	–	–	32
TOTAL Science	1058	75.4	294	20.9	46	3.3	5	0.4	1403
Arts oriented studies	1934	86.0	226	10.0	84	3.7	6	0.3	2250
GRAND TOTAL	2992	81.9	520	14.2	130	3.6	11	0.3	3653

Table 9.4. continued

1969–70 Course of Study	Sinhalese No. %	Tamil No. %	Moor-Malay No. %	Others No. %	TOTAL
1975					
Phy. Sc., Bio-Sc. &					
Architecture	535 77.3	135 19.5	22 3.2	– –	692
Engineering	241 83.4	41 14.2	7 2.4	– –	789
Medicine	195 78.9	43 17.4	8 3.2	1 0.4	247
Dental surgery	33 66.0	16 32.0	1 2.0	– –	50
Agriculture	75 73.5	24 23.5	3 2.9	– –	102
Vet. science	22 71.0	9 29.0	– –	– –	31
TOTAL Science	1101 78.0	268 19.0	41 2.9	1 0.1	1411
Arts oriented studies	1781 85.6	211 10.1	79 3.8	9 0.4	2080
GRAND TOTAL	2882 82.6	479 13.7	120 3.4	10 0.3	3491
1976					
Phy. Sc., Bio-Sc. &					
Architecture	519 72.9	174 24.6	16 2.2	2 0.3	711
Engineering	204 76.1	60 22.4	3 1.1	1 0.4	268
Medicine	158 65.8	73 30.4	7 2.9	2 0.8	240
Dental surgery	28 56.0	20 40.0	2 4.0	– –	50
Agriculture	71 74.0	21 21.9	3 3.1	1 1.0	96
Vet. science	14 46.7	14 46.7	– –	2 6.6	30
TOTAL Science	994 71.3	362 25.9	31 2.2	8 0.5	1395
Arts oriented studies	2071 86.3	208 8.6	114 4.7	6 0.3	2399
GRAND TOTAL	3065 80.8	570 15.0	145 3.8	14 0.4	3794
1977					
Phy. Sc., Bio-Sc. &					
Architecture	566 73.0	179 23.1	26 3.4	4 0.5	775
Engineering	229 79.5	55 19.1	4 1.4	– –	288
Medicine	164 68.0	67 27.8	9 3.7	1 0.4	241
Dental surgery	38 76.0	12 24.0	– –	– –	50
Agriculture	76 74.5	24 23.5	2 2.0	– –	102
Vet. science	16 55.2	13 44.8	– –	– –	29
TOTAL Science	1089 73.3	350 23.6	41 2.8	5 0.3	1485
Arts oriented studies	2139 85.8	229 9.2	112 4.5	14 0.6	2494
GRAND TOTAL	3228 81.1	579 14.6	153 3.8	19 0.5	3979

Source: University Grants Commission, Colombo.

Table 9.5. University Admissions — 1974: Statistics of students selected on district basis and on order of merit

(A) District basis selections

	Population %	MEDICINE Vacancies 225			DENTAL SURGERY Vacancies 50			BIOLOGICAL SCIENCE Vacancies 320			ENGINEERING & APPLIED SCIENCE Vacancies 290			PHYSICAL SCIENCE Vacancies 330			ARTS-ORIENTED STUDIES Vacancies 2225	
		(a)	(b)	(c)	(a)	(b)	(c)	(a)	(b)	(c)	(a)	(b)	(c)	(a)	(b)	(c)	(a)	(c)
1. Colombo	70.54	46	23	70	10		21	66	17	84	60	9	72	68	13	79	457	449
2. Kalutara	5.77	13	5	18	3		2	18	5	23	17	2	20	19		23	128	129
3. Kandy	9.77	22	11	33	5		9	31	8	39	28	3	32	32	6	37	218	214
4. Matale	2.47	6	3	7	1			8	2	10	7	1	8	8	2	11	55	64
5. Nuwara Eliya	3.65	8		1	2			12		4	11		7	12		2	81	82
6. Galle	5.91	13	7	20	3		7	19	5	25	17	2	19	20	4	25	132	138
7. Matara	4.92	11	6	15	2			16	4	20	14	1	15	16	3	19	110	109
8. Hambantota (Tangalle)	2.65	6		1	1			8	2	10	8		7	9		8	59	65
9. Jaffna	5.76	13	6	19	3		6	18	5	22	17	2	20	19	4	23	128	128
10. Mannar	0.59	1		1				2		–	2		2	2		1	13	14
11. Vavuniya	0.69	2		–				2		1	2		2	2		1	15	15
12. Batticaloa	1.96	4	2	5	1			6		5	6	1	7	6	1	7	44	39
13. Amparai	2.11	5		2	1			7		–	6	1	7	7		5	47	48
14. Trincomalee	1.40	3		3	1			4		–	4		1	5		1	31	31
15. Kurunegala	8.17	18		5	4			26		24	24	2	26	27	5	32	182	186
16. Puttalam (Chilaw)	2.97	7		3	1			9		3	8	1	7	10	2	12	65	63
17. Anuradhapura	2.80	6		2	1			9		5	8		4	9		4	62	61
18. Polonnaruwa	1.13	3		–				4		4	8		1	4		2	25	25
19. Badulla (Bandarawela)	5.00	11		1	2			16		6	14		7	17		9	111	115

Table 9.5 continued

	Popula-tion %	MEDICINE Vacancies 225			DENTAL SURGERY Vacancies 50		BIOLOGICAL SCIENCE Vacancies 320			ENGINEERING & APPLIED SCIENCE Vacancies 290			PHYSICAL SCIENCE Vacancies 330			ARTS-ORIENTED STUDIES Vacancies 2225	
		(a)	(b)	(c)	(a)	(c)	(a)	(b)	(c)	(a)	(b)	(c)	(a)	(b)	(c)	(a)	(c)
20. Moneragala	1.34	3		–	1	–	4		2	4		1	4		2	30	30
21. Ratnapura	5.14	12		8	3		16		11	15		15	17		8	114	113
22. Kegalle	5.31	12		6	3	3	17	4	21	15	2	17	18		17	118	118
Total	100.00	225	63	220	48	45	318	52	319	290	27	297	331	44	328	2225	2236
(B) No. taken in order of merit																	
Colombo			–	23		–			13			–			15		
Jaffna			–	22					–			10			–		
Total				45		3			13			10			15		
TOTAL ADMITTED (A) & (B)				265		48			332			307*			343		

(a) Quota on population percentage
(b) Additional No. allocated out of unfilled places
(c) No. finally selected

Note: Due to the non-availability of qualified students in certain districts, it was not possible to fill the quota of places allocated to them. These unfilled places were reallocated among districts which had a surplus of qualified students, in proportion to the population of those areas.

*Including 7 opting for Physical Science.

Note: Selection of students in the Arts group was done on district basis only.

Source: University Grants Commission, Colombo.

Table 9.6. University Admissions—1975: Statistics of students selected on district basis.

District	Population %	MEDICINE				DENTAL SURGERY				BIOLOGICAL SCIENCE				ENGINEERING & APPLIED SCIENCE				PHYSICAL SCIENCE				ARTS			
		(a)	(b)	(c)	(d)	(a)	(b)	(c)	(d)	(a)	(b)	(c)	(d)	(a)	(b)	(c)	(d)	(a)	(b)	(c)	(d)	(a)	(b)	(c)	(d)
1. Colombo	21.03	94	94	265	38.1	38	38	255	76.0	69	68	258	23.8	71	71	289	24.6	110	112	269	26.7	442	447	246	21.3
2. Kalutara	5.76	21	15	–	6.1					19	19	240	6.7	19	19	274	6.6	30	30	255	7.2	121	122	249	5.8
3. Kandy	9.34	35	24	–	9.7					30	30	243	10.5	31	32	258	11.1	49	51	240	12.2	196	195	248	9.3
4. Matale	2.49	9	7	–	2.8					8	10	242	3.5	8	9	255	3.1	14	15	235	3.6	52	51	236	2.4
5. Nuwara Eliya	3.57	9	1	–	0.4					10	3	–	1.0	8	6	–	2.1	15	3	–	0.7	75	75	224	3.6
6. Galle	5.80	26	26	239	10.5	9	2	–	4.0	19	20	246	7.0	19	20	278	6.9	30	30	259	7.2	122	113	254	5.4
7. Matara	4.63	11	7	–	2.8					15	17	238	6.0	15	15	275	5.2	25	26	250	6.2	97	98	260	4.7
8. Hambantota	2.68	7	1	–	0.4					9	9	213	3.2	8	8	–	2.8	11	8	–	1.9	56	54	247	2.6
9. Jaffna	5.54	25	26	272	10.5	10	10	265	20.0	19	19	260	6.7	18	18	296	6.2	29	31	274	7.4	116	117	247	5.6
10. Mannar	0.61	2	1	–	0.4					2	2	239	0.7	2	1	–	0.4	3	–	–	0.0	13	13	212	0.6
11. Vavuniya	0.75	2	–	–	0.0					2	1	–	0.4	2	–	–	0.0	3	1	–	0.2	16	16	225	0.7
12. Batticaloa	2.03	8	6	–	2.4					7	7	212	2.4	–	7	256	2.4	11	11	228	2.6	43	43	210	2.0
13. Amparai	2.14	5	–	–	0.0					6	1	–	0.4	6	1	–	0.4	9	7	–	1.7	45	44	228	2.1
14. Trincomalee	1.51	4	3	–	1.2					4	1	–	0.4	5	5	263	1.7	6	6	–	1.4	32	33	223	1.6
15. Kurunegala	8.09	20	12	–	4.9					27	27	227	9.5	27	28	241	9.7	42	41	–	9.8	170	170	253	8.1
16. Puttalam	2.99	7	3	–	1.2					9	9	226	3.2	10	10	247	3.5	16	17	236	4.1	63	64	232	3.0
17. Anuradhapura	3.06	8	2	–	0.8					9	7	–	2.4	4	4	–	1.4	13	1	–	0.2	64	64	236	3.0
18. Polonnaruwa	1.29	3	1	–	0.4					4	–	–	0.0	1	1	–	0.4	5	1	–	0.2	27	27	229	1.3
19. Badulla	4.84	12	2	–	0.8					14	7	–	2.4	14	6	–	2.1	20	5	–	1.2	101	102	228	4.8
20. Moneragala	1.51	4	–	–	0.0					4	2	–	0.7	4	1	–	0.4	6	–	–	0.0	32	33	243	1.6
21. Ratnapura	5.21	13	10	–	4.1					15	8	–	2.8	15	9	–	3.1	22	4	–	1.0	109	111	240	5.3
22. Kegalle	5.13	13	6	–	2.4					16	18	223	6.3	17	17	233	5.9	22	19	–	4.5	108	110	251	5.2
TOTAL	100.00		247		99.9		50		100.0		285		100.0		288		100.0		419		100.0		2101		100.0

* Basis of selection: 100% district-quota system based on population percentage.

(a) Quota on district basis: include unfilled vacancies which were re-distributed among districts which had a surplus of qualified students.

(b) No. actually selected.

(c) Lowest mark of student selected. Absence of this statistic indicates that all qualified students in that district have been selected. All marks are standardised marks.

Note: In addition to the above numbers 76 students (44 from Colombo and 32 from Jaffna) selected in order of merit in 1974 but whose admission was deferred due to a shortage of places were also admitted to Biological Science courses. 29 other students (14 from Colombo and 15 from Jaffna) were also admitted on the same basis for engineering and applied science.

Source: University Grants Commission, Colombo.

Table 9.7. University Admissions—1975: Statistics of candidates who have obtained minimum requirements for university admission but who have not been selected (by ethnic group)

District	BIOLOGICAL SCIENCE					PHYSICAL SCIENCE					ARTS				
	Sinhala	Tamil	Muslim	Others	Total	Sinhala	Tamil	Muslim	Others	Total	Sinhala	Tamil	Muslim	Others	Total
1. Kegalle	17	—	—	—	17	25	—	—	—	25	590	2	29	—	621
2. Ratnapura	5	2	—	—	7	10	2	—	—	12	346	2	1	—	349
3. Anuradhapura	2	—	—	—	2	5	1	—	—	6	187	5	5	—	197
4. Polonnaruwa	4	—	—	—	4	2	—	—	—	2	60	—	2	—	62
5. Galle	69	—	—	—	69	56	—	—	—	56	774	6	1	—	781
6. Matara	26	—	—	—	26	22	—	2	—	24	774	2	17	1	794
7. Hambantota	7	—	—	—	7	7	—	—	—	7	286	—	2	—	288
8. Badulla	2	1	—	—	3	7	—	—	—	7	101	16	2	—	119
9. Moneragala	1	—	—	—	1	2	1	—	—	3	92	—	3	—	95
10. Kurunegala	23	—	1	—	24	8	—	—	—	8	1180	3	40	7	1230
11. Puttalam	7	4	1	—	12	18	1	1	—	20	181	3	10	2	196
12. Matale	15	3	—	—	18	11	—	—	—	11	116	9	8	—	133
13. Kandy	63	9	8	—	80	46	4	3	—	53	769	18	94	4	885
14. Nuwara Eliya	3	2	—	—	5	4	1	—	—	5	132	13	4	—	149
15. Jaffna	—	329	—	—	329	—	192	—	—	192	—	449	—	—	449
16. Vavuniya	2	8	—	—	10	1	2	—	—	3	12	22	—	—	34
17. Mannar	—	2	—	—	2	—	—	—	—	—	1	14	6	—	21
18. Batticaloa	—	5	—	—	5	—	12	1	—	13	2	31	12	—	45
19. Trincomalee	—	7	—	—	7	1	5	—	—	6	20	14	8	—	42
20. Amparai	1	—	—	—	1	1	2	1	—	4	52	18	5	1	76
21. Kalutara	26	1	2	—	29	49	—	3	—	52	537	2	8	1	548
22. Colombo	380	74	9	6	469	216	34	4	3	257	1536	50	56	6	1648
Total	653	447	21	6	1127	491	257	15	3	766	7748	679	313	22	8762
Percentage	57.94%	39.66%	1.86%	0.54%	100%	64.10%	33.55%	1.96%	0.39%	100%	88.43%	7.75%	3.57%	0.25%	100%

Source: University Grants Commission, Colombo.

Table 9.8. University Admissions—1975: 100% selected on district quota

District	Highest mark of candidate/candidates failing to get selected in Colombo and Jaffna and the lowest mark of candidate/candidates qualifying for selection in other districts: standardised marks	
	MEDICINE	ENGINEERING
Colombo	262	289
Kalutara	226	273
Kandy	229	259
Matale	220	263
Nuwara Eliya	260	246
Galle	232	278
Matara	237	264
Hambantota	245	240
Jaffna	268	294
Mannar	262	218
Vavuniya	—	—
Batticaloa	227	256
Amparai	—	303
Trincomalee	221	276
Kurunegala	225	248
Puttalam	250	248
Anuradhapura	240	244
Polonnaruwa	248	268
Badulla	231	244
Moneragala	—	229
Ratnapura	211	231
Kegalle	246	237

Source: University Grants Commission, Colombo.

Table 9.9. University Admissions—1976: Statistics of students selected on district basis and on order of merit

District	MEDICINE			DENTAL SURGERY			BIOLOGICAL SCIENCE			ENGINEERING AND APPLIED SCIENCE			PHYSICAL SCIENCE		
	(1)	(2)	(a)	(1)	(2)	(a)	(1)	(2)	(a)	(1)	(2)	(a)	(1)	(2)	(a)
1. Colombo	13	83	272	5	15	267	13	109	257	13	101	285	26	163	262
2. Kalutara	3	5	264	1	—	263	5	12	252	4	11	284	7	20	259
3. Kandy	6	12	267	2	—	264	5	16	255	6	13	274	11	9	256
4. Matale	1	2	255	—	—	—	1	3	253	1	2	284	3	5	261
5. Nuwara Eliya	1	—	—	—	—	—	4	1	—	3	—	—	3	1	—
6. Galle	3	8	274	1	5	266	4	14	255	5	19	283	7	40	260
7. Matara	3	3	269	1	—	268	3	7	254	2	2	284	6	7	258
8. Hambantota	2	1	—	—	—	—	9	—	236	8	—	—	6	—	—
9. Jaffna	3	33	273	1	15	268	5	39	257	3	37	287	8	76	264
10. Mannar	3	—	—	—	—	—	1	—	232	2	—	256	6	—	—
11. Vavuniya	9	—	—	—	—	—	3	—	216	3	—	241	6	—	—
12. Batticaloa	1	1	266	—	—	—	1	3	251	3	2	286	3	5	255
13. Amparai	1	—	—	—	—	—	6	—	—	5	—	—	4	—	—
14. Trincomalee	5	1	—	—	—	—	5	—	—	9	2	231	12	—	—
15. Kurunegala	5	10	261	2	—	260	5	15	253	6	3	271	10	10	255
16. Puttalam	2	3	257	1	—	253	3	—	255	1	2	268	3	3	261
17. Anuradhapura	2	—	—	—	—	—	6	0	—	3	—	—	6	—	—
18. Polonnaruwa	1	—	—	—	—	—	2	0	—	—	—	—	2	—	—
19. Badulla	2	—	—	—	—	—	16	1	218	8	1	—	8	—	—
20. Moneragala	1	—	—	—	—	—	—	—	—	1	—	—	1	—	—
21. Ratnapura	3	3	264	1	—	264	5	2	250	3	1	264	7	1	226
22. Kegalle	3	—	—	—	—	—	3	3	253	2	2	282	6	4	257
Total	73	165		15	35		105	226		89	199		151	344	

(1) No. on district basis
(2) No. on merit
(a) Lowest mark of student admitted on district basis. All marks are standardised marks.
Note: Absence of lowest mark of student selected indicates that all qualified students in that district were selected.
Source: University Grants Commission, Colombo.

10 PUBLIC POLICIES RELATING TO BUSINESS AND LAND, AND THEIR IMPACT ON ETHNIC RELATIONS IN PENINSULAR MALAYSIA

Mavis Puthucheary

Malaysia[1] is unique in that it is a plural society where political power is concentrated in the hands of one ethnic group, whereas economic power is in the hands of another. Although all ethnic groups have voting rights, the delineation of constituencies and the weightage given to rural seats results in a large number of constituencies with a majority, or sizeable number of Malay voters; because voting tends to be along communal lines, these constituencies return Malay candidates to Parliament. Since independence, the ruling party has been a coalition of three ethnically-based parties that claim to represent Malays, Chinese, and Indians;[2] in actual fact, however, it is the Malay party, the United Malay National Organisation (UMNO), that has majority representation in Parliament and therefore dominates the political coalition.

UMNO has long been concerned about the economic position of the Malay community *vis-à-vis* other communities in the country. In fact, UMNO was created in 1946 as a protest against an attempt by the colonial government to extend the franchise to everyone, regardless of ethnic background. UMNO did not accept the view that the other ethnic groups should have equal political rights with the Malays, since it regarded the country as belonging to the Malay sultans and the Malay people. Because Britain had been given the right to rule by treaties with the sultans, UMNO argued that the country should revert to the Malays when Britain relinquished power. Thus, even after independence, when it was decided to allow Chinese and Indians to become citizens of the country and thus to share political power with the Malays, UMNO continued to make a sharp distinction between Malaysian citizens of Malay origin who were considered genuine 'sons of the soil', or Bumiputras,[3] and other Malaysian citizens, mainly of Chinese and Indian origin.

The distinction was rationalised on the grounds that the Malays were dispossessed of their land and deprived of economic advantages during colonial rule; they therefore needed to be given special attention by the government to help them improve their economic position. In particular, post-independence governments have concentrated on improving the standard of living and quality of life of the rural people, the majority of whom are Malaysians of Malay origin. At the same time, the government continued to encourage private investment in the country. Since private investment was mainly foreign, with some local participation by Chinese and Indian entrepreneurs, differences in wealth and income continued to widen not only between but within ethnic groups. Intra-racial differences, however, were muted as the government, afraid of losing Malay votes to the more extremist Malay opposition parties, continued its emphasis of inter-racial inequality and formulated policies to correct the imbalance.

Since 1970 the government has given these policies new direction and focus. Called the New Economic Policy (NEP), the policy embarked on by the government attempts to introduce rapid changes in society so that the Malay community will be more directly involved in the modern agricultural sector as well as in the commercial and industrial sectors of the country. Within twenty years the government hopes to create a Malay entrepreneurial community that will own at least 30 per cent of the wealth in the country and occupy positions at all levels of economic enterprise. A Malay capitalist class was envisaged within the framework of a free enterprise system in which all private enterprise would continue to function, more or less unimpeded, but in which Malay private enterprise would be given a special push by the state. The government made it clear that its policy of expanding Malay ownership would be carried out within the framework of a growing economy so that no one would be deprived of anything already possessed.[4]

The objectives of the NEP were outlined in the Fourth Malaysia Plan:

1. Increase the productivity and enhance the quality of life of the rural poor through rural modernisation.
2. Reduce, in progressive steps and through overall economic growth, current imbalances in employment so that employment in the various sectors of the economy and by occupational level will reflect the racial composition of the population.
3. Increase progressively and through overall growth of the economy the share of Malaysians in the ownership of productive capital in the economy, including corporate stock, and in particular improve the position of the Bumiputras who currently account for a particularly low share in comparison with their representation in the population.
4. Ensure the creation of a commercial and industrial community among the Bumiputras, in order that, within one generation, they will own and manage at least 30 per cent of the total commercial and industrial wealth of the country and will become full partners in the economic life of the nation.[5]

Land reform policies were not explicitly formulated in the various statements of government policy except in terms of opening up new land for Malay settlement; there is no doubt, however, that the government is concerned about the concentration of plantation land and urban land in non-Malay hands, and is attempting to increase Malay ownership by various strategies.

The strategies designed to advance the objectives of the NEP, especially those relating to business and land, their implementation and impact on ethnic relations in Malaysia, are investigated in this paper.

NEP Goals and Strategies

The NEP has two primary goals—the eradication of poverty and the restructuring of society to correct inter-ethnic economic inequalities. The basic instruments expected to influence achievement of the goal of the eradication of poverty are:

- provision of adequate credit and technical assistance to farmers and fishermen;
- introduction of input subsidy schemes and price-support programmes for rice;
- replanting grants for rubber;
- improved marketing and infrastructure facilities;
- better education and health facilities in rural areas;
- new land-settlement projects for moving Malays from traditional subsistence agriculture to modern plantation methods.

Policies designed to induce change in the economic structure of society are:

- monetary policies that influence the lending behavior of commercial banks so that they will extend credit to Malays in larger amounts and on easy repayment terms, especially for setting up new businesses or expanding existing ones;
- tax incentives aimed at encouraging private investment in particular areas so that restructuring targets related to equity and employment can be achieved;
- development policies designed to encourage greater Malay participation in the economy and to bring about more balanced regional development;
- policies to increase the equity stock held by Malays by having public corporations invest directly in the corporate sector, either on a project basis or through acquisitions and mergers;
- provision of credit and technical services to small-scale Malay entrepreneurs.[6]

Land Policies

Land policies in the agricultural sector are designed to reduce pressure on existing land use by opening new land for settlement and by shifting from rice to plantation crops. Between 1971 and 1980 a total of 731,587 hectares of new land in peninsular Malaysia was developed by various federal and state government agencies.[7] This is an increase of about one-third of the country's total cultivated land. Another 470,182 hectares have been allocated for new development in 1981–5. It has been the unwritten policy of the government to reserve all available, new cultivable land for Malay ownership. Almost all the land in the new land-settlement projects is owned by Malays.[8] This policy is justified on the grounds that in 1970, 49.3 per cent of the total households in peninsular Malaysia were classified as poor;[9] 86.3 per cent of these poor households were in rural areas. Of the 791,800 poor households in the country, 584,200, or 73.8 per cent, were Malay.[10] The Third Malaysia Plan indicated that while the incidence of poverty was 49.3 per cent for the entire country, the highest percentage was among Malays—64.8 per cent compared with 26.0 per cent for the Chinese and 39.2 per cent for the Indians. Poverty was considerably more severe for rural than for urban households, with the rural–urban differential being especially large for Malays.

Apart from the fact that Malays need more land because they constitute the largest and poorest section of the rural population, there exists the view (though not as openly expressed) that the Malays are the rightful owners of the land and as such should not be dispossessed of their own land. It is generally recognised that the constitutional provision assigning the right to allocate land to state governments is rooted in the proposition that the country is the native land of the Malays and that 'given the self-conscious racial attitudes in Malaysia it would invite political disaster if Malays were dispossessed by Chinese'.[11] It was this attitude that led to the creation of Malay reservation land areas which could not be transferred to non-Malays. However, as a result of political bargaining between the British government and various political leaders representing ethnic groups in the country, constitutional restrictions were placed on the establishment of Malay land-reservation areas.[12] In fact, by 1969 only some 13 per cent of the total alienated land for cultivation was estimated to be in Malay reservation areas.[13] Meanwhile, large tracts were alienated to foreign and Chinese ownership for rubber cultivation early in the twentieth century, and, though little new agricultural land was alienated to non-Malays after independence, the damage had been done, in the sense that the choicest tracts of land, in terms of size and location, were alienated to foreigners and Malaysians of Chinese and Indian origin. In a study conducted in two districts near Kuala Lumpur, it was shown that Malay ownership in terms of acreage was only 16.3 per cent, whereas

Chinese ownership was 42.2 and European 28.5 per cent. The study also showed that the lots were much larger for Chinese and European plantation companies than for Malaysian. The average size of European lots was 83.4 hectares, compared with 7.1 hectares for Chinese and only 1.6 for Malays (see Table 10.1). It is likely that a detailed study would reveal that in the case of European ownership individual owners owned several lots.

Table 10.1. Land Alienation by Ethnic Ownership in Seminyih and Ulu Seminyih, 1960

	Hectares	%	No. of lots	Average size of lot
Planting companies	1,035	9.1	39	26.5
European	3,251	28.5	39	83.4
Chinese	4,817	42.2	678	7.1
Malay	1,863	16.3	1,172	1.6
Indian	434	3.8	73	5.9
Mixed	8	0.1	3	2.7
Total	11,408	100.0	2,004	5.7

Source: Phin-Keong Voon, 'Evolution of Ethnic Patterns of Rural Land Ownership in Peninsular Malaysia: A Case Study', *South East Asian Studies,* vol. 15, no. 48 (March 1978).

Much of this land, on the urban fringe of Kuala Lumpur, has now become extremely valuable for building purposes. By 1968, Malay ownership of the modern agricultural sector (excluding FELDA schemes) was only 0.8 per cent as compared with 42.2 per cent non-Malay ownership and 56.8 per cent foreign ownership. (Details of acreage by crop are given in Table 10.2.)

The government's strategy for increasing Malay ownership of agricultural land for growing plantation crops was to inaugurate new land-settlement projects throughout the country. Projects were begun by federal and state agencies. Between 1960 and 1979 the area of rubber estates under private ownership decreased by 34 per cent while individual smallholdings remained about the same. The expansion in land settlement was meteoric, rising by more than 3,000 per cent since 1960, and has more than offset the substantial loss in the estate sector, as shown in Table 10.3.

In urban areas, however, there was no restriction on non-Malay ownership. As land in the centre of the main towns and cities became scarce, urban land became a major source of wealth. Because Chinese and

Table 10.2. Estimated Total Estates Acreage for Rubber, Oil Palm, Coconut and Tea, by Race, as at End of 1968

Crop	Total Acreage	Malaysian-owned						Non-Malaysian-owned	
		Malays	%	Non-Malays	%	Total	%		%
Rubber	1,507,716	14,081	1	726,776	48	740,857	49	766,659	51
Oil Palm	380,680	41	–	83,182	22	83,196	22	297,484	78
Coconut	56,563	831	1.4	13,918	24.6	14,731	26	41,832	74
Tea	7,492	NIL	–	3,353	45.3	3,353	45.3	4,139	54.7

Source: The Report of the Economic Committee National Consultative Council on the Problems of Racial Economic Imbalance and National Unity, Kuala Lumpur, Jabatan Perpaduan Negara, October 1970, p. 41.

Table 10.3. Total Planted Area under Rubber in Peninsular Malaysia, 1979, and Changes in Area since 1960 by Sector

Sector	Area (000s hectares)	Average size (hectares)	Percentage of total	Area changes since 1960 (%)
Estates	516.8	309	30.2	–34
Individual smallholdings	815.4	2.6	47.6	–3
Land-development projects	379.6	1.4–3.7	22.2	+3117
Total	1,711.8	–	100	+5

Source: Lim Sow Ching, 'The Role of the Malaysian Rubber and Rubber-based Industries in the 1980s', paper presented at Sixth Malaysian Economic Association Convention, May 7–10, 1980, Penang.
(1 hectare equals 2.47 acres)

Indian-Malaysians lived mostly in urban areas, especially on the west coast of peninsular Malaysia, inevitably their proportion of land ownership was higher than that of Malays. Data of foreign ownership is not available, but data on the ownership of urban land in certain towns indicate that Malay ownership in the capital city of Kuala Lumpur and in Georgetown, Penang is very low, whereas their proportion of ownership in the major towns of the north and east coast is much higher. (The distribution of land ownership in certain major towns and cities is given in Table 10.4.)

From the figures given in table 10.4, it can be seen that by 1970 Malay ownership of land was small in terms of both size and value. In Kuala Lumpur, for example, the average value of Malay property was roughly one-fourth that of non-Malay property. What was perhaps more disturbing was that Malays appeared to be selling urban land at a faster rate than they were buying new land, while the reverse was true of the Chinese; thus, between 1960 and 1977, Malays experienced a net loss of 233.3 hectares, while Chinese experienced a net gain of 598 hectares. [14]

Since 1970, the state has adopted policies designed to increase Malay ownership of urban land, especially land suitable for commercial and industrial use. The Urban Development Authority (UDA) was established to acquire urban property with the right to sell or rent such properties to Malays at prices below market rates. The UDA has powers to compulsorily acquire land for urban development, but to date it seems to prefer to purchase land at market prices from non-Malay owners. Another strategy used by the UDA is to form joint ventures with private housing developers to construct houses for sale to all ethnic groups but with a specified quota

Table 10.4. Land Ownership (by Area) in Selected Towns, by Ethnicity (in %), 1974

	Malays	Chinese	Indians	Others
Georgetown	5	70	6	19
Butterworth	8	77	14	1
Bukit Mertajam	13	77	5	5
Kulim	29	53	17	1
Alor Star	61	20	12	7
Kota Bharu	86	9	1	4
Kuala Lumpur*	15	70	12	3

*Calculated on number of properties owned by each ethnic group, 1968 figures.
Source: Goh Ban Lee, 'Patterns of Landownership: Case Studies in Urban Inequalities', in Cheong Kee Cheok, Khoo Siew Mun and R. Thillainathan, 'Malaysia, Some Contemporary Issues in Socio-economic Development', *Persatuan Ekonomi Malaysia, Kuala Lumpur,* January 1979, p. 66. Kuala Lumpur figures are from Karl von Vorys, *Democracy without Consensus,* Oxford University Press, 1976. p. 242.[15]

reserved for Malays who could purchase the houses at prices below the market rates. The state also requires private-housing developers to obtain licences for each housing project; the licences are approved on the condition that a certain number of houses are reserved for sale to Malays.

In addition to these measures, the government provides housing loans to government officers that carry low interest rates and easy repayment terms. Although loans are available to all civil servants regardless of race, a large proportion of senior civil servants who qualify for large loans are Malays. Measures have also been taken to increase the salaries of government officers so that they have more savings available to invest in land and commercial ventures.

Business Policies

Business policies are designed to encourage economic growth while at the same time ensuring greater participation by Malays. Public policies have concentrated on restructuring the corporate sector, especially the ownership of equity and employment. The equity-ownership targets of the NEP for 1990 are to be achieved by steady progress over a twenty-year period, from 1970 to 1990.

Table 10.5 shows ownership and participation in the industrial and commercial sectors by race. It will be seen that Malay ownership in all sectors except road transport was tiny.[16] In road transport, as far back as 1958, the Licensing Board was directed to give preference to applications from Malays or Malay companies. When the NEP was formulated, in which the government made clear its determination to expand Malay

Table 10.5. Peninsular Malaysia: Ownership and Participation in Industrial and Commercial Sectors, 1970 and 1975 (% share in selected sectors)

Activity	1970					1975				
	Malay	Chinese	Indian	Others	Foreigner	Malay	Chinese	Indian	Others	Foreigner
Industry (fixed assets)	1.0	33.3	0.4	8.8	56.5	3.5	23.6	0.3	28.3	44.4
Mining	0.8	24.9	–	11.1	63.2	2.1	32.3	0.2	13.3	52.0
Manufacturing	0.9	32.5	0.4	8.6	57.6	3.6	19.7	0.3	31.8	44.5
Construction	3.8	88.5	1.0	0.8	5.9	4.5	59.2	0.7	7.0	28.6
Trade (turnover)	1.2	69.5	3.5	0.2	25.5	2.2	58.4	5.7	2.9	30.7
Wholesale	0.7	66.2	2.5	0.2	30.4	1.7	53.3	5.8	3.3	36.0
Retail	3.0	81.2	7.3	0.4	8.2	4.2	77.3	5.5	1.6	11.4
Transport (fixed assets)	18.0	56.5	3.2	14.3	8.0	31.2	37.0	2.6	28.2	1.0
Taxi	47.7	37.5	12.5	2.3	–	65.5	21.8	4.6	8.0	–
Bus	18.0	52.8	1.7	18.0	9.5	18.6	34.2	0.6	46.6	–
Haulage	14.5	69.4	6.0	4.8	5.3	39.9	41.3	4.4	12.4	2.0

Source: Fourth Malaysia Plan, 1981–85, p. 64.

participation in the economy as a matter of urgent priority, further amendments were added to the Road Traffic Act to remove 'most legal obstacles to the rapid expansion of Malay participation in the transport industry'.[17] Many safeguards provided to existing non-Malay operators were removed and the Malay preference clause was extended to other areas. The participation of Bumiputras in road transport increased significantly from 1970 to 1978. About 67 per cent of total licences to operate taxis and rented cars were issued to Bumiputras. In lorry transport, the Chinese still dominate, with 83 per cent participation, although in Type A lorries, Bumiputra participation was 60 per cent.[18]

It was felt that Malay equity ownership in other sectors could be increased in the same way, that is, by regulation and direction. The Industrial Coordination Act (ICA) was aimed at the manufacturing sector, the prime mover of the economy, which had registered the highest growth rate and was the one sector where the disparity between Malays and non-Malays was most significant.[19] The primary purpose of the ICA was to control the development and growth of the manufacturing industry through the issue of licences. When a licence was issued, new conditions were imposed. These conditions were not stated in the Act, but government has indicated that the conditions relate to such matters as equity structure, composition of the board of directors, employment and training, distribution patterns, and marketing arrangements. Concerning equity participation, companies were required to submit long-range plans so as to comply with the state's request for at least 30 per cent Malay ownership by 1990. Companies, while not expected to comply immediately with these conditions, were required to submit long-term plans indicating how they would take specific measures to achieve the NEP target 'over a reasonable period of time'.

Thus, through administrative and regulatory measures, the state hoped to increase Malay ownership in the corporate sector. In the same way, proposals to expand business in a particular field or move into new business ventures required government approval; here again, conditions are laid down requiring a certain quota of new shares to be reserved for Malays. The government also set up numerous administrative units and committees to carry out, on the one hand, the regulation and control of private enterprises and, on the other, to provide special assistance to Malays who wish to set up or to expand their businesses. In addition, regulations gave preference to Malays in such areas as government contracts and the purchase of new shares.

At the same time, the government realised that Malay savings were insufficient to absorb the equity stock reserved for Malays. During the Second Malaysia Plan, therefore, public corporations increasingly took up these shares and invested them directly in the corporate sector. In the Third Malaysia Plan, the government allocated approximately M$1.7 billion to increase the equity stock of Malays. The urgency of government priorities is reflected in the amount of government funds allocated to the agencies, including the National Corporation (PERNAS), the Peoples Trust Council (MARA), the State Economic Development Corporations (SEDCs) the Urban Development Authority, the Development Bank and the Bumiputra Investment Fund. These allocations by the government amounted to M$4197 million, or 77 per cent of the allocation of public development funds for commerce and industry. The government has also set up a special investment company, Permodalan Nasional Berhad (PNB; National Investment Company), to consolidate public-sector investment in private companies and make investments on behalf of the government. At the same time, a special trust company was set up to mobilise Malay savings and invest savings on behalf of the company's Malay members. The administrative expenses of running many of these agencies were paid from the annual budget of the federal government. The government also guaranteed at least a 10 per cent dividend on investment in the PNB.

The function of the PNB was to invest funds received from the government and from the National Unit Trust in private-sector companies considered to be financially sound. The PNB bought shares in private plantation companies and mining companies, sometimes acquiring shares large enough to have a controlling interest in the companies. It also acquired shares in companies partially or fully-owned by public corporations—companies purchased at cost. Naturally, the PNB has been interested only in purchasing companies that are financially sound, whether they are owned by the private sector or by public corporations. The government thus bears the full cost of all public-sector projects that are not profitable. As soon as they become profitable, the beneficiaries will almost entirely be Malays and not the public as a whole. In effect, only one segment of the population benefits from government investments, although all segments must bear the financial burden. In other words, government resources are used to finance the bulk of Malay-share capital acquisition.

The establishment of the PNB and the National Unit Trust Scheme has the advantage of spreading the benefits to all classes of the Malay community rather than to only one; this would have happened if the companies had been sold directly to private Malay individuals and companies. It has also resulted in ensuring goals of both ownership and control; thus, while ownership is dispersed among numerous holdings, control is concentrated in the hands of the trustees, or, effectively, those of trust fund managers. In effect, control falls into the hands of government. The government, through ownership of shares, is said to control about 60 per cent of the plantation and mining sectors and 70 per cent of the banking sector.[20] The government now controls 56.6 per cent of the Malaysian Mining Corporation, the world's largest tin conglomerate in terms of annual output. Through shares in plantation companies, the government is thought to control at least half of the estate acreage under rubber and oil palm. For the time being, the government is content to concentrate on acquiring ownership but not actively participating in the management and control of companies in which it has ownership. It is possible, however, that the control that such ownership gives can be used to further the government's aim of increasing Malay ownership of wealth in the corporate sector.

The Implementation of the NEP and Its Impact on Ethnic Relations

There is no doubt that the NEP, and particularly the policy of poverty eradication, has contributed significantly to reducing rural poverty. As shown in Table 10.6, the incidence of poverty for all ethnic groups fell from 49.3 per cent in 1970 to 35.1 in 1976. Income improvement is seen particularly among the Malays, where the poverty levels fell from 64.8 to 46.4 per cent, due largely to government efforts to improve the standard of living of paddy farmers, rubber smallholders, and fishermen through various measures to increase productivity and through subsidies and price-support schemes. The incidence of poverty has also fallen noticeably for the other ethnic groups despite the absence of a conscious effort on the part of government to improve their socio-economic position; in fact, income improvement among Chinese and Indians is greater than for Malays, so that poor Malay households have increased from 73.8 to 75.5 per cent of the total poor households.

Data given in Table 10.7 on the mean monthly household income of the poorest section of society by race indicate that the annual growth rate was highest for the Chinese between 1971 and 1976 but was highest for the Malays between 1971 and 1979. Clearly, without these affirmative measures by the government, the poverty levels would not have fallen.

No figures are available showing how land-ownership patterns have changed, reflecting government policy of increasing Malay ownership of urban land; but significant improvements have been made in Malay ownership of agricultural land through land settlement (Table 10.8). FELDA has become the single largest grower of oil palm in the world. By 1979 the total area developed by FELDA alone was 1,194,000 acres, with 53,000 families settled on FELDA projects.[21] If we include all new land for agriculture opened up during the last ten years by federal and state agencies, including land-development agencies and regional development

Table 10.6. Peninsular Malaysia: Households in Poverty, by Race, 1970 and 1976

	1970				1976			
	All households (000s)	Poor households (000s)	Poverty incidence (%)	Percentage of total poor households	All households (000s)	Poor households (000s)	Poverty incidence (%)	Percentage of total poor households
Malay	901.5	584.2	64.8	73.8	1,119.4	519.4	46.4	75.5
Chinese	525.2	136.3	26.0	17.2	628.8	109.4	17.4	15.9
Indian	160.5	62.9	39.2	7.9	197.1	53.8	27.3	7.8
Others	18.8	8.4	44.8	1.1	14.7	5.7	33.8	0.8
TOTAL	1,606.0	791.8	49.3	100.0	1,960.9	688.3	35.1	100
All rural	1,166.7	683.7	58.6	86.3	1,417.5	606.2	42.8	88.1
All urban	439.3	108.1	24.6	13.7	543.4	82.1	15.1	11.9

Source: Third Malaysia Plan, p. 180; Fourth Malaysia Plan, pp. 46–7.

Table 10.7. Peninsular Malaysia: Mean Monthly Household Income of
the Lowest Four Deciles for 1970, 1976 and 1979

	1970 ($)	1976 ($)	1979 ($)	Annual growth rate	
				1971–76 (%)	1971–79 (%)
Malay	56.76	101.95	140.35	10.3	10.6
Chinese	135.93	247.27	280.11	10.5	8.4
Indian	112.48	197.21	263.43	9.8	9.9
Others	44.72	107.08	154.37	15.7	14.8
TOTAL	75.90	142.19	186.19	11.0	10.5

Source: Fourth Malaysia Plan, 1981–5, p. 37.

Table 10.8. Malaysia Progress in Land Development 1971–80 and
Target Acreage 1981–85 (hectares)

Agency/Programme	Target 1971–80	Achievement 1971–80	Target 1981–85
Federal programmes			
FELDA	365,587	373,705	149,798
FELCRA	60,729	50,710	32,662
RISDA	101,215	31,463	15,409
	527,531	455,878	197,869
State programmes			
Peninsular Malaysia	75,911	155,662	143,872
Sabah	67,611	57,816	56,680
Sarawak	90,202	76,655	16,599
	233,724	290,133	217,151
Joint venture/private sector	134,615	120,047	128,441
TOTAL	895,870	866,058	543,461

Source: Fourth Malaysia Plan, 1981–85, p. 270.

agencies, we get an increase of about 2,100,000 acres of new land opened up for agriculture, or an increase of about 22 per cent of land earmarked for agriculture since 1969. Most new land-development projects are owned either by Malays or by public agencies acting in trust for Malays.

Regarding changes in equity ownership, Table 10.9 shows that Bumiputra ownership has increased from M$279.6 million in 1971 to M$3,273.7 million in 1980, primarily because of the substantial inflow of government funds to public enterprises. The individual Malay share in the corporate ownership sector, however, increased in slow stages from 4.3 per cent in 1971 to 12.4 per cent in 1980. The growth in the economic development of the country as a whole that resulted in the expansion of the corporate sector exceeded even the expected rate of growth envisaged by government planners.

The country's impressive economic growth rate has made it possible for the state to redistribute incomes and restructure society without openly resorting to discriminatory measures against particular ethnic groups. Certain adverse consequences of the NEP, however, may aggravate tensions between and within racial groups. The NEP has not been able to solve the problems of urban unemployment or rural under-employment. There has been no definite industrialisation policy to absorb excess labour from the land; land-settlement schemes thus far have not opened up new land at the rate necessary to absorb this excess labour. In addition, the amount of new land that can be made available for cultivation is finite—something that several writers have pointed out—for example, S. Nair and L. J. Fredericks:

While FELDA is recognised as having pioneered a model of land development much admired in the region, its impact on rural employment creation and on reducing rural unemployment and under-employment is less than impressive. By the early 1970s, the total number of settler families absorbed by FELDA was only 2,740 per annum as opposed to the increase in rural population of 150,000 per annum. Over 1970–80, the labour force in Malaysia increased from 3.7 million to 5.4 million, while 286,500 people were unemployed. The total number of settler families absorbed by FELDA during the same period was only 42,200. Thus FELDA's impact on employment in a microcontext does not appear to be substantial.[22]

What is perhaps more disturbing, favourable rubber prices in 1980 had much to do with the dramatic drop in poverty among rubber smallholders, whereas the government's price-support and input subsidy schemes were crucial to reducing poverty among paddy farmers.[23] A recent study of land tenure in the MUDA area showed how the fragmentation and subdivision of paddy land has increased over the fifteen years, resulting in more than two-thirds of the farms being less than six relongs in size (1 relong equals approximately 0.7 of an acre) and about one-third being

Table 10.9. Malaysian Corporate Ownership and Control of the Corporate Sector ($ millions)

	1971	%	1980 (target)	%	1980 (estimated actual)	%	1990 (target)	%
Malaysian residents	2,512.8	38.3	11,574.8	56.4	13,817.8	52.5	52,193.9	70.0
Bumiputra individuals	168.7	2.6	695.4	3.4	1,128.9	4.3	3,891.4	5.2
Bumiputra trust agencies	110.9	1.7	2,589.9	12.6	2,144.8	8.1	18,477.4	24.8
Other Malaysian residents	2,233.2	34.0	8,290.5	40.4	10,544.1	40.1	29,825.1	40.0
Foreign residents	4,051.3	61.7	8,952.5	43.6	12,505.2	47.5	22,368.8	30.0
TOTAL	6,564.1	100	20,528.3	100	26,323.0	100	74,562.7	100

Source: Third Malaysia Plan, 1976–80, p. 86, table 4:16; Fourth Malaysia Plan, 1981–85, p. 62, table 3.14 and p. 176, table 9.7.

less than three relongs.[24] It is clear that the incidence of poverty among paddy farmers would have been much higher had the government not provided assistance in the form of subsidies and price supports. In the same way, temporary commodity upswings cannot be relied upon for the sustained reduction of poverty in the long run, as the effects of recent downward trends in rubber price have dramatised.[25]

Another adverse effect of the NEP on ethnic relations is its tendency to shift government attention from the eradication of poverty to the creation of a small group of wealthy Malays. As is pointed out by Sundram, since the inception of the NEP, the state's commitment, as reflected by expenditure allocation, has shifted increasingly from eradication of poverty to restructuring. The ratio of allocations for restructuring, compared to poverty eradication, rose steadily from 0.216 under the Second Malaysia Plan to 0.373 under the Third Malaysia Plan, and to 0.472 under the Fourth Malaysia Plan.[26]

Two dangers arise from this shift in emphasis. First, there is the danger that government efforts, in terms of both funds and manpower, are being diverted from tackling the major problem of poverty, which, as the NEP itself says, is the fundamental cause of inter-ethnic conflict. In particular, Malay poverty juxtaposed with what is seen as non-Malay affluence is the most serious challenge to ethnic relations in the country. For this reason, efforts to improve the standard of living of the Malay majority are a positive contribution to national harmony.[27] So far, there are positive indications that the standard of living of the Malay majority has improved, but to what extent this is due to outside factors, such as favourable commodity prices, is not clear. Some observers are concerned that, with a decline in world commodity prices, not only will the income of farmers fall but reduced revenue will deprive the government of the funds necessary to maintain the improvements already achieved. If this happens, a deterioration in ethnic relations in the country is likely.

Second, there is the danger that a large proportion of government resources is being channelled into creating a small group of wealthy Malays at the expense of the rest of the population. It has been estimated that at most 5 per cent of the Bumiputra population is in a position to benefit from restructuring-oriented expenditures, compared to the 46.4 per cent of the Malay population officially considered poor in 1976.[28] As Chandra Muzzafar points out, it is not clear how the creation of a small Malay wealthy class can solve the problem of Malay poverty:

That the creation of Malay millionaires, or Malay capitalists and entrepreneurs, is of no consequence at all to national unity is only too apparent. We could in fact turn the argument around: is the present paucity of Malay capitalists one of the fundamental sources of Sino–Malay tension? We know for certain that none of the ethnic riots in the entire history of the country·had anything to do with this question. By and large, Malay apprehensions are linked to the poverty of the majority of Malays in relation to what is perceived as non-Malay affluence and the extent of non-Malay political participation in relation to existing Malay political pre-eminence. It is true that Malay poverty juxtaposed with what is seen as non-Malay affluence is easily the most serious challenge to ethnic relations in the country. It is an issue which can be and has been exploited by politicians. For that reason any endeavour to improve the standard of living of the Malay majority can be interpreted as a positive contribution towards national unity. But resolving problems of Malay poverty is quite different from creating Malay capitalists. Even if Malay capitalists are created but Malay poverty persists, the problem of national unity will remain.[29]

The focus on ethnic differences in the corporate ownership of wealth and on creating a class of Bumiputra entrepreneurs and capitalists has made ethnicity a key issue in all public policy matters. It has blurred the attitude of society to such broader socio-economic challenges as land reform, credit and marketing systems, the co-operative movement, clearance of slums, better wages and working conditions, more employment opportunities, proper housing and social amenities, fair prices for goods and services, and the elimination of corruption. All this has nothing to do with ethnicity.[30] Instead, it has left the economic system continuing to operate within the framework of a free enterprise system with no effective safeguards to ensure fairer distribution of income between rich and poor segments of society. Several studies indicate that wealth is concentrated in the hands of a small group, while the rest of the community remains poor. In fact, evidence exists showing that from 1957 to 1970 the distribution of income among all ethnic groups became more unequal. The total income of the upper 10 per cent of households rose from 48 to 56 per cent. Within the Malay community, differences between rich and poor increased more markedly than in the other communities, with the total income of the top 10 per cent rising from 42 to 53 per cent.[31]

Even within the capitalist class, there are significant differences in the ownership of wealth. A study of the 98 largest manufacturing companies in the country reveals that 214 shareholdings, 0.3 per cent of the total number, are worth M$36,700,400, or 23 per cent of the total value.[32] Significant differences also exist in the average value of shareholdings among ethnic groups. As shown in Table 10.10, the average value of Malay shares is smaller than the average value of Chinese shares, but the average value of Malay small, medium and large shareholdings is larger than the average of the Chinese shareholdings in these categories. Only in the very small category is the average value of Malay shareholding smaller than the Chinese shareholding. There are, however, seven shareholdings in the very large category, valued at M$10,734,100 owned by Chinese.

The concentration of corporate wealth in a capitalist system is not surprising. As pointed out by Moore, equity ownership in most capitalist

Table 10.10. Distribution of Number and Value of Malaysian Personal Ordinary Shareholdings, by Race and Size

Size of Shareholdings (No. of shares)	Malays			Chinese			Indians			Others			Total		
	No. of share holding	Value of share holding ($000s)	Average value of share holding	No. of share holding	Value of share holding ($000s)	Average value of share holding	No. of share holding	Value of share holding ($000s)	Average value of share holding	No. of share holding	Value of share holding ($000s)	Average value of share holding	No. of share holding	Value of share holding ($000s)	Average value of share holding
Very small	5,993	3412.0	569.3	30,426	22,238.0	730.9	4,577	2696.9	589.2	934	601.1	643.6	41,930	28,948.0	690.4
Small	1,535	3751.6	2,444.0	17,824	42,588.7	2,389.4	1,946	4499.2	2,312.0	527	1,285.9	2,440.0	21,832	52,125.4	2,387.6
Medium	316	3929.6	12,435.4	2,981	33,828.7	11,348.1	209	2304.2	11,024.8	116	1,369.8	11,808.6	3,622	41,432.3	11,439.1
Large	17	2471.6	145,388.2	181	22,565.1	124,669.0	7	596.2	85,171.4	2	333.4	166,700.0	207	25,966.3	125,441.1
Very large	—	—	—	7	10,734.1	1533,442.8	—	—	—	—	—	—	7	10,734.1	1,533,442.8
TOTAL	7,861	13564.8	1,725.6	51,419	131,954.6	2,566.3	6,739	10096.5	1,498.2	1579	3,590.2	2,273.7	67,598	159,206.1	2,355.2
%	11.6	8.5		76.1	82.9		10.0	6.3		0.3	0.3		100	100	

Source: Sieh Lee Mei Ling, 'The Structure of Ownership and Control of Manufacturing Companies in Malaysia'. Ph.D. thesis, University of Sheffield, 1978, vol. **2**, pp. 179–82.

countries tends to be highly concentrated, with the top 10 per cent of households holding 90 per cent or more of total equities. Lower- and middle-income groups invariably hold lower wealth-income ratios and prefer to hold the bulk of their wealth in such tangible assets as consumer durables—for example, automobiles, TV sets and real estate. To the extent that they hold financial assets, they are primarily high-liquid currency and savings deposits.[33] True, the government has encouraged more lower and middle groups to own shares through government investment trust companies, but the companies at the bottom of the income scale still cannot participate. In 1973 nearly 85 per cent of Malays lived in rural areas, and 35 per cent of Malay households had a per capita income of less than M$300 per year. It is difficult to see how they could become shareholders. Thus, by concentrating on the target of equity ownership, the NEP has yielded in an even more skewed distribution of wealth in the country than earlier. Moore emphasises this point:

Given the fact that in all capitalist countries share-ownership is extremely highly concentrated it is not conceivable how increasing Malay share ownership could benefit the Malay kampong dweller, the [paddy] farmer, or [the] fisherman. Even if shares were distributed evenly among the Malay community, they would be resold by the poorer members, who would prefer to hold their wealth in other forms. A closed-end mutual fund restricted to Malays could at least keep the wealth share within the Malay community. But even if shares were initially equally distributed, their resale by the poorer classes to finance consumption expenditures would soon operate to increase the inequality of wealth distribution.[34]

The NEP tends to view the country's economic problems in racial terms. Comparing the progress of the Malay community in terms of the other communities, it has failed to tackle successfully the economic problems of the country as a whole, resulting in ambiguities and contradictions in its policy. For example, on the one hand, the state depends on foreign investment to raise the growth rate of the Malaysian economy, while, on the other, aiming to reduce the share of corporate wealth owned by foreigners from 60 per cent in 1970 to 30 per cent by 1990. Another example of a conflict requiring resolution is the need for a clear distinction between the role of the Bumiputra entrepreneur and the public corporation in the corporate sector. There have been cases where Bumiputras felt that public corporations were competing against them for public-sector contracts, which was not the intention of the NEP. Another example is the conflict between policies that are discriminatory in practice against Malaysians of Chinese and Indian origin despite the expressed non-discriminatory intention of the NEP.

By measuring economic growth in terms of communities and by fixing arbitrary targets based on a percentage of ownership of wealth in racial terms, the NEP has created other problems which, if not solved, can exacerbate rather than reduce ethnic conflict. The other danger arising from the view of economic problems in racial terms is that such a view tends to create ethnic stereotypes. Thus, all Malays are regarded as poor and all Chinese as rich. In particular, the highly visible wealth of the Chinese in urban areas contrasts with Malay poverty in rural areas. This over-simplified view tends to blur the fact that almost 60 per cent of the wealth of the country, in terms of equity capital, is in foreign hands and that the highest profit rate is to be found in foreign-controlled firms.[35] Also, that view tends to ignore the fact that a considerable number of the Chinese and the Indians are poor and just as much in need of government assistance as poor Malays. For example, 55 per cent of poor urban households are Chinese and Indian.[36] One study revealed that in 1972 the extent of squatting and slum dwelling in major urban centres of the country was 10.15 per cent of the total urban population. The percentage of squatters was even greater in Kuala Lumpur, where the figure was about 45 per cent of the city's population. Of 174,000 squatters living in Kuala Lumpur, 64.5 per cent were Chinese.[37]

The participation of the Indian community, in terms of capital ownership in the modern agricultural sector and the industrial and commercial sectors, is negligible (table 5). Only in the coconut and tea plantations (a very small sector in terms of planted acreage in the modern plantation sector) and the professional establishments, is Indian participation significant. (In the transport industry it is assumed that Indian ownership has declined because of the government's discriminatory policy). Most Indians are wage labourers working on estates and in urban employment; but it is they who have suffered most under the NEP. Their rate of unemployment is the highest among the ethnic groups, although the percentage has fallen significantly from 11 in 1970 to 7.5 per cent in 1980.[38] Of 525,000 new jobs created in 1970-5, 58.9 per cent were taken by Malays, 32.4 per cent by Chinese, and 8.4 per cent by Indians. The Chinese and Indian share was lower than their proportion in the population. Because a significant proportion of Indians depend on employment to earn a living, this means considerable hardship. Already they constitute 16 per cent of poor urban households, though their population is only 10.5 per cent of the total.

The danger of the NEP is that in concentrating on inequalities between the races it tends to assume that the economic problems of Malays are a national problem, whereas those of other communities are not, and must be resolved by each particular community. This tendency was hinted at by a Chinese minister:

We have sometimes tended to look at the economic problems of communities by sectors, comparing their progress or lack of it with others. Measuring economic growth by communities alone can lead to a situation [where] some politicians may feel that only the problems of their own community are a national problem, whereas those of another community are one for that particular community to resolve as best it can. It is precisely because we must avoid this incipient danger that economists and politicians together need to measure growth that will cut across such narrow perceptions if we are to ensure the adoption of a set of policies that will keep us stable politically and grow steadily.[39]

The NEP target is supposed to be achieved within twenty years. Ten years have already passed, but, while great progress has been made in increasing the corporate wealth of Bumiputras, it is far behind in its stated goal. Despite the large government funds pouring into public corporations classified as Bumiputra trust agencies—which have resulted in an annual growth rate between 1972 and 1980 of 31.4 per cent for Bumiputras, compared with an annual growth rate of 18.8 per cent for other Malaysians and 13.3 for foreign residents[40] —the Malay share of the corporate wealth increased to 12.4 per cent in 1980, whereas the Chinese and Indian target of 40 per cent was achieved by 1980. Of course, the achievement of the Bumiputras is much greater as it was able to increse its share from 4.3 per cent in 1971 to 12.4 per cent in 1980, whereas the share of Chinese and Indian communities rose from 34 per cent in 1971 to 40 per cent in 1980. The fact that Bumiputras have not yet achieved even half their target, while non-Bumiputras have already achieved theirs, has resulted in a considerable amount of frustration and inter-ethnic conflict.

The youth wing of UMNO, known to express Malay extremist views, has played an active part in influencing the government to restrict the economic growth of other Malaysians, to allow Malays to catch up. In March 1981 the UMNO youth wing opposed the proposed purchase of substantial shares in the United Malayan Banking Corporation (UMBC) by a Chinese company, on the ground that since 30 per cent of UMBC shares were already owned by the government, the move 'was threatening Malay interests'. The government then intervened, increasing its share ownership of UMBC to maintain a balance of Malay and non-Malay ownership in the bank. More recently, a move by a Chinese company to purchase substantial shares, which would give controlling interest in Dunlop Estates, a plantation company, was opposed by the UMNO youth wing on the grounds that 'any sale of shares by big foreign companies should rightly be offered to Bumiputra companies before it [is] offered to anybody else'.[41] Since several public corporations owned by the government are considered to be Bumiputra companies, it was not difficult to get the necessary funds from the government to purchase the shares.

Definite signs of increased inter-ethnic conflict are evident among middle-class urban groups. The emerging Malay middle class is in the best position to use government policy to better itself, whereas the non-Malay middle class is afraid to lose what it has already gained. Both groups tend to make aggressive demands ostensibly on behalf of their own ethnic community. Under slogans of communal interest and unity, they advance particular class interests as the concern of the entire ethnic community.[42] The policies they advocate are different. Malay middle-class groups—concentrated in the civil service, statutory bodies, public enterprises, and the military' usually advocate increased salaries for government officers, greater opportunities and privileges for Malays (so they can improve their economic position *vis-à-vis* the other communities), and more controls over private non-Malay enterprise. Non-Malay middle-class groups, on the other hand, emphasise the importance of free enterprise and less government intervention in what they consider normal business trans-actions within a free-enterprise system. It is this group that is most affected by the state's educational policies.

Thus the NEP has done little to reduce income inequalities, either between ethnic groups or within an ethnic group. To be sure, the incidence of poverty has fallen, especially among the poorest sections of society; but the country has a long way to go towards reducing or eradicating poverty. In a country that is relatively rich in per capita income, it is imperative that something be done immediately to correct the differences in wealth between the rich and the poor, especially when the majority of the rich are of one ethnic group and the majority of the poor are of another. This is what the NEP has attempted to do; but in emphasising the ethnic differences between the races, it has tended to provide benefits and privileges to Malays whether they are poor or not while denying assistance to members of other ethnic groups even when they are poor and need assistance. In particular, the NEP's emphasis on creating a Malay capitalist class has done little to reduce inter-ethnic tension, and may intensify inter-ethnic rivalry and competition, since poor Malay peasants feel that other ethnic groups are becoming richer while their own situation has not improved significantly; besides, urban non-Malays feel that they are not given the same opportunities as other citizens, especially in employment, housing and social services, and education and business opportunities. Thus there is the danger that the NEP may succeed in its short-term policy of achieving the target of 130 per cent Bumiputra ownership and wealth in the modern sectors of the economy while failing in its long-term policy designed to achieve inter-ethnic harmony and national unity.

Notes

1. Malaysia consists of the peninsula of Malaya (West Malaysia) and Sabah and Sarawak (East Malaysia). This chapter deals only with peninsular Malaysia. The population of peninsular Malaysia is 53.9 per cent Malay, 34.9 per cent Chinese and 10.5 per cent Indian.

The remaining 0.7 per cent consists of Sri Lankans, Eurasians, and other smaller groups. *Fourth Malaysia Plan 1981-5*, p. 74.

2. The ruling party since independence is the Alliance Party, made up of the United Malay National Organization, the Malayan Chinese Association, and the Malayan Indian Congress. In 1972 the coalition was expanded to include several other political parties, and the name of the coalition party was changed to Barisan National (National Front). All prime ministers since independence have been of Malay origin.

3. The term *Bhumiputra* is used to cover Malays and other indigenous groups in peninsular Malaysia, Sabah and Sarawak. In peninsular Malaysia, Malays make up the majority of *Bhumiputras*.

4. See the speech by Sri Dato' Muhammad Ghazalie Shafie (Minister with Special Functions and Minister of Information), in the Dewan Negara, August 2, 1971, introducing the Second Malaysia Plan.

5. The Fourth Malaysia Plan 1981-5, p. 53.

6. Dr Mahathir Mohamad's Theme Address on the official opening of the Economic Convention sponsored by the Malaysian Economic Association on 19 May 1977 at the University of Malaya.

7. The Fourth Malaysia Plan, 1981-5, p. 270.

8. According to the Third Malaysia Plan, 1976-80, p. 183, 96.2 per cent of all land in FELDA schemes was owned by Malays.

9. The Plan does not indicate how poverty is measured.

10. The Third Malaysia Plan, 1976-80, p. 180.

11. Dorothy Guyot, 'The Politics of Land: Comparative Development in Two States of Malaysia', *Pacific Affairs*, vol. **44**, no. 36 (Fall 1971), p. 370.

12. Article 89(1) of the Constitution of Malaya restricts the amount of land that can be declared as Malay Reservation Areas, stipulating that for every acre of land declared a Malay reservation, an equal amount of land must be available for general alienation and the total area declared as Malaya Reservation cannot exceed the total area for general alienation.

13. Tunku Shamsul Bahrin, P. D. A. Perera, and Lim Heng Kow, *Land Development and Resettlement in Malaysia*, Department of Geography, University of Malaya 1979, table 1:1.

14. *Fourth Malaysia Plan*, p. 63.

15. Calculated from data given in table 9.6 of Karl von Vorys, *Democracy without Consensus*, Oxford University Press, 1976, p. 242.

16. Ownership figures by themselves tell only part of the story. It is well known that the government's control of the economy through share ownership is much larger than the figures indicate. For example, the minister of finance recently confirmed that *Bhumiputras* controlled up to 60 per cent of the mining industry and over 70 per cent of the equity in the financial sector. *Bhumiputras* also controlled 60 per cent of the plantation sector in terms of acreage, if FELDA schemes are included in the plantation sector. *Business Times*, November 28, 1981.

17. J. H. Beaglehole, 'Malay Participation in Road Transport—A Study of Public Policy and Administration in a Multi-racial Society', *New Zealand Journal of Public Administration*, vol. **38**, no. 1 September 1975), p. 48.

18. Bhumiputra Economic Congress, 1980, Working Paper on Transport.

19. The ownership of share capital in limited companies in the manufacturing sector showed that Malay ownership was only 2.5 per cent. *Mid-Term Review of the Second Malaysia Plan*, table 4.7.

20. *Business Times* (27 November 1981) and *New Straits Times* (1 January 1982).

21. Raja Muhammad Alias, FELDA Officers' Conference, 1979, Working Paper No. 1.

22. Nair and Fredericks, 'Rural Employment Income and Equity Issues in Malaysia', paper presented at Fourth Agricultural Economics Association of South East Asia Conference, Singapore, November 1981.

23. Jomo Sundram, 'Prospects for the New Economic Policy in Light of the Fourth Malaysia Plan', paper presented at the National Seminar on the Fourth Malaysia Plan, sponsored by the Malaysian Economic Association, Kota Kinabalu, October 1981, p. 4.

24. Land Tenure in the Muda Irrigation Area, Final Report, Part 2, findings by D. S. Gibbons, Lim Teck Ghee, and G. R. Elliston, Centre for Policy research, University of Sains, Penang, Malaysia, 1981.

25. Sundram, 'Prospects for the New Economic Policy in Light of the Fourth Malaysia Plan'.

26. Ibid.

27. Chandra Muzaffar, 'Some Political Perspectives on the New Economic Policy', paper presented at the Fourth Malaysian Economic Convention, sponsored by the Malaysian Economic Association, Kuala Lumpur, May 1977, p. 25.

28. Sundram, 'Prospects', 8–9.

29. Muzaffar, 'Some Political Objectives,' pp. 24–5.

30. Chandra Muzaffar, 'The New Economic Policy and the Quest for National Unity', paper presented at the Fifth Malaysian Economic Convention, sponsored by the Malaysian Economic Association, Penang, May 1978, p. 20.

31. D. Snodgrass, 'Trends and Patterns in Malaysian Income Distribution, 1957–70', quoted in Basil Moore, 'Restructuring Wealth Ownership', Discussion Paper No. 2, Centre for Policy Research, University of Sains, Penang, Malaysia, 1975, p. 56.

32. Sieh Mei Ling, 'The Structure of Ownership and Control—Manufacturing Companies in Malaysia', 1978, Ph.D thesis, University of Sheffield, vol. 2, tables 4.10a and 4.10b.

33. Basil J. Moore, 'Restructuring Wealth Ownership', Discussion Paper No. 2, Centre for Policy Research, University of Sains, Malaysia.

34. Ibid., p. 54.

35. Ibid., pp. 30–1.

36. *Fourth Malaysia Plan*, p. 48.
37. M. K. Sen, 'Rehousing and Rehabilitation of Squatters and Slum Dwellers with Special Reference to Kuala Lumpur', in Tan Soo Hai and Hamzah Sendut, *Public and Private Housing in Malaysia*, Heinemann Educational Books, Kuala Lumpur, 1979.
38. *Fourth Malaysia Plan*, p. 57.
39. Chong Hon Nyan, 'Economics and Political Realities', paper presented at the 1977 Annual Lecture of the Malaysian Economic Association, 20 October 1977.
40. *Fourth Malaysia Plan*, p. 62.
41. *Sunday Star*, 11 October 1981.
42. Sundram 'Prospects' p. 10.

11 ETHNIC REPRESENTATION IN CENTRAL GOVERNMENT EMPLOYMENT AND SINHALA–TAMIL RELATIONS IN SRI LANKA: 1948–1981

S. W. R. de A. Samarasinghe

Sri Lanka is a multi-ethnic society in which the Sinhalese form the majority and the Tamils the most important ethnic minority. The Tamils themselves are conventionally divided into two groups. The first group are the Sri Lankan Tamils who have shared the island with the Sinhalese since ancient times.[1] The bulk of the Sri Lankan Tamils live in the northern and eastern parts of the country. The second group, the Tamils, are the descendants of south Indian immigrant workers who came to the country soon after 1830 to work on the plantations developed by the British. The majority of the Indian Tamils inhabit the central and south-western parts of the country, where the plantations are located.

Historically, relations between the Sinhalese and the Sri Lankan Tamils have been coexistence punctuated by conflict form time to time. In many years of British rule (1796–1947), however, the occasion for such conflict was seldom present. Initially, when the struggle for constitutional reform and eventual self-rule began, there was some unity among elite groups of the two communities involved in the struggle. Before long, the effort turned into mutual suspicion and then open conflict.[2] The growth of Sinhala-Buddhist nationalism, which began to have a strong impact on the nation's political, economic, and cultural life in the 1950s, exacerbated the division.[3] Generally, the Sinhalese-Buddhists viewed this merely as a process that helped them gain their 'rightful' place in national life; but the Tamil minority began to view Sinhala-Buddhist nationalism as a threat to their political, economic, and cultural survival. The tension and mutual suspicion that developed between the two communities after 1948 resulted in periodic outbursts of violence, the most recent in July 1983. Such violence can, and does, contribute to further widening the gap between the two ethnic groups. Nevertheless, violence with ethnic undertones essentially is a symptom and not a cause of socio-economic, political, and cultural conflicts that can arise in multi-ethnic societies. Employment has emerged as a major area of conflict between the Sinhalese and the Tamils. In this chapter we focus our attention on employment in the central government service within the context of conflict between the two communities.

This analysis can be justified on several grounds. First, there has been bitter debate on this issue in Sri Lanka's political discussions in post-war years. Second, trends in employment by the central government probably reflect trends in public-sector employment in general. A study of this nature is, however, invariably constrained by lack of published data; published data were more readily available with regard to central government services than were other services in the public sector.

The general perception among the Sinhalese is that the Tamils occupy an 'unduly high proportion' of government jobs, a proportion not warranted by their proportion of the population. Indeed, this perception was stronger and more widespread in the 1940s and 50s.[4] A recent debate in Parliament indicated that it is a belief that still persists among at least some sections of the Sinhalese leadership.[5] The Tamils, for their part, complain that they are not getting their due share of state employment.[6]

Employment and the Economy

Sri Lanka has often been cited as a success story *vis-à-vis* the quality of life of its people in general, despite their being economically poor when measured in conventional terms such as GNP per capita.[7] Sri Lanka, however, failed to increase its productive capacity at a rate adequate to absorb its rapidly-growing labour force. Thus, in 1948 the labour force was calculated at 2.69 million, of whom 320,000 (11.9 per cent) were estimated to be unemployed.[8] Twenty-five years later, in 1973, the labour force was estimated at 4.17 million (an increase of 55 per cent) and it was estimated that no less than 1 million (24 per cent) were unemployed.[9] Since employment in the state service was much sought after because the state is the largest employer, competition is keenest and has taken on distinct political overtones.

First, as Table 1 shows, the State has become a major employer in Sri Lanka. Today employment in the state sector accounts for almost 25 per cent of total employment. Even more important is the fact that the state accounts for a high proportion of formal jobs, which are greatly valued by job seekers. Second, in the context of the relatively slow-growing economy job opportunities in the state sector grew more rapidly than elsewhere, partly because of a rapid expansion of administrative services and partly because of state involvement in the economy. To some extent the state came under increasing pressure to provide employment for the growing labour force. The inevitable solution was to create job opportunities in the state sector even at the expense of overmanning and a loss of efficiency. Third, employment in the government sector was desired

Table 11.1. Labour Force and Employment: 1953–79

	1953	1968	1979
1. Labour force ('000)	2,886	3,631	5,827
2. Employed ('000)	2,535	3,181	4,953
3. Unemployed ('000)	351	450	874
as % of labour force	12.2	11.0	15.0
4. State employment ('000)	156*	419†	1,218
as % of employed	6.2	13.2	24.6
of which central govt. ('000)	123*	304†	409
as % of employed	4.9	9.6	9.5

* 1951 figure from DGS, *Report of the Census of Government and Local Government Employees 1951*, Colombo, 1952. Figures for 1951 from Donald J. Snodgrass, *Ceylon: An Export Economy in transition*, 1966, pp. 100–1.

† DGS, *Statistical Abstract* (Annual). All remaining figures from the Central Bank, *Annual Report 1979*, Colombo, 1980.

because it carried a high status, especially where white-collar jobs were concerned; the relatively attractive remuneration and other fringe benefits offered by the government[10] and the job security enjoyed by government employees were still other factors. Fourth, and most important, the bias towards academic training and qualifications in the educational system drove qualified people to seek white-collar jobs, most of which only the government could provide.[11]

In seeking government employment, Sri Lankan Tamils from the north were influenced by two important factors. One was the 'push' factor. There was a relatively unfavourable man–land ratio in Jaffna district (Table 11.2).[12] It is also generally acknowledged that in the Jaffna peninsula, climate and other environmental and physical factors are less favourable than elsewhere in the country for agricultural production. Thus, the incentive and drive of the Sri Lankan Tamil from Jaffna to educate himself for employment outside Jaffna especially in government service is explained. In this, he was fortunate to have better educational facilities, especially for an education in English, unmatched by those elsewhere in

Table 11.2. Population per acre of agricultural land

	1946	1962
Sri Lanka	1.56	2.24
Jaffna district	2.78	3.63

Source: DCS, *Report on the Census of Agriculture, 1962* Colombo, 1965, p. 7.

the country, with the exception of Colombo district. For instance, in 1948, Northern Province, where Jaffna district is located, accounts for 7.2 per cent of the island's population but 25.9 per cent of total school enrolment in schools with facilities for teaching English.[13] The educationally-privileged position of Jaffna (and Colombo) was partly the result of the establishment of numerous Christian missionary schools during the colonial period.

Even as recently as 1980, Jaffna district managed to maintain a certain educational advantage, especially in the highly-desirable science streams. That year, for every 3,869 school pupils in Jaffna there was a school in the district equipped with laboratories to teach science at the General Certificate of Education (Advanced) level, i.e. university admission grade, whereas the average figure for the entire country was 6,907 and even for the relatively developed Colombo district it was only 4,237.[14]

Ethnic Composition in Central-Government Employment

S. J. Tambiah, in 'Ethnic Representation in Ceylon's Higher Administrative Service, 1870-1946'[15] noted that between 1870 and the 1920s there was an 'over-representation' of the Burgher (Eurasians with Dutch or Portuguese ancestry) and the Jaffna Tamil communities and an 'under-representation' of the Sinhalese. During the 1930s, however, a transition took place, and by 1946 the Sinhalese dominated the administrative service. Tambiah also noted that, relative to their proportion in the total population, the Jaffna Tamils (and the Burghers) in 1946 still enjoyed disproportionately high representation in the higher administrative services.

From where Tambiah stopped, we have assembled further data (Tables 11.3, 11.4, and 11.5) for analysing the period after independence. We have not, in this, restricted ourselves to the higher administrative grades, but instead extended the data base to cover the lower echelons of the service as well.

The most important generalisation to be made is that since independence in 1948 there has been an overall shift in the ethnic composition of central government employment in favour of the Sinhalese. Wriggins, using the *1951 Census of Government and Local Government Employees*, estimated that in 1951 Tamils probably accounted for only about 22 per cent of the total.[16] Unfortunately, similar data are not available for more recent years. Nevertheless, a rough estimate can be made. The General Clerical Service, where recruitment of Tamils fell sharply after independence retains about 16 per cent Tamil representation. At the higher level, near the end of 1979, Tamils accounted for 45 per cent of those in the Sri Lankan Administrative Service, Government Accountants Service, Shroffs (intermediary bankers between the Bank (British) and the natives in the

Table 11.3. Ethnic Representation in Selected Central Government Employment Categories, 1948-1981

Category		1948 No.	1948 %	1955 No.	1955 %	1963 No.	1963 %	1979 No.	1979 %	1981 No.	1981 %
Ceylon Civil Service	S	83	53.9	104	57.4	—	—	—	—	—	—
	T	38	24.7	47	26.0	—	—	—	—	—	—
	O	33	21.4	30	16.0	—	—	—	—	—	—
Sri Lanka Administrative Service	S	—	—	—	—	506	71.6	1,316	85.2	—	—
	T	—	—	—	—	165	23.4	203	13.1	—	—
	O	—	—	—	—	35	5.0	26	1.7	—	—
Irrigation Department (Engineers)	S	14	31.1	30	43.4	47	45.2	—	—	85	57.1
	T	19	40.0	32	46.1	50	48.1	—	—	58	38.9
	O	13	20.9	7	10.1	7	6.7	—	—	05	3.7
Police (Rank of ASP and above)	S	23	39.0	—	—	68	62.3	143	75.7	—	—
	T	3	5.1	—	—	21	19.2	33	17.4	—	—
	O	33	55.3	—	—	20	18.3	13	6.9	—	—
Police (Rank of Inspector and below)	S	—	—	—	—	—	—	951	55.3	—	—
Department of Health (Doctors)	S	244	57.3	437	55.3	652	54.7	1,140	55.5	—	—
	T	136	32.4	279	35.3	484	40.6	900	43.5	—	—
	O	43	10.1	74	9.4	56	4.7	19	0.9	—	—
Government Accountants Service	S	27	40.5	30	36.5	72	42.6	233	60.8	—	—
	T	31	46.2	32	59.9	95	56.2	148	38.6	—	—
	O	3	13.4	4	3.6	2	1.1	2	0.6	—	—
General Clerical Service	S	—	—	—	—	—	—	—	—	—	—
	T	—	—	—	—	—	—	3,989	18.0	—	—
	O	—	—	—	—	—	—	—	—	—	—

S: Sinhalese; T: Tamil; O: Other.

Ceylon Civil Service: *Ceylon Civil List* (Annual)

Sri Lanka Administrative Service: 1963 from the *Ceylon Civil List* (Annual); 1979 from *Hansard*, Vol. 15, No. 10, 24 July 1981, col. 1412.

Irrigation Department Engineers: 1948-63 from the *Ceylon Civil List* (Annual): 1981 from the Department of Irrigation.

Police: (rank of ASP and above): *Ceylon Civil List* and *Ferguson's Ceylon Directory* (Annuals): note that figures shown under 1963 and 1979 refer to 1965 and 1977 data respectively.

Police: (rank of Inspector and below): Police Department (1960 figure).

Department of Health: (doctors), 1948-63 from the *Ceylon Civil List* (Annual); 1979 from *Hansard*, vol. 15, no. 10.

Government Accountants Service: same as doctors above.

General Clerical Service: *Hansard*, vol. 15, no. 10.

Table 11.4. Recruitment to Selected Employment Categories in
Central Government Service: 1949-1981

		S		T		O	
		No	%	No	%	No	%
Irrigation Department	1971–77	52	58.4	34	38.2	3	3.4
(Engineers)	1978–79	40	67.8	15	25.4	4	6.8
Department of Health	1956–59	237	57.1	148	35.6	23	7.2
(Doctors)	1960–65	305	54.9	209	37.6	42	7.6
	1966–70	567	59.4	393	34.8	64	5.7
	1971–77	792	47.5	777	46.6	97	5.6
	1978–79	212	65.0	99	30.4	15	4.6
General Clerical	1949	805	53.7	610	40.7	84	5.6
Service	1955	422	65.9	191	29.8	27	4.2
	1963	703	92.4	52	6.8	9	0.9
	1965	384	95.8	13	3.2	4	1.0
	1966–67	863	80.6	168	15.3	44	4.0
	1970–77	6,949	87.0	881	11.0	160	2.0
	1978–81	4,870	93.6	279	5.4	53	1.0
School Teachers	22.7.1977 to 12.10.1979	22,399	89.3	1,516	6.1	1,164	4.0
of which graduate teachers		365	100.0	0	0.0	0	0.0
Graduates from the Police Training School (1980 March Batch)		343	91.7	17	4.5	14	3.7
Translators	1970–77	159	81.1	29	14.6	8	4.1
	1978–81	6	50.0	5	41.5	1	8.5
Stenographers	1970–77	506	89.4	33	5.6	27	4.7
	1978–81	269	70.1	78	20.3	37	9.6
Typists	1970–77	1,290	89.6	129	9.0	20	1.4
	1977–81	643	89.4	64	9.8	7	0.8

Notes and sources:
S:Sinhalese; T:Tamil; O:Other.
Irrigation Department (Engineers): From the Department of Irrigation (note that
those Engineers who have resigned from service are not included).
Department of Health (Doctors): from the Ministry of Health.
General Clerical Service: 1949–67 from *Ceylon Government Gazette* (various
issues); 1970–81 from Ministry of Public Administration.
School Teachers; *Hansard*, vol. 9, no. 5, Col. 364.
Translators, Stenographers and Typists: Ministry of Public Administration.

Table 11.5. Recruitment to the Sri Lankan Administrative Service: 1970–81

	Sinhalese		Tamil	
	1970–77 No. %	1978–81 No. %	1970–77 No. %	1977–81 No. %
Open Competitive Examination	433 91.5	159 100.0	34 7.2	0 0.0
Limited Competitive Examination	208 83.5	39 92.9	39 15.7	3 7.1
Merit Appointment	148 82.2	48 77.4	27 15.0	12 19.4
Total	789 87.4	246 93.5	100 11.1	15 5.7

Source: Ministry of Public Administration.

British colonial empire, who guarantee the native application for loans) and Doctors taken together. On the other hand, it is likely that in recent years in the lower grades, Sinhalese recruitment would have been even more pronounced than in the clerical grades.[17] Moreover, the lower grades are heavily weighted in central-government employment.[18] It is possible that the overall strength of Tamil representation in Sri Lanka's central-government service is 10 to 15 per cent, more or less approximating the percentage of Sri Lankan Tamils in the total population.[19]

Aggregates have a tendency to mask important details which often help throw a great deal of light on the issue being probed. The present subject is no exception. First, it is evident that the Sinhalese have increased their share considerably in such non-technical fields as the Administrative and the Clerical services. In some technical services (for example, doctors), Tamil recruitment has fallen only marginally. Even where Sinhalese representation has increased (for example, irrigation engineers), it has been more at the expense of the 'other' category (chiefly the Burghers and the Europeans) and not necessarily at the expense of the Tamils.

The crux of the Sinhala–Tamil ethnic conflict, in so far as employment is concerned, lies in the data given in Tables 3–5. The Tamils have already lost the relative position in central government employment that was enjoyed in the past. Apart from the obvious economic loss this entails, there is the psychological adjustment that many Jaffna Tamil families must make in the wake of this change. There is the fact that government jobs are no longer as easily obtained as they were a generation or two ago. The Sinhalese, on the other hand, are bound to view the change as a natural and inevitable adjustment which bestows on them their 'due' share. Clearly, these are two different perceptions of the same phenomenon. The result is, the Tamils have begun to feel they are 'discriminated' against and the Sinhalese feel recent changes have simply reversed the 'discrimination' they had been subjected to in the past. Such irreconcilable positions tend to contain the seeds of future conflict, including violence. The avoidance of such unfortunate consequences depends on seeking solutions to the problem at hand, based on a proper appreciation of the factors behind the changes discussed above.

'Discrimination'?

In the present context the term *discrimination* can be defined as unequal treatment of equals, where the person who is treated less favourably receives such treatment because of the group he or she belongs to.[20] Given this definition, several problems arise. First, can a declining percentage of Tamils in central-government job recruitment be construed as discrimination? Second, if discrimination does exist, are the Tamils the only group which is being discriminated against? Third, if there is discrimination, what are the motives behind it? Fourth, what solutions are available for resolving the problem?

The answer to the first question is that a declining percentage of Tamil representation in central-government employment does not in itself consti- tute discrimination against the Tamils. The expansion of educational facilities in the more backward Sinhalese areas has greatly increased the number of 'educated' Sinhalese. At a higher level, since 1959, university degree courses have been available in the Sinhalese (and Tamil) media. This is especially true of course in the fine arts. As a result of changes made in the past three decades, more and more Sinhalese have become academically qualified to seek government employment. Therefore, relative to the position in 1948, a rise in Sinhalese representation in central-government service in the post-independence period was inevitable. This argument is confirmed by the fact that, generally, Sinhalese representation has risen greatly in non-technical areas of employment, such as administrative and general clerical services, and least, in the technical areas of doctors, irrigation engineers, and accountants. The Sinhalese are known to have made rapid gains in general education and in the arts at the universities. On the other hand, Tamils claim a relatively low proportion of places in technical courses at institutions of higher learning, and the proportion is declining.[21]

The chances of Sinhalese entry into government service were improved after Sinhalese was made the official language in 1956, since admission to any post in government service could be sought through that language. Tamils are also permitted to seek entry to government service through the Tamil language; but upon admittance they are usually required to gain proficiency in Sinhalese within a stipulated time.[22]

These arguments notwithstanding, recently influential Tamil opinion in Sri Lanka has repeatedly focused attention on 'discrimination against the Tamils in government employment'.[23] The basis of this complaint is the relatively low level of recruitment of Tamils in recent years to certain grades in government service. For example, Table 4 shows that Tamil recruitment to the General Clerical service has fallen sharply since the early 1960s. The table also shows that less than 5 per cent of a recent group of police recruits were Tamils and that only 6.1 per cent of the teachers recruited in 1977-79 were Tamils. Table 5 shows that Tamil recruitment to the Administrative Service has also fallen in recent years. Several other similar examples were highlighted in recent parliamentary discussions on the question; in most instances cited, Tamil recruitment has fallen to less than 10 per cent of the total.[24] The stated assumption in such complaints is that non-recruitment of Tamils, at least in proportion to the Tamil population, constitutes discrimination. There is, of course, the general proposition made by the Tamils that recruitment should be independent of ethnic origin.

Motives for Discrimination

The motivation for such discrimination, if it is discrimination in the sense defined above, seems partly political and partly economic. Given the fact that governments in Sri Lanka have increasingly come to be guided by electoral considerations in their conduct of business it is not surprising that awarding jobs to one's own voters (mostly Sinhalese) takes precedence. The importance governments attach to this level of political patronage is evidenced by the fact that over the past decade or so, in several instances, relatively impartial systems of recruitment through examination and interview have been abandoned in favour of an interview alone or simply a recommendation by a member of Parliament. For example, the constitution of the First Republic (1972) replaced a seemingly independent Public Service Commission with the State Services Advisory Board and the State Services Disciplinary Board and made the Cabinet of Ministers—a purely responsible body—'responsible for the appointment, transfer, dismissal, and disciplinary control of state officers.'[25] The 1978 Constitution of the Second Republic gives similar powers to ministers.[26] The pressures that brought about this change to political appointments are mainly economic: the scarcity of job opportunities. Indeed, in such a context, Tamils may well not be the only group discriminated against. There is evidence that in the present situation, where the demand for jobs far exceeds the supply, schemes such as the Job Bank are designed to discriminate in favour of political supporters of the government as against its political foes.[27]

The ideal solution would be to establish recruitment mechanisms that take account of merit only. In the present political and economic context, however, that may not be so possible. If the present recruitment patterns, which often offer less than 10 per cent of the available places to the Tamils, is continued, it will almost certainly aggravate inter-ethnic tension. One solution may be to set a quota for each ethnic group. There are some indications that Sri Lankan Tamil political leaders might consider such a proposal as a second-best solution. Just before the October 1982 presidential elections an influential section of the Sinhala–Buddhist leadership publicly demanded an ethnic quota system not only for government jobs, but also for other spheres, such as university admissions. However, several objections can be raised against such a scheme.

First, it could entrench ethnic divisions when the long-term goal should, in the view of many, be to narrow such divisions. Second, the ethnic division is not the only division in Sri Lankan society. There are divisions based on class and caste. Moreover, the ethnic groups themselves have subdivided themselves. The Sinhalese have a low-country–Kandyan division, and the Tamils have a Sri Lankan–Indian Tamil division. Thus, once the quota principle is accepted, quotas could be demanded by various deprived groups. Third, once the quota principle is accepted in employment, demands will inevitably be made to extend the principle to other spheres. The Sinhalese, for example, might argue that the same principle should apply to university admissions—particularly in the pure and applied sciences—Sri Lankan Tamils continue to secure places in proportions that exceed their proportion in the total population.

Conclusions

Given the considerations discussed in this paper, the only practicable long-term solution for easing Sinhala–Tamil relations in employment is vigorous economic development. In this, the recent attempt to decentralise administration and economic management through district development councils and a decentralised budget provide a partial answer to the problem. Such agencies will have to be utilised to distribute available resources equitably. Although more jobs in Tamil areas will ease the demand for government jobs, in the forseeable future, employment in government is bound to remain an attractive proposition for the average Sri Lankan. Thus, both the Sinhalese and the Tamils will demand to have their fair share of the employment cake. This is a question that cannot be resolved by merely setting quotas, it also requires sensible political accommodation on both sides.

Notes

1. Cf. K. M. de Silva, ed., *Sri Lanka: A Survey*, London, Hurst, 1977, p. 37.
2. Ibid., pp. 79–84.

3. About 94 per cent of the Sinhalese are Buddhists and 85 per cent of the Tamils are Hindu (source: same as Table 1). See B. H. Farmer, *Ceylon: A Divided Nation*, London, 1963; W. Howard Wriggins, *Ceylon: Dilemmas of a New Nation*, Princeton University Press, 1960, pp. 211–70.

4. Wriggins, *Ceylon*, p. 235.

5. *Hansard*, 24 July 1981, cols. 1547–1572.

6. Amirthalingam, in *The Island*, 29 November 1981, p. 5.

7. See, for example, Hollis Chenery and Associates, *Redistribution with Growth*, London, Oxford University Press, 1974.

8. Donald J. Snodgrass, Ceylon: *An Export Economy in Transition*, Illinois, Richard O. Irwin, 1966, pp. 100–1.

9. Central Bank of Ceylon, *Review of the Economy*, Colombo, 1979, p. 95.

10. See International Labour Office, *Government Pay Policies in Ceylon*, Geneva, 1971, p. 75.

11. International Labour Office, *Matching Employment Opportunities and Expectations*, Report, Geneva, 1971.

12. According to the 1981 Census of Population, 42 per cent of the Sri Lankan Tamils lived in Jaffna district.

13. Acting Director of Education, *Administration Report*, 1948. Note that about 87 per cent of the population of Northern Province, as well as almost all the English schools, were in Jaffna district.

14. *Hansard*, vol. 19, no. 6.

15. *University of Ceylon Review*, vol. 13, (1955), pp. 113–34. See also P. T. M. Fernando, 'The Ceylon Civil Service: A study of Recruitment and Policies, 1880–1920', *Modern Ceylon Studies*, vol. 1 (1970), pp. 64–83.

16. Department of Census and Statistics, Colombo, 1952.

17. For example, beginning in January 1979, almost all recruitment to the lower grades of the state sector was through the Job Bank scheme. Under this plan, each Member of Parliament was allowed to recommend a thousand jobseekers. The seventeen Members of Parliament of the Tamil United Liberation Front were also invited to recommend applicants (at the same rate). It is generally acknowledged, however, that no more than a thousand applicants found jobs.

18. Central Bank, *Review of the Economy 1980*, Colombo, 1981: Statistical Appendix, Table 55.

19. It is generally acknowledged that the Indian Tamils are very poorly represented in government employment, partly because as non-citizens they are denied such employment and partly because even those among them who are legally eligible lack the requisite educational qualifications.

20. See H. H. Blalock, Jr., *Toward a Theory of Minority-Group Relations*, New York, Wiley, 1967, p. 18.

21. For example, here are the percentages of candidates admitted in the Tamil medium to the various professional courses in Sri Lankan

universities in the academic year 1982–3:
Medicine 26.3%
Dental Surgery 38.3%
Veterinary Science 35.6%
Agriculture 23.4%
Engineering 30.8%
(Note: a few Tamil-speaking Muslims are included in the figures.)
Source: *Hansard*, vol. 21, no. 9.
For a fuller discussion of this issue, see C. R. de Silva's article in this volume.

22. There is evidence suggesting that this constitutes a disincentive to Tamil applicants for government jobs. In theory, officers who fail to gain proficiency in Sinhalese may be subject to certain penalties; in practice, it appears that in the recent past only a few have lost their jobs. According to information supplied to Parliament in respect of 26 ministries and semi-government agencies functioning under those ministries (these, together, covered well over 90% of state-sector employment). During the term of the present UNP government up to 1 March 1982, only two ministries have had the services of employees terminated (a single employee in one and 28 in another) for failing to acquire proficiency in Sinhalese (*Hansard*, vols. 21, 22, various issues). In practice, however, penalties are not often imposed, since the law prescribes them especially when exigencies of service arise.

23. See note 6 and *Hansard*, vol. 15, no. 10, p. 24, July 1981.

24. See, for example, *Hansard*, vol. 7, no. 8; vol. 10, no. 16.

25. *The Constitution of Sri Lanka (Ceylon)*, Colombo, 1972, Section 106.

26. *The Constitution of the Democratic Socialist Republic of Sri Lanka*, Colombo, 1978, Section 59.

27. In a reply to a letter from the Tamil United Liberation Front (TULF) and opposition leader A. Amirthalingam, President J. R. Jayewardene admitted that the present government has failed to give Tamils their due share of jobs through the Job Bank Plan. (Between January and November 1981 no person who applied to the Job Bank through a Jaffna district TULF MP secured a job. By 20 May 1982, out of a total of 11,000 such applicants only 1,470 had secured jobs. (*Hansard*, vol. 20, no. 5, col. 453). The reason given by the President for the government action is that in the context of the TULF demand for a separate state ('*Eelam*') the government could not have complete confidence in those recommended by TULF MPs for government jobs. This may be true. The fact, however, is the UNP, under great pressure to provide jobs for its own supporters, would have readily used the quota that could have gone to the TULF. (See President J. R. Jayewardene's reply, dated 16 July 1979, to TULF and opposition leader A. Amirthalingam's letter dated 11 July 1979; unpublished manuscript.)

12 ETHNICITY AND RESOURCE ALLOCATION

Neelan Tiruchelvam

> The deepest source of all calamity in history is misunderstanding.
> For where we do not understand, we can never be just.
> *Rabindranath Tagore*

In a plural society, with limited resources, access to higher education, employment, and land are viewed as indices of group advancement. In this context the principles of allocating the benefits of development are drawn into the vortex of inter-ethnic conflict and confrontation. Little empirical inquiry has been directed towards analysis of the politics of resource allocation in Sri Lankan society. This paper examines the competing conceptions of injustice and relative deprivation as articulated by an 'achieving minority' and an ethnic majority which believed that it had been historically deprived. These perceptions have shaped and defined the parameters within which there exists competition for scarce resources and limited economic opportunities. We will therefore have to look at the politics of patronage which grew out of the processes of representational democracy and their more specific implications for inter-ethnic relations. In this respect, our inquiry is of a general nature and complements the more specific papers relating to higher education and employment. Finally, we look at the techniques of political bargaining that were resorted to in reaching inter-ethnic accommodation in sharing resources.

Competing Perceptions of Injustice

A central grievance of the Tamils since independence is related not merely to the erosion of their political base through linguistic policies and citizenship laws, but to the denial of access to employment, economic, and trading opportunities. The complaint is that Sinhala-dominated governments consciously pursued policies of ethnic preference with regard to recruitment and the distribution of government benefits. The language policies of the 1950s were perceived as a conscious effort to drastically alter the terms under which ethnic groups competed for power, influence, and economic opportunity.[1] While providing the Sinhala-educated majority with opportunities for upward mobility, it excluded an 'achieving

Tamil minority' from access to similar opportunities. The conflicts arising from language and employment were aggravated by the confrontations arising from restrictions on educational opportunities.

In view of the traditional importance attached to education, and recruitment to public service, the new policy of ethnic preference posed a serious threat to both the material well-being of the Tamil community, as well as the preservation of their cultural identity. The chief motivating force behind the push for government employment was pressure on land in the densely populated peninsula.[2] Closure of these opportunities for personal advancement led to an economic crisis in Tamil areas. Although in 1977, the United National Party conceded that Tamil grievances relating to employment, education, and colonisation needed urgent resolution, the government was incapable of reversing the discriminatory policies on recruitment. In 1979, Tamil leaders complained that 'the government in its employment policies had been more discriminatory than any previous government'.[3] It was said that, of the 140,000 jobs allegedly given by the government in 1978, less than 1,000 went to Tamils. To highlight the magnitude of Tamil grievances, detailed statistics were provided on recruitment to certain illustrative categories in the higher and intermediate grades of the public service (see Table 12.1). Although these figures provide a

Table 12.1. Recruitment in public service employment in 1977-78

	No. recruited	No. of Tamils
C.A.S. Open Competitive Examination	140	0
Assistant postmasters	98	4
Assistant medical practitioners	–	–
Pharmacists, radiographers	480	7
Survey learners	318	5
Sri Lanka Navy	2,170	146
Graduate teachers	1,000	0
Untrained teachers	17,000	700
General Clerical Service	1,000	2

fragmented, incomplete picture of the pattern of recruitment, the imbalances are confirmed by Samarasinghe's inquiry into more general trends.[4] Samarasinghe's study reveals that Tamil recruitment to the General Clerical Service declined from about 40.7 per cent in 1949 to 6.8 per cent in 1963, to 11 per cent in 1970-77 and 5.4 per cent in 1978-81. Similarly, in recruitment of schoolteachers, Tamil teachers accounted for only 6.1 per cent of the total in 1977-79. No Tamil graduate teachers were recruited during this period; on the other hand, 385 Sinhalese graduate teachers were given employment. Samarasinghe, however, makes the point that the increase in the intake of Sinhalese into public service was more pronounced in the non-technical and administrative grades. Sinhalese recruitment to the Administrative Service expanded from 87.4 per cent in 1970-77 to 93.5 per cent in 1978-81.[5] In the recruitment of doctors, the Sinhalese proportion increased from 57.1 per cent in 1956-59 to 65 per cent in 1978-79. Similarly, Sinhalese irrigation engineers increased from 58.4 per cent in 1971-77 to 67.8 per cent in 1978.

Similar complaints were voiced about locating major programmes of public investment and identifying projects for external funding. With regard to 'Integrated District Development Programmes', it was pointed out that, at the time of this writing, not one district in the Northern or Eastern provinces was included. On the subject of irrigation projects, A. Amirthalingam, leader of the Tamil United Liberation Front (TULF) stated:

we are not complaining that [Mahaveli development] is not in the Northern Province . . . But what about other schemes . . . the Kerendenita Irrigation and Settlement Project, Inginimetiya Irrigation Dam Project, Dry Zone Project, Muttu Kandiya Reservoir Scheme, Teaching Hospital Scheme in Peradeniya, Sewenagall Sugar Development Project, Kurunegala Area Development Project, Colombo Dockyard Project, Regional Planning Study, Lower Uva Project . . . [?] Not one in the North or East.[6]

Amirthalingam added that in economic development 'the government has discriminated against Tamil areas and neglected them completely.'

Many forces interacted to shape Sinhalese-Buddhist perceptions of injustice and deprivation. One force grew out of the pre-independent Buddhist Revivalist Movement of the early part of this century. Anagarika Dharmapala, architect of Sinhalese-Buddhist identity, deplored the fact that Tamils and Muslims 'were employed in large numbers, to the prejudice of the people of the island—'sons of the soil'.[7] Dharmapala thus shaped a conception of the national polity permeated by notions of 'Dhamma dipa and Sinha dipa', notions founded on the belief that the Sinhalese are the legitimate inheritors of the island and that they are destined to preserve the Buddhist dhamma in its pristine purity. The Sinhalese-Buddhist consciousness thus viewed Tamils 'as late entrants, invaders, mercenaries, and traders' who could not legitimately be regarded as the people of the island. These concepts of Sinhala-Buddhist revivalism fused with the more modern conceptions of the nation-state, thus propelling the 'sons of the soil' theory into a dominant political force.

Another powerful force was related to a perception of historical deprivation. The Buddhist Revivalist Movement highlighted the indignities

Sinhala–Buddhists suffered during the period of Christian and colonial dominance. According to this perception, Tamils were consciously favoured particularly during the British occupation. A Member of Parliament forcefully expressed this view recently.

Tamils in Sri Lanka are a privileged lot. They received all the benefits under the British during the colonial days. The Sinhalese were fighting for . . . independence against the foreign yoke. . . . Even after the annexation of the Kandyan Territory, the last of the Sinhala Kingdoms, in 1815, the Sinhalese made two attempts, [one] in 1818 and [another] in 1848, to win back their independence. In these struggles the Sinhalese lost their leaders. . . . and thousands . . . had to lay down their lives. They lost their houses, their crops, and their land. But the Tamils in the north gained all the benefits of missionary education—English education—and they became heir to all the plums of public office under the British.[8]

S. J. Tambiah in his study of ethnic representations in the Higher Administrative Service concedes that between 1870 and 1920, there was an overrepresentation of the Burgher and Jaffna Tamil communities. He points out, however, that in the period 1930–46, the Sinhalese consolidated their domination. With the spinoffs from economic nationalism that came their way (from the partial autonomy gained under the Donoughmoure constitution), coupled with the abolition of communal representation and the introduction of universal suffrage, several measures were introduced designed to expand Sinhala-Buddhist control of the economy. Even the Co-operative Movement was viewed as an effort to displace Tamils *and* Muslims from trade.

Since plantation enterprise, nascent industry, and the island's trade were dominated by foreign capitalists, and minorities were disproportionately influential within the indigenous capitalist class, Buddhist pressure groups viewed socialism as a means of redressing the balance in favour of the majority group. Every extension of state control was justified on the ground that it helped [gain] the influence of foreigners and . . . minorities.[9]

Despite the fact that language and economic policies had radically altered the conditions in which ethnic groups competed for access to the bureaucracy, professions, land-owning, and trade and industrial opportunities, Sinhalese leaders continued to view themselves as relatively deprived. 'If any injustice is done, it is to the majority Sinhalese. . . . It is the Sinhalese majority who have to agitate for their rights. Even today the majority is demanding its due place in all spheres.'[10] As a social historian observed, 'Sinhalese nationalists gird their loins for battle in the seventies for grievances of the forties'.[11]

The third force that helped shape Sinhalese perceptions of injustice has to do with the majoritarian principle. The Sinhalese formed 71 to 72 per cent of the population, and with universal adult franchise and the political processes that were thereby set in motion, larger segments of the political population entered the political life of the country. As the base of political participation expanded, ethnic identities were exploited to gain electoral support and were therefore accentuated. The insinuation of Sinhala-Buddhist dominance in political and socio-economic areas was thought to enjoy a democratic sanction. With the disenfranchisement of the Indian Tamils in 1948–49, the Sinhalese expanded their share of representation to about 80 per cent. This move gave the majority community an exaggerated sense of political dominance, which in turn fed their determination to exercise control of the economy and play a decisive role in shaping Sri Lankan society.

Perceptions of relative deprivation had important implications for the view that a Sinhala-Buddhist identity was the equivalent of being sons of the soil. It was only natural that Sinhala leaders would articulate preferential policies that would give expression to this identity. The increasing politicisation of the electoral process and the corresponding shrinkage of the Tamil political base strengthened these perceptions. Sinhala-Buddhist dominance in economic spheres was perceived to draw its moral authority and sanction from what appeared to be a distorted version of the Western majoritarian principle; whereas in the West the majority cut across various barriers, here the majority was identified with the majority ethnic group. The process aroused feelings of deprivation and injustice among members of the Tamil community, perceptions that profoundly influenced the shaping of the militant Tamil view and Tamil aspirations for equality and self-determination.

The Politics of Patronage

No inquiry into the allocation of resources can safely disregard the politicisation of discretionary decision-making concerning developmental benefits. The Wilmot Perera Commission in 1961 deplored 'the extent of political patronage and influence' in matters of public service and day-to-day administration.[12] More recently it has been noted that 'the MP's chit has become the password for employment, for transfer in the public or the semi-public sector, in claims of public assistance, or even in such pedestrian matters as admitting a child to a school or obtaining a bed in hospital'.[13]

The pervasive impact of the spoils system on administrative decision-making has important implications for the varying access of different ethnic groups to socio-economic benefits. Some writers believe the patronage system is a successor to the systems of government that prevailed in the pre-colonial period and the political practices of the Donoughmore period (1931–47). During the latter period, elections were conducted primarily along lines of caste, family, and ethnicity. The gift of a vote had to be reciprocated by the distribution of rewards to one's primordial group. The exective committees of this period frittered away their energies in *ad hoc* interference in administrative and private matters. A more recent phenomenon was the growth of political parties organised around a common programme and political ideology. But the tradition of political interference was so deeply ingrained in the system that even the emergence of a multi-party system did little to reverse the process. In fact, the opposite process was seen in the 1960s and 1970s. With the periodic transfer of power from one political party to another, the spoils system assumed a more exclusionary and discriminatory form. Constituents began to look to representatives of the party in power for mediation with the bureaucracy in pressing almost every conceivable demand relating to the provision of government and municipal services. 'It is not an uncommon sight to see crowds seeking interviews with the MP, filling the waiting room and porch of his residence, and indeed, overflowing into the garden and adjacent roadside!¹⁴ Most significant, they looked to members of Parliament for jobs, the means by which they might satisfy their basic needs and contribute to the general welfare of their families. Commissions of inquiry into the Postmaster General's department and the Co-operative Wholesale Establishment revealed that departmental heads and corporation executives had received thousands of letters and telephone calls from members of Parliament requesting appointments 'in any capacity' for specific constituents.

As noted, state control of critical economic sectors through public enterprises and redistributive policies in respect of land and housing opened up new and unprecedented opportunities for the distribution of favours. In a controlled economy the discretionry power to issue import quotas, release foreign exchange for industrial ventures, or provide credit for trading operations provided enormous scope for dispensing political favours. With the liberalisation of the economy and the massive expansion of public investment, new avenues were opened for the distribution of favours. The increase in government procurement, the award of tenders for large-scale building and construction contracts, the inflow of foreign capital and external assistance—all these resulted in the forging of new links between the political elite and the indigenous entrepreneurial and professional classes.

We now consider the implications of the patronage system for inter-ethnic competition for governmental benefits. One of the most significant characteristics of the spoils system as it has evolved in recent decades is its exclusion of opposition political groups and their adherents. For the major Sinhala parties, which periodically changed places, this meant at most a temporary denial of their share of developmental benefits;

but for the ethnic groups that did not share power at the centre, it meant almost permanent exclusion from sharing in the spoils of office.

With the political patronage system now more formally integrated into administrative decision-making, the discriminatory impact of the system became more marked. Recently, the issue of employment has raised considerable controversy. Despite the dismantling in 1977 of controls on exchange and imports, the one sector where the government strengthened its control was employment. Control was institutionalised through the job bank scheme, by which data banks were set up at central and district levels for processing the qualifications of unemployed youth. Entry into the job banks was regulated by members of Parliament, who were given a thousand job bank forms for distribution among their constituents.

The seventeen TULF members of Parliament were given job bank forms for distribution; but, on a directive from the Centre, the forms were later excluded from consideration. The opposition leader complained that as a result, 'Tamil youths of these electorates [were] denied chances of employment'.[15] It was argued that Tamil youths had been denied recruitment as trainee surveyors, levellers, and clerical servants. Similar controversy surrounded the recruitment of teachers, where TULF members of Parliament alleged that, while their job bank forms were disregarded, appointments of unqualified people were made 'on the payment of Rs.6,000 to Rs.8,000'. The opposition leader protested that such appointments had imprinted on young minds 'a cynical disregard of all moral values'.[16]

It is thus clear that politicisation of resource allocation had a discriminatory impact on Tamil youths from electorates in the north and east which since 1956 had consistently been represented by opposition members from Tamil parties. A recent justification offered was the government's belief that, given the demand for a separate state, such appointees would prove disloyal to the government. A TULF leader countered that this was a vicious circle, 'since the demand for a separate state grew out of the discriminatory denial of such employment'. Tamil youths outside the north and east encountered even greater difficulty in securing benefits from members of Parliament from Sinhala parties, since the members tended to give preference to youth drawn from the members' own ethnic political bases. No doubt, it was possible for a few individuals to surmount the barriers of politics and ethnicity through informal links to people in authority: but the vast majority of Tamils felt excluded. Finally, it should be noted that the discriminatory impact of spoils was to some extent mitigated at the district level by new opportunities for sharing power. The decentralised budget of the 1970–77 period was directly made available to each member of Parliament, which enable even parliamentary representatives in the north to disburse limited funds for repairing school building, roads, minor irrigation works and as grants to local authorities.

Toward New Techniques of Political Bargaining

The analysis in this paper reveals that preferential policies relating to development benefits emerged from perceptions of injustice among majority ethnics who believed they had for a long time been deprived. Tamil perceptions of injustice and self-identity were antagonistic to, and in conflict with these perceptions. It has also been argued in this chapter, that the politics of patronage reinforced exclusion of Tamils from equitable sharing of the spoils of power. We now look to the process of political bargaining instituted to reach an acceptable accommodation on sharing resources. The most difficult problem, however, is the over-politicisation of the electors, which makes it problematic whether the opposing elite could arrive at an overarching accommodation.

Many would concede that two of the most significant achievements in the development of political institutions have been the continuity of universal adult franchise and the emergence of the multi-party system. Although the system has repeatedly been challenged by working-class agitation, youth insurrection, abortive *coups d'état* of both the left and the right and Tamil parties (the FP and the TULF), the institutions of democracy remain intact. In fact, the democratic political process may have minimised the propensity for violence and instability latent in the socio-economic structures. Social and political conflicts traditionally the source of structural violence were submitted to bargaining and accommodation within the parliamentary process. Social welfare and equity-oriented economic policies thus surfaced.

These very processes, however, have proved inadequate in resolving the conflict and violence arising from inter-ethnic competition for positions of power and wealth. The electoral process reinforced, stabilised and sanctioned Sinhala-Buddhist predominance in the political and socio-economic spheres. The legislative forums, instead of becoming arenas for accommodation, often served to assert the dominance of the majority. The disproportionate representation of the Sinhalese community in the legislature would have aggravated an already exaggerated numerical superiority. More recently, the legislative forum has proved an arena of ethnic confrontation rather than reconciliation. Whatever reconciliation there is usually occurs outside the legislature.

Neither did the paralysis in the legislature encourage the judiciary to become more activist and interventionist in extending equal opportunity to Tamils. Tamil political groups have in general been reluctant to invoke the fundamental jurisdiction over rights of the superior courts. When the infrequent contentious issues of equal opportunity in higher education have been presented to the courts, the Supreme Court ended up by affirming the admission formulas Tamil parents and students vigorously resisted. The superior courts, with their conservative orientation and restrictive and textual approach to constitutional interpretations, were incapable of asserting a societal vision that was radically at variance with the vision of the population at large or of the more populist legislature.

If the modes of political discourse and judicial challenge within the parliamentary framework proved inadequate, to what extent was agitation possible outside this framework? In the years 1956–58 and 1961, *satyagraha* campaigns were instituted for non-violent agitation in favour of linguistic equality. The mob violence inflicted on peaceful protestors in Colombo and the repressive measures the state directed against the campaign clearly indicated that this form of protest and dissent would not be tolerated. A similar *satyagraha* campaign by the United National Party in the 1970s ended in violent confrontations with supporters of the government. This was in part the result of the growth of political parties as the principal actors in competitive politics. Political parties effectively appropriated dissent and discouraged its expression outside the parliamentary framework. Further, they prevented or co-opted grass-roots organisations and political movements that endeavoured to operate outside party control or regulation. With the experience of the *satyagraha* campaigns of the 1950s and 60s, Tamil political leaders recognised that even non-violent campaigns outside the parliamentary framework would not prove effective instruments for exerting political pressure.

As the fabric of the pluralistic society deteriorated, a serious threat to the stability of the political system came from the political violence of militant Tamil youth and the retaliatory collective violence of militant Sinhalese forces in the south. The police excesses in Jaffna in May and June 1981 and the racial disturbances in August 1981 confirmed that individual acts of political violence against the police and the armed forces could de-stabilise not merely the north but be felt throughout the country. Some Tamils may even believe that the violence of Tamil militant groups would strengthen the bargaining power of the Tamil community. Violence has also been part of the political armoury of the majority. '[It] has formed part of the political strategy of the majority to both intimidate the minorities and contain their communal demands.[17] More recently, both Sinhalese and Tamil leaders have unequivocally dissociated themselves from acts of violence, both in the north and in the south. Tamil leaders have declared that non-violence was a 'central article of their political faith' and that violence as an instrument of political pressure or bargaining is morally unacceptable. It is in this context that the search for alternative techniques of political bargaining assumed critical importance.

Both the government and the TULF were constrained from engaging in direct negotiations toward achieving an enduring solution. It would not do for TULF leaders to be perceived by their supporters as negotiating lesser solutions to the demand for a separate state. On the other hand, the government could not be seen by its supporters as having conceded that separation was a negotiable issue. In this environment direct negotiations were fraught with immense difficulties and uncertainty.

In working out the structural arrangements relating to devolution and decentralisation, negotiators resorted to the technique of working through an honest broker and a trusted intermediary. As we have seen, elsewhere, this political strategy was effective in working out institutional arrangements that had proved elusive for half a century.[18] The flaw in this strategy was the attempt to balance the 'unconventional' political intermediary against the conventional device of a presidential commission. The majority of the commission even suspected what seemed a compromise; it was deadlocked for months over the issue of the scope of its functions. The delay set back implementation of the scheme by almost a year.

The technique for direct negotiations evolved from the crises in Sinhala-Tamil relations resulting from political violence in the Tamil north and retaliatory police violence and mob violence in the second half of 1981. A formal meeting took place between the leaders of the government and the TULF, primarily to 'condemn all forms of violence'. Such statements helped develop a climate of goodwill essential to the continuance of exchanges and the diffusion of ethnic tensions throughout the country and for reviewing the delicate national situation with regard to protecting people and property. Thereafter it became institutionalised in a forum for direct negotiations on a wider range of issues relating to devolution of power, in financing development programmes in the north and east, and in the issues of employment and education. Many of the issues directly bear on such problems as sharing resources, preferential policies in employment, allocation of housing, and implementation of developmental programmes.

Although it may be too early to predict the outcome of these processes, it is impossible to overstate the importance of the process of bargaining in the context of ethnic tensions in Sri Lanka. The leaders of the Tamil United Liberation Front, in commenting on the process, have stated that, while agreements were readily reached on specific issues, delays and setbacks in implementation have been frustrating. Both UNP and TULF leaders continue to face severe criticism from Sinhala and Tamil militants for sustaining a process of what the latter call 'continuing compromises'. The significance of the Inter-Party Committee between the government and the TULF rests on the ability of both sides to evolve a framework for bargaining on specific grievances where mutually antagonistic identities and aspirations had rendered inadequate regular modes of political discourse.

Notes

1. Michael Roberts, 'Meanderings in the Pathways of Collective Identity and Nationalism', in *Collective Identities, Nationalism, and Protest in Modern Sri Lanka*, ed. Michael Roberts, 1979, p. 8.
2. S. Arasaratnam, 'Nationalism in Sri Lanka and the Tamils', in Roberts, ed., *Collective Identities*, pp. 500–23.
3. A. Amirthalingam, in *Hansard*, 26 November 1976, p. 1,842.
4. Ibid.
5. See Chapter 11, Table 11.3 to 11.5.
6. A. Amirthalingam, *Hansard*, 26 November 1976, p. 1,855.
7. Anagarika Dharmapala, 'Message to the Young Men of Ceylon', in Ananda Guruge edition *Return to Righteousness*, 1965, p. 515.
8. W. J. M. Loku Bandara, *Hansard*, 24 July 1981, p. 1556.
9. S. J. Tambiah, 'Ethnic Representation in Ceylon's Higher Administrative Service, 1870–1946', *University of Ceylon Review*, vol. 13 (1955), pp. 113–34.
10. K. M. de Silva, *Sri Lanka since Independence* 1974, p. 465.
11. Loku Bandara, *Hansard*, 24 July 1981, p. 1556.
12. Michael Roberts, *Collective Identities, Nationalisms and Protest in Modern Sri Lanka*, Chapter 1.
13. Sessional Paper 4, of 1961, p. 101.
14. G. R. Tressie Leiton *Local Government and Decentralized Administration in Sri Lanka*, Colombo, 1979, p. 203.
15. Ibid.
16. A. Amirthalingam in unpublished letter to His Excellency the President of Sri Lanka dated 26 September 1979.
17. See chapter 'Violence in Development', in 'Extra Dilemmas of Development, 1982', Marga Institute study, 1982, unpublished..
18. See Neelan Tiruchelvam, Chapter 13.

13 THE POLITICS OF DECENTRALISATION AND DEVOLUTION: COMPETING CONCEPTIONS OF DISTRICT DEVELOPMENT COUNCILS IN SRI LANKA

Neelan Tiruchelvam

> The proposal [for the establishment of District Ministers and Development Councils] will strengthen the representative character of the democratic system by grafting onto it a scheme for self-management by the people of a district.
>
> > White Paper on the appointment of district ministers,
> > 22 June 1978

> The District Development Councils of Sri Lanka may be considered a compromise between the . . .' demand for a separate state of Eelam and an undiluted and highly centralized unitary form of government.
>
> > Professor A. J. Wilson, member of the Presidential
> > Commission on Development Councils;
> > *Morning Star*, 5 June 1981

> Since time immemorial this country has had a unitary system of government and the people all along regarded this one country, and that a Buddhist country. If these development councils are set up, the Buddhists have great fears not only as to the loss of their rights and privileges as citizens of the land, [but] also for their survival. . . .
>
> > Siri Perera, Q.C.

I

The recent Development Councils Law enacted by the Sri Lankan legislature is one of the most controversial pieces of legislation of post-independent Sri Lanka. Although some welcomed the legislation as a response to the need for regional autonomy among Tamils in the north and east, others consider the measure an attempt to deflect the drive for a separate state and legitimise further inroads into the 'traditional areas' of the Tamils. On the other hand, some Sinhalese have condemned the scheme as an attempt to undermine the unitary character of the constitution.

The plan for development councils, therefore, must be viewed as a structural arrangement designed to ease the ethnic tensions that have eroded the multi-ethnic polity of Sri Lanka. A proper appraisal of this can take place only against a backdrop of the evolution of Sinhala-Tamil relations in the socio-political history of Sri Lanka.

Although no attempt is made to provide a comprehensive view of this process, the chapters by professors K. M. de Silva and C. R. de Silva (Chapters 8 and 9) provide useful insights into specific aspects of the process. We do endeavour, however, to draw attention to the conceptual transformations that have taken place in the character of Tamil aspirations, with a view to comprehending the significance of the new arrangement. We can thus look briefly at the shaping of the policy decision for institutionalising development councils within the government and at the various political actors and interest groups involved and/or accommodated in the decision-making process. The analysis is concluded by outlining some major elements of the new institutional arrangements, as well as some of the forces that may seek to thwart effective implementation of the law.

II

We begin by going back to 24 May 1972, two days after the enactment of the first Republican constitution. The Tamil Federal Party participated in the deliberations of the Constituent Assembly but withdrew in despair after its attempts to insert certain amendments in some basic resolutions were dismissed by the government. Despite the mood of pessimism among Tamil leaders, an effort was made to formulate a programme that would incorporate the lowest denominator of Tamil needs and aspirations. The programme, later called the Six-Point Plan, contained six elements.

The first element called for equal constitutional status between the Tamil and the Sinhala languages. Second, the plan called for the extension of citizenship to all who had settled in Sri Lanka and who had been rendered stateless by the citizenship laws. Third, a commitment to a secular state was called for, one ensuring equality of religions. Fourth, the Six-Point Plan called for constitutional guarantees of fundamental rights and freedoms, based on equality of citizens on ethnic and cultural grounds. The fifth element of the plan involved abolition of caste and untouchability. Most important was a call for a decentralised structure of government that would enable participatory democracy to flourish, and where 'power would be people's power rather than state power'.

The six elements presupposed a commitment to constitutionalism. They represented a desire among Tamil leaders to work towards equality within a pluralistic society. The refusal of the government to negotiate these proposals seriously shattered the expectations of even the most optimistic exponents of the plan. Becoming embittered, party leaders sought to demonstrate to the government the complete rejection of the

Republican constitution by the Tamil people. S. J. V. Chelvanayakam, the leader of the Federal Party, resigned his seat in the National State Assembly with a view to seeking a mandate for the Six-Point Plan.

During this period other forces were contributing a dramatic escalation of Tamil demands. Tamils complained of a conscious policy of discrimination in access to employment and education and the conduct of developmental programmes in the north and east. The language concessions contained in the regulations framed under the Tamil Language (Special Provisions) Act were not implemented. In land use and land settlement, the government was accused of pursuing a policy directed towards transforming the demographic composition of Tamil areas. When Indian estate labour displaced by the land-reform policies of the government were voluntarily settled in the Eastern province, emergency laws were enacted to eject the labourers. The government, however, is alleged to have regularised the illegal settlement of thousands of Sinhala squatters in the traditional Tamil areas of the north and the east.

Political resistance to and agitation against such discrimination were further repressed through preventive detention and harassment of Tamil youth in the north. The politics of hostility, supported by repression and the arbitrary exercise of emergency powers, hardened Tamil resistance to the government.

These events had an important bearing on the emergence of a new Tamil awareness. The Kankesanthurai by-election of 1975 became the focal point of agitation for the emerging aspirations of the Tamil people. The Tamil Federal Party fought the election on the issue of the Six-Point Plan; but it was the government coalition which contended—irresponsibly, many felt—that support for Chelvanayakam would accelerate the processes of separation. The overwhelming majority of the vote received by Chelvanayakam enabled Tamil leaders to appropriate this argument. After the results, Chelvanayakam said: 'I wish to announce to my people and the country that the Eelam Tamil Nation should exercise the sovereignty already vested in the Tamil people and become free'. By this historic statement the conceptual transformation and the demands of the Tamil people were crystallised. Chelvanayakam's statement represented a shift from the struggle for equality to an assertion of freedom, from the demand for fundamental rights to the assertion of self-determination, from the acceptance of the pluralistic experiment to the surfacing of a new corporate identity.

Two other events helped consolidate the transformation. First was the Vaddukoddai Resolution, which sought to translate these vague, disconnected aspirations into a concrete political programme. Second, in the trial-at-bar (where three Tamil members of Parliament and a former Tamil member of Parliament were charged with sedition), a legal challenge was made to the validity of the Republican constitution. This trial provided an opportunity for strengthening the juridical and historical underpinnings of the new corporate identity of the Tamil people. The refusal of the Tamil United Liberation Front (TULF) to participate in the deliberations of the Select Committee constituted an extension of the juridical argument articulated in the trial.

III

In its election manifesto of 1977, the United National Party took due account of the continuing escalation of the grievances and discontent of the Tamil-speaking people. Their manifesto stated:

The United National Party accepts the position that there are numerous problems confronting the Tamil-speaking people. The lack of a solution to their problems has made the Tamil-speaking people support even a movement for the creation of a separate State. In the interest of national integration and unity so necessary for the economic development of the whole country the Party feels such problems should be solved without loss of time. The Party when it comes to power will take all possible steps to remedy their grievances in such fields as—
(1) Education
(2) Colonisation
(3) Use of the Tamil language
(4) Employment in the public and semi-public corporations.
   We will summon an All-Party Conference, as stated earlier, and implement its decisions.

One of the new government's first steps was to constitute a select committee to draft a new constitution. The three recognised political parties represented in Parliament were invited to participate in the committee's deliberations. It was later pointed out that a select committee thus constituted would have been the equivalent of the all-party conference envisioned in the manifesto. Despite efforts by some government leaders to persuade the TULF to join the committee, its leader, Appapillai Amirthalingam, declined to do so. He summarised the TULF's refusal to participate in forming the constitution thus: 'The United National Party had a clear, unequivocal mandate to assert the sovereignty of the Sinhala nation and enact a new constitution. The mandate of the majority of the Tamil nation pointed to a different duty'.

The statement symbolised the major conceptual transformation from 1972 to 1977 that resulted in a questioning of the relevance of 'constitutionalism' to the problems of a multi-ethnic society. The conceptual transformation was related to the assertion of a corporate identity by the Tamil people which was shaped by their perception of a distinct history, language, and culture. This identity was seen by others, however, as incompatible with, and antagonistic to, the corporate, collective identity of the Sinhala people, causing ideological and political crises in Sinhala-Tamil relations.

The Constitutional Select Committee reached a remarkable degree of consensus on several matters relating to the rights of the Tamil people: recognition of Tamil as a national language and a language of the courts and administration in the north and east; removal of the insidious distinction between citizens by descent and those by registration; recognition of justiciable fundamental rights; and establishment of an ombudsman vested with jurisdiction over fundamental rights. An attempt was made during the committee's deliberations to give some recognition to Tamil concerns about colonisation. The proposal was to provide in the chapter on fundamental rights or the directive principles of state policy a provision prohibiting the state from pursuing a policy of state settlement that sought to alter the demographic composition of a district. This proposal did not receive due consideration by the committee, however. Even Amirthalingam, the TULF leader, conceded during the debate on the new constitution that the government had gone further than any previous regime in recognising the Tamil language. He despaired that the constitutional assurance of non-discrimination and ethnic equality was diluted by the primacy that was accorded to the Sinhala language and Buddhism, the religion of the majority of Sinhalese.

Despite these constitutional advances, Tamil discontent rose to serious proportions. Tamil leaders continued to complain about discrimination in state employment and non-enforcement of the language safeguards in the constitution. The issue of university admissions continued to be a source of racial antagonism and ethnic friction. The government's formula of district quotas and preferential treatment of backward areas caused bitter resentment among Tamil university aspirants in Jaffna and Colombo.

In a climate of communal antagonism and increasing pressure on the government by its more chauvinistic elements to combat 'terrorism by terrorism', the government introduced a state of emergency in Jaffna and passed a harsh Prevention of Terrorism Law. The Movement for Interracial Justice and Equality viewed these developments as 'the logical outcome of two parallel, but complementary developments ... The betrayal of promises to solve the "Tamil Problem" at successive stages proceeded hand in hand with the uninterrupted induction of chauvinistic anti-Tamil hysteria in the country ... followed by the emergency and military intervention'. [See *Report on the Emergency*, 1979].

IV

It was in this climate that the government considered structural arrangements that could provide a measure of self-government to Tamil areas.

The need for such an approach was reiterated by other party Leaders. N. M. Perera, leader of the Trotskyist Lanka Sama Samaja Party, argued that the language provisions of the constitution (Chapter IV(Language)) were no longer satisfactory. 'What might have satisfied the Tamil community twenty years ago cannot be adequate twenty years later. Other concessions along the lines of regional autonomy will have to be in the offing if healthy and harmonious relations are to be regained'. Informal discussions were initiated with political leaders of the United National Party on regional arrangements that might be responsive to Tamil needs.

Government leaders were alert to the extreme sensitivity of this issue. Previous accords with Tamil leaders on schemes for decentralisation of authority had been thwarted by Sinhala extremism. The intensification of the campaign for a separation, as manifested in the activities of the expatriate community and the militant youths in the north, had further estranged the Sinhalese. Strong antipathy toward Tamils was felt even among the bureaucracy and the professional and middle classes, which formed the core of the liberal Sinhala constituency. An equally powerful constraint operated within the Tamil community. Political solutions mooted in the 1950s and 1960s no longer seemed durable or viable, given rising Tamil aspirations. Also, the TULF could not be perceived by its members as abandoning its electoral mandate to work for a separate state. Even moderate Tamils were wary of political compacts that depended on the goodwill of the majority community for effective implementation.

In this sensitive political climate, discussions on alternative structural arrangements proceeded cautiously. Two alternative proposals were under consideration. The first, based on the models of devolution in Scotland and Wales, was designed to respond to the special economic and political needs of the north and east. The second proposal was designed to strengthen and democratise the existing district ministry scheme, which recognised the government's political commitment to a system of district ministers as representatives of the executive president and which endeavoured to work within the framework of that commitment.

The district ministry scheme was formally instituted in March 1978, but no specific assignment of functions had taken place. The district minister presided over decentralised budget meetings and meetings of district co-ordination committees. He assumed some of the ceremonial functions of the government agent but had no authority to interfere with the agents' statutory duties. The district minister in some districts was equated with an ombudsman who mediated between public and officials in district administration; but his influence varied with the relationship he was able to develop with the government agent. The district minister scheme was a direct descendant of the system of district political authority instituted by the UF government of 1970–77.

The District Political Authority plan, however, was seen as a system of political mobilisation rather than a genuine devolution and decentralisation. It has been faulted for its politicisation of decision-making in the distribution of rewards and benefits and for its lack of formal or informal accountability to the people—the intended beneficiaries of governmental programmes. There was no formal machinery for redress of abuses of discretion or the arbitrary deprivation of sections of the community of their equitable share of the benefits of development. In addition, the capacity of the District Political Authority to take decisive decisions was impeded by lack of clarity in the demarcation of the powers and responsibilities of the district minister. Blurring of the lines of responsibility between the political and the bureaucratic heads of a district led to encroachment by the former into the latter's sphere, thereby weakening the morale and confidence of public officials. The District Political Authority had no legal or constitutional status; it was no more than a projection into the periphery of the formal authority and influence of the office of the prime minister.

The district ministry system was placed on a more formal constitutional footing in the second amendment to the First Republican constitution, which provided for the appointment of ministers other than cabinet ministers. There was concern, though, that in the absence of proper procedures for ensuring accountability to the people of a district, this institution would be overtaken by the same abuses that had eroded the effectiveness of the district political authorities. Thus a more positive response to the second proposal was made, which was directed towards integrating the district ministry scheme with a more comprehensive programme of decentralisation.

A major initiative of the government was a comprehensive White Paper on district ministers, presented to Parliament by the prime minister on 4 June 1978, a few weeks before the debate on the Second Republican constitution began. The White Paper received little public attention at the time. It outlined some of the major concepts that would serve as building blocks for the institutional changes to follow. The White Paper stated that its purpose was to strengthen the representative character of the democratic system by grafting on to it a scheme of self-management by the people of a district. The objectives of the district ministry scheme were to:

(a) Enable the people to participate in the administration at the district level through their elected representatives and through institutions established in the district;
(b) Enhance the accountability of the district minister to the president, the cabinet of ministers, and parliament;
(c) Facilitate control and co-ordination and secure the expeditious functioning of administrative functions at the district level.

It was this White Paper that set forth the concept of the district development council—its representative character, powers, functions, and devolved subjects over which it would enjoy jurisdiction. The White Paper envisioned direct allocation of resources to a development council, including the decentralised budget and other funds voted by Parliament.

The institution of the district minister provided for an independent secretariat and the appointment of a secretary as the executive head of the district, subject to political control by the district minister. The need for additional secretaries responsible for implementation of technical and other programmes was also emphasised. The district minister was regarded as essentially a link between the district and the centre. He was called upon to co-ordinate all developmental activities within the region by identifying bottlenecks in the implementation of governmental programs and directly supervising inter-departmental activities.

The White Paper, however, did not define precisely the relationship between the district minister and the development council. Instead, it envisioned the district minister as a member of Parliament drawn from the Government Parliamentary Group. It was thought that whenever possible, the district minister would be appointed to a district other than the one in which his electorate formed a part and the district minister should be one who enjoys the confidence of a majority of development council members in the district.

With the issue of the White Paper on 22 June 1978, critical discussion of the organisational form within which the district minister should function received the active consideration of senior public servants. It was pointed out that if district ministers were to be responsible for the political co-ordination and direction of work programmes in the district, it would be necessary for the authority to give the required direction to public officials. This would be achieved without intervention by the district minister in the flow of administrative and technical direction from the centre to district heads of departments. It was emphasised that the success of the district minister scheme depended entirely on the extent to which the sectoral minister was prepared to decentralise powers. Also, it was pointed out that any reluctance on the part of the ministers to promote the shifting of power and authority would jeopardise the entire scheme.

V

Despite the internal debate, no meaningful steps were taken to strengthen the district minister scheme through assignment or delegation of functions by sectoral ministers, nor the creation of a participatory organisation at the district level to complement the de-centralisation of executive power.

Dr A. Jeyaratnam Wilson, a political scientist, played a critical role in this process. Wilson, who enjoyed the confidence of the major political figures, was in a unique position to initiate discussion of the issues that divided the government and the TULF. Wilson's understanding of the workings of alternative political arrangements enabled him to direct his energies to how decentralisation of authority and devolution of power could be institutionalised in a manner that would be acceptable to the Sinhalese and the Tamils. As a result of Wilson's efforts, the government decided to appoint a presidential commission on devolution and to consult the country's major political parties on its composition. A critical, though uncertain, element was related to the response of the Sri Lanka Freedom Party and the Tamil United Liberation Front to the offer made by the government, that each party should nominate a representative to the commission. The Sri Lanka Freedom Party declined to participate in the process, which it characterised as only 'a ruse to translate into action by means of a commission the very regional council system [that] was rejected by the people in 1957 and 1968'. Although this was a major setback, political commentators were somewhat relieved when the TULF decided to nominate a member.

In its composition the commission reflected the ethnic balance of the country. The Commission was headed by a former Chief Justice who was a Kandyan Sinhalese. The commission included three other Sinhalese representing various social interests, three Tamil members and three Muslims. Of the three Tamil members, one was considered the representative of the Batticaloa Tamils; the second (the author of this paper) was the TULF representative; and the third was Dr Wilson.

In the letter of invitation to the members of the commission, the president outlined some policy considerations that had influenced the government's decision. In 'appreciating the advantage of democratic decentralisation for accelerating development and promoting participatory democracy, the government had decided to constitute a Presidential Commission to make recommendations regarding a scheme of devolution and decentralised administration'. The terms of reference of the commission outlined the institutional framework, which would be capable of advancing 'the ideals of accelerated development and participatory democracy'.

The commission, in recognising the importance and sensitivity of the issues it was required to inquire into and report on, called for public representations. It received detailed memoranda from several groups, including religious and ethnic organisations, delegations of district ministers, local bodies, public interest groups, trade unions, and voluntary bodies. Limited, direct oral representations were also permitted. Right from the beginning, it was clear that these groups had conflicting views of the commission's terms of reference. Some Buddhist religious organisations warned that any change in the existing system of district administration could 'gravely threaten the security of the State, endanger the religion of the majority, and seriously jeopardise the lives of the people'. On the other hand, organisations from the Tamil north voiced expectations of a different order. They argued that 'except for matters such as defence, external affairs, and money, all other subjects should be handled by the district authority'. Others emphasised the need for 'regional autonomy, preferably on the federal pattern'. These representations pointed to deep controversy over the proposed scheme of devolution and decentralisation.

Some felt that the commission should, at the very inception, dissociate the development councils contemplated in their terms of reference from the regional and district councils envisaged in 1957 and 1968, arguing that it was difficult to comprehend how the commission's terms of reference could be interpreted as authorising such a degree of freedom from control by the centre in all twenty-four districts when there was no demand or need on the part of most districts to adopt such a course, whether in the name of separatism or decentralisation. The differences were reflected in the work of the commission. Although it was originally thought that the broad concepts of the scheme had been determined in the terms of reference, and that the commission would concentrate on the details of the mechanism, there was little agreement on fundamentals. The disagreement concerned such issues as the powers and functions of development councils, the subjects to be devolved, and the borrowing and taxing powers of the councils. These differences were reflected in the commission's final report. The eight commissioners who submitted the majority report left many issues unresolved. Clearly, the majority report was a compromise between those who viewed the development councils as an advisory body and those who wanted it clothed in the powers of a decision-making body. The TULF representative (the author of this paper) dissented and submitted a separate report. During the legislative debate on the bill, the Sri Lanka Freedom Party issued a statement rejecting the plan. The statement alleged that the legislation had rejected the views of the majority of the commission and that it had adopted the concepts and proposals in the dissenting report. The statement also expressed the fear that implementation of the legislation would contribute to the division of the country and undermine the unitary character of the constitution.

VI

As we have pointed out, there were competing and conflicting conceptions of the decentralisation scheme, of which the district development councils formed a part. Some, in urging that the unitary character of the state be strengthened by reinforcing the district ministry scheme, felt that such a scheme would enable the centre to project itself more effectively at the periphery. Others called for more authentic devolution through democratically constituted institutions at the district level. A review of the main elements of the legislation illustrates the accommodations reached between these competing conceptions. First, we examine the representative character of the development councils. The development council is a democratically constituted decision-making body; there was no provision for nomination of members or appointment of officials. Most members of the council would be members of Parliament elected from the districts. The remainder would be elected directly on the basis of proportional representation, which would ensure that the council reflected the interplay of diverse social forces and group interests. The only exceptions were the councils in the districts of Vavuniya, Mullaitivu, and Mannar, where there was only one member of Parliament; provision was therefore made for the election of four other members in each of these districts. The chairman of the council was the candidate whose name appeared first in the list of the political party which received a majority in the district development council elections. The district minister was not a member of the council, but he could on appropriate occasions send messages to the council.

The majority weighted in favour of members of Parliament was severely criticised by the opposition parties. It was pointed out that the weighting would, in effect, ensure that in twenty of the twenty-four districts the UNP, which had a five-sixths majority in the legislature, would exercise control of the councils. This aspect was identified as one factor influencing the Sri Lanka Freedom Party, the Communist Party, and the Lanka Sama Samaja Party not to participate in the elections to the councils, held in late May 1981. Squabbles within the Sri Lanka Freedom Party may also have affected the party's capacity to adopt a consistent position on the elections. The Tamil United Liberation Front, however, did not allow this to influence its decision to participate in the elections, though in the seven districts in which it presented candidates it enjoyed a weighted majority only in Jaffna District. It was felt as well that such a weighted majority was a temporary phenomenon which would end in 1983 when the term of the present Parliament was due to expire (since extended by a referendum specified in the constitution for a further period of six years). In their composition, the district development councils manifested two conflicting representational systems. Their members, who were members of Parliament, were elected on the principle of 'first past the post', while district council elections were conducted on the principle of proportional representation. When this anomaly is removed, a more balanced representation is inevitable. The development councils were to be regarded as mini-parliaments, with subordinate law-making authority and standing orders framed to regulate debate and provide for the appointment of select committees. Provision is also likely to be made for publication of the proceedings of the development councils in the form of district *'Hansards'*.

The second aspect relates to reconciliation of the roles, functions, and responsibilities of the district ministers (the 'central government functionary') with that of the development councils (a body that 'derived authority from the people of the District'). As noted above, the White Paper sought to resolve this difficulty by stipulating that a district minister should enjoy the confidence of the council. It was found difficult, however, to incorporate this concept into the legislation, partly because the president's power to appoint district ministers is derived directly from the Constitution. The need thus arose to formulate a solution that would minimise the potential for conflict and re-enforce complementarity of roles of the respective institutions.

Such a solution was found in the institution of the executive committee. This institution facilitated a clearer demarcation of responsibilities and powers between legislative and executive components of the district development council scheme. Implementation of the plan and the mobilisation of resources would be under the development council, while those of implementation and execution would be under the executive committee. The development council would be headed by an elected chairman and the executive committee by a district minister. Both the district minister and the chairman were made ex-officio members of the committee, with one or two other members being appointed by the district minister in consultation with the chairman.

An important provision that underscored the interrelation of the executive committee and the district development council was the provision specifying that 'executive committee members were individually and collectively accountable to the council'. It was thus anticipated that the executive committee would be the political executive at the district level, collectively responsible and answerable to the people for implementation of the district development plan. The council, on the other hand, was the 'collective conscience of the district—directing, guiding, and humanizing the development process so that benefits accelerating development shared would be equitable'. The plan thus envisages replication at the district level of the institutions of the presidency, cabinet and legislature, with the district minister, committee and council playing corresponding roles.

The third aspect central to the scheme is the district development plan. Such a plan represented a compromise between those seeking to devolve certain limited and specific subjects to the exclusive control of the council and those advocating a more flexible approach. Those who advocated the latter approach argued that it would be more satisfactory to define the devolved subjects in general terms, so takeover of the district administration by the council would be a progressive, evolving process. The pace at which greater responsibility would be appropriated would be determined by the role of local resource mobilisation. Therefore, the district development plan provides a compromise between these concepts. The legislation expressly defined the devolved subjects as including agriculture and food; land use and settlement; animal husbandry; co-operatives; small- and medium-scale industries; fisheries; rural development; housing; education; health services; cultural services; irrigation of an intra-district nature; and agricultural marketing, social services, and employment. The council, however, was required to formulate a plan for a programme of development in the district relating to each devolved area. The draft plan would include a detailed statement of technical feasibility and a financial estimate. The plan (formulated initially by the executive committee) will need to be debated and voted on by the council. Thereafter, it will be submitted to the centre for appraisal and approval. Once the plan had been approved, the executive authority can assume responsibility for administration of the matters referred to in the plan. In addition to the devolved areas, the council has the power to formulate any scheme on other matters and ask the government to transfer the scheme to the council.

The fourth aspect concerns the district fund. A district fund is to be established to which all grants and loans as well as the revenue of the council is to be credited. An important component of the district fund is direct grants made by the central government under the decentralised budget. It was pointed out, however, that this system of financial allocation does not adequately take note of the developmental potential, varying financial needs, and implementation capacity of various districts.

Undeveloped areas with dispersed population had hitherto been denied the special consideration that was required. Some argued, therefore, that an independent grants commission was needed to develop objective criteria for resource allocation based on area, stage of development, and revenue-raising potential. The proposal was resisted by others contending that it would be more advantageous for backward districts to negotiate directly with political leaders at the centre. They added that, in any case, a grants commission could not be insulated from political and other parochial considerations in resource allocation. In addition, the legislation also vested in the Council the authority to tax and borrow from both local and external financial institutions. The council might also receive grants or gifts from any source. Exercise of these powers, however, requires the concurrence of the ministers in charge of local government and finance.

The fifth aspect is that of the district service. It was felt that the development councils, through executive committees, should develop a body of experts and officials who primarily meet the district's administrative needs. The district service would have two categories of officers— servants and employees appointed by the council, and public servants and members of the local government service who were seconded to the council. Members of the district service are subject to the direction and supervision of the executive committee, which is exercised through the district secretary.

The institutional arrangements outlined in this paper call for concerted action by the political executive, district administration, and local government to resolve the developmental crisis facing several districts in Sri Lanka. They provide a framework for the integration of institutions that have worked in isolation for decades. No doubt, the potential for conflict exists; but complementarity in institutional roles and interests could provide the framework for collaboration and concerted action.

Some social scientists emphasise that the tendency toward centrepetal authority in the political culture of the Sinhalese aborted previous efforts to achieve devolution of power and authority. The system of the executive presidency instituted in 1978 reinforces these tendencies in such a way that power inevitably gravitates towards the centre; the district development councils represent a trend in the opposite direction. It could prove to be a bold experiment in participatory democracy, and even redress some of the grievances of the Tamil areas of the north and the east if sustained by an abiding commitment to the sharing of power.

14 LEGISLATIVE RESERVATIONS FOR SOCIAL JUSTICE: SOME THOUGHTS ON INDIA'S UNIQUE EXPERIMENT

Upendra Baxi

I

India's experiment in providing political participation for her most depressed groups through a system of political reservations is unprecedented in its aims, nature and scope. Based on the idea of a just distribution of political power, it represents a crucial aspect of the massive, ongoing endeavour to reverse India's Hindu past. A close look at this experiment reveals numerous unexpected complexities. Yet this is a much neglected area of compensatory discrimination; mainstream research has more closely followed policies and programmes of employment and education reservations and quotas that lend themselves more readily to cross-cultural comparisons. In general, the linkages between political reservations and other related policies and programmes of compensatory discrimination seem to have been overlooked.

II

The first debate after adoption of the Constitution on the justification of political reservations occurred in Parliament in 1959. Essentially, the debate focused on the claim that political justice for the scheduled communities justified the political reservations. Also, representation through reservations is essential for securing a speedy amelioration of the plight of the untouchables and the tribals.

Only through a system of reservations could the scheduled castes and tribes acquire 'a voice in the administration', a 'mighty platform to ventilate their grievances' and a political status denied them by Hindu stratification.

This argument was vehemently met by opponents of reservations. In particular, members of the Republican party argued that conditions had changed dramatically, that there had been a political awakening among the scheduled castes, even if the social structure remained repressive. Therefore, proponents of this view argued, reservations could only have the negative effect of arresting the growth of the new political consciousness, and it might even paralyse that growth. The argument was also advanced that the reservations, instead of providing political power, would give 'political charity'. Reservations would make scheduled groups dependent on the dominant classes. Dr Ambedkar's insistence that reservations be abolished was repeatedly endorsed on these grounds. Furthermore, it was suggested that the best way to verify these contentions was to consult the scheduled groups themselves; opponents undertook to withdraw their opposition if even 50 per cent of the scheduled castes expressed themselves in favour of the reservations.

The justification that adequate representation to scheduled groups was a necessary, though not sufficient, condition for ameliorating their depressed conditions, was also questioned, on both political and theoretical grounds. Taking the latter justification first, opponents asked whether reservation of seats in the legislature would 'really add substance' to the caste as a whole. How could the presence of a few members of a caste in the legislature help all the members of that caste?

At the political level, the argument was made that even representatives of the scheduled castes had agreed in the Constituent Assembly to accept the principle of reservation for a period of ten years only, although Dr Ambedkar himself disapproved of the concept. Some claimed that extension of reservations was not being carried out at the instance of, or in adequate consultation with, the scheduled groups, particularly the scheduled castes. Others openly doubted that members elected from reserved constituencies on the Congress ticket were the true representatives of the scheduled castes. Further, it was alleged that the reservations were demanded not so much by the groups affected as by the groups that were the recipients of an imposition of reservations. One member was brutally frank: 'the Congress talks about a casteless society, but entrenches it in politics'.

The extension of reservations by another decade in 1970 was marked by an air of inevitability. The time allotted for discussion was about six hours. Most members could not bring themselves to support the modest proposal that the bill be circulated in order to generate public opinion and for discussion in early February 1970.

Interestingly enough, the principal argument in favour of extending the legislative reservation until 26 January 1980 was that the overall positions of the protected classes had not improved significantly or substantially. Statistics on literacy, education, job reservations, land redistribution and the overall social and economic conditions of scheduled tribes and castes were cited in support of extension for another decade. Predictably, much of the discussion reflected allocation of blame for the situation to the present government. Equally predictably, spokesmen for the government said the problem was a massive one, that the government needed support of all parties and groups in this vast enterprise. Predictably, members held that what was needed was the elimination of the caste system; without it, untouchability would never be truly abolished.

Given the inevitability of extension, the time span for continuation of the reservations became crucial. Quite a few members thought a decade too short; they desired two or three decades as a minimum. It would take 106 years to modestly improve the conditions of the scheduled castes and 329 years for the scheduled tribes. Dr Ambedkar therefore moved an amendment that the reservations would continue until these groups reached 'the same level of advancement as the other people, economically, socially and politically'.

The impact of continuing the reservations was of concern to only one member—M. R. Masani—who drew attention to the costs of continued legislative reservations for the scheduled groups, arguing that the policy had an 'opiate effect', that it has 'put the conscience of the upper class and upper castes to sleep'. He said it also had a 'doping effect' on the scheduled groups and 'put to sleep the instinct for social justice and the dynamism that should come from an underprivileged class'. Masani argued that the government had not made a good case for the policy being truly beneficial to the scheduled groups; rather, the policy had become a sort of 'crutch' for them. Accordingly, he favoured progressive abolition of legislative reservations within thirteen years, the reduction rate to be 33.3 per cent after each general election. This suggestion, however, also went virtually unheeded.

In the event, the only reason for supporting the extension of reservations by another decade was that there had been no significant change in the condition of the scheduled group. One member expressed the matter in sharp terms: 'Whatever concessions have been offered, they are just a drop in the ocean. We have completely failed to uplift these people'.

III

Soon after the second extension of reservations, Parliament was forced to consider the manner of electing representatives from the scheduled groups. In the first two elections, the system of double-member constituencies (DMC) was used. Under the DMC system, wherever a constituency could be demarcated in which either of the two scheduled groups was in a majority, that would become a single-member constituency. Where the scheduled groups were in a minority, the constituency would be doubled in size and two seats would be created, one to be reserved and the other left open to all. When the votes were counted, the leading candidate from the scheduled caste or tribe would receive the reserved seat. Thereafter, all other candidates, including the scheduled groups, were considered to be in competition for the general seat, which was awarded to the candidate who polled the most votes. Thus, if the scheduled groups polled the largest number of votes in the second category, the system would produce two of their representatives, instead of one, as in the system of a reserved constituency.

The DMC system could be justified on several grounds. One was that the 'geographical distribution of the scheduled groups [was] relatively so even that they [formed] less than half the votes in all the constituencies from which members [were] elected to Lok Sabha . . . and in all but three constituencies at the state assembly level'. Also, 'in some reserved constituencies their proportion [dropped] below 10 per cent and there [were] many constituencies with over 20 per cent Scheduled Castes [that were] not reserved for them. In any case, the great majority of the scheduled caste voters, like the great majority of other voters, live in unreserved constituencies'.

The DMC system could be justified on still another ground: reservation of constituencies in most cases where the scheduled groups constituted even less than 10 per cent of the population would inevitably result in a situation where the 'vast majority of the electorate in the constituency would be denied their right to representation, of setting up one of their members as a candidate at any election'. (These observations are continued in the report of the Election Commission on the Second General Elections.) The commission was of the view, therefore, that any attempt to move towards a single-member constituency must be preceded by careful deliberation.

The third ground was that the DMC system encouraged electoral integration, whereas the single-reserved-constituency system encouraged electoral separation. If the eventual ending of reservations was the goal, it would be necessary to retain the DMC system. Some insisted as early as 1959 that if reservations were extended a decade or more, the DMC system must be continued; that would give the scheduled groups an opportunity not merely to represent their specific constituents but to represent the larger electorate as well. The scheduled-group legislators would then more cogently feel themselves to be the 'genuine representatives of the people'.

The actual member of scheduled-group members returned from unreserved seats was not large. The defeat in 1959 of V. V. Giri, in the tribal constituency of Parvatipuram, in Andhra, dramatised the potential of the DMC system. In that election, two tribal members received more votes than the two non-tribal candidates, and thus were declared elected.

One must agree with Lelah Dushkin that the fact that the DMC, set up to 'favour' election of the scheduled groups, could *actually* do so 'seems to have given the non-scheduled-caste politicians a nightmare'. (Dushkin, p. 192). In fact, a private-member bill was introduced in Lok Sabha at the end of 1959, calling for the abolition of the DMC on the grounds that the system was cumbersome and confusing to the voters. In 1960 the Congress party considered the matter in detail, and in December 1960 the Congress Parliamentary party (CPP) met and resolved to abolish the DMC. Only 229 of 555 members of the CPP attended the meeting, however; the motion to introduce a bill to change the system was marked by substantial division of opinion, manifest in the voting. The motion was carried by a vote of 124 to 94. It is hard to resist the conclusion that the debate was 'confined mainly among the politicians directly concerned' (Dushkin, p. 193). In addition to all this was the rude fact that the third general elections were imminent. It is in this context that a bill to abolish the DMC was introduced and passed in February 1961.

The principal justification proposed in both houses of Parliament was that the DMC system was cumbersome in all respects. Some members suggested that scheduled groups in the DMCs could not hold their own against caste candidates—rather that they served merely as 'shadows' or 'appendages' of the latter. Therefore, these members argued, it would be in the interest of the scheduled groups for their candidates to separate and for reserved constituencies to be free from the necessity of electoral trade-offs.

Thus, the arguments in favour rested mainly on administrative and electoral convenience. Otherwise, the argument that the interests of the scheduled groups would be better served by single-member constituencies was not substantiated.

Opposition to the motion was widespread and intense. It was said that as the scheduled groups worked hard and began to win victories, the caste Hindus would present this set of legislative proposals. The DMC system was justified in terms of electoral integration, given that the reservations were viewed as a temporary phase. It was maintained that the scheduled groups were indeed much better served by the DMC system than the proposed SMC system could ever serve them.

The other major thrust of the critique was that the SMC system would deprive many people (estimated then at 55 million) of their right to put up candidates of their own choice without regard for caste factors. The SMC would deprive the non-scheduled-group population of the opportunity to field their own candidates.

It was further argued that reservations made sense only when a plurality of seats existed. When only one was available in the single-member constituency, Shri Kamble asked, 'what is to be reserved'? It was pointed out that elections in 1937 had produced 125 DMCs out of 151 seats.

Others argued in the same vein, though with restraint. 'If you want to abolish DMCs', Shri Khadilkar said, 'the logical process would be to abolish reservations'.

Aside from the merits of the various arguments, many members, both in the Congress party and among the opposition, felt that wider consultation was necessary before the DMCs were abolished. Members felt that although the matter fell within the purview of Union legislative power, it affected the states as much as it did the Union; thus, there should be maximum consultation.

As things turned out, there was little public discussion. According to Dushkin, the press gave to it 'absent-minded coverage, not making it clear that the bill would simply bifurcate the constituencies, leaving [one] member reserved and [one] member unreserved'. The impression was widespread, even among the experts, that the new SMCs would be in the 'Harijan majority areas', and that 'such areas are almost non-existent'. Some felt the new system meant the end of reservations—and so soon after the renewal, by another decade, of reservations. It was only after the bill was passed that 'eventually, some citizen groups in the constituencies involved began to speak up, universally, against the bill' (Dushkin, p. 193).

IV

In reviewing the empirical studies of reservations in operation, it must be noted, first, that there are few studies, and second, that those that do exist vary in their focus. Some provide general analyses of elites among the scheduled castes, while others discuss the profiles of legislators from the scheduled castes. Some deal with the politics of untouchability; still others focus on the behaviour of the scheduled-caste electorate. No nationwide study has been made of what scheduled-caste legislators *do* to advance the interests of their constituents. Yet some features begin to emerge.

1. In so far as the scheduled-caste composition of the Lok Sabha is concerned, there is a wide gap between scheduled-caste masses and their representatives, in terms of education, occupational affiliation and rural-urban balance. More than half the scheduled-caste members in the Third, Fourth and Fifth Lok Sabha were in the age group 25–40, whereas the bulk of the scheduled tribes and general members were in the age group 41–55. In terms of education, we find that most scheduled-caste members 'were drawn from 0.3 per cent of [educated] scheduled-caste population'. Thus the 'elite-mass gap in terms of education was more among the scheduled castes than among the more general members'. While 72.2 per cent of the scheduled-caste people are agricultural workers, only half that percentage of their representatives in Parliament come from this rural

population. On the other hand, while only 1.2 per cent of their total population is engaged in trade and commerce, the share of this group in Lok Sabha is as high as 9.2 per cent. It was found that the 'occupational background of the scheduled-caste members does not reflect the occupational structure of the scheduled-caste population'. Similarly, whereas the rural-urban balance, relatively high for the general members, has not significantly changed for them, there is a clear trend among the reserved scheduled-caste members to the effect that people with more 'urban background were replacing the rural members'. If this trend continues, 'there will be no significant difference left with regard to places of residence between the general and scheduled-caste members'. It is also striking that in terms of previous Lok Sabha experience, more scheduled-caste members have been 'continuously elected' than the general or tribal members.

In other words, the gap between the scheduled-caste Lok Sabha members and their population is 'wider as compared with the gap between the two other groups (tribals and all others) and the population they represent'. At the same time, there is increasing evidence of the 'emerging homogeneity' of the political elite.

These general profiles are substantiated by regional studies. Thus, the Republican party of India and other political groupings of the scheduled castes have often been caste-dominated. For example, the party is known as Mahar-dominated in Maharashtra and Jatav-dominated in western Uttar Pradesh. There seems to be no serious attempt to 'consolidate the scheduled castes' under the party. And scheduled-caste people, particularly of the non-dominant castes, are not drawn to 'their parties and organis-ations'. A recent study of the scheduled-caste elite in Andhra Pradesh also attests to the hegemony of some better-off castes among the scheduled castes. It was found that members from only five sub-castes form the political elite, out of a total of sixty caste groups in the state. Interestingly, of five politically dominant castes (a term used rather loosely, for purposes of emphasis), the majority of the elite group is formed by only one caste—the Mala sub-caste.

2. It is clear from the fluctuating fortunes of the Republican party that the scheduled castes have not been able to organise successfully as an effective political party or even as an effective conglomeration of assorted groups. The Table below gives an idea of the level of electoral success the party has had in the six general elections to the Lok Sabha.

The problems of the Republican party are many. In a system of reserved seats, the dominant political parties pre-empt the scheduled-caste candidates. Many scheduled-caste people consider it undesirable to belong to opposition parties. It has been observed that to 'belong to an opposition party is worse than being a scheduled-caste person'. For example, of

Table 14.1. Seats won by the Republican party at six general elections to the Lok Sabha

Elections	Seats won
First	2
Second	7
Third	3
Fourth	1
Fifth	1
Sixth	2

Seventy-seven reserved seats for the scheduled castes in the 1967 elections, the Republican party won only one, whereas the Congress party won forty-seven. Many members of the Republican party are Buddhists and thus are ineligible to contest the reserved seats. Other organisational and functional factors affect the fortunes of the party. The identification of the party with one dominant caste group not only generates fear of domination but resistance, factionalism and divisiveness as well. Frequently, there is poor leadership aggravated by 'empty coffers or the lack of money'. Lynch found that the party in Agra was, on the whole, 'the party of the poverty-stricken'.

No funds [are] available to maintain an office or to keep a full- or even part-time staff; nor are there [sufficient] funds for conducting election campaigns. Without an office and a staff, there is no visible formal locus of continuity. . . . Also, the party's sources of patronage are very limited. In such a situation, its appeal is restricted to caste and party loyalty.

In this context, leaders of the party who have an 'independent means of support' or who have acquired one are liable to accusations of corruption. This, in turn, weakens the rank and file's confidence in the leadership and produces a climate conducive to a politics of corruption.

3. Scheduled-caste politicians have chosen (or inherited) the strategy of working with and through well-established political parties, particularly the party in power. This system has several advantages. The problems of election-funding and of campaigning, plus related organisational needs, are accommodated through a system of alliances and alignments. By the same token, the bargaining power of scheduled-caste politicians has been reduced significantly. This diminution of bargaining power has generally meant that scheduled-caste politicians and legislators lack the capacity to force initiation or attainment of swift structural changes—even the limited objective of ensuring effective implementation of policies and programmes to ameliorate the plight of their countrymen. There is not a priori reason

why this should happen; but the fact remains that it has happened despite the substantial number of representatives the scheduled castes possess in the Lok Sabha and the state legislatures. Perhaps the organisational and leadership infirmities that frustrate their attempt to achieve a united political front, let alone a party, also preclude the achievement of an effective voice in the forums of the party. It remains true that, despite the number of people they lead, scheduled-caste leaders 'have not extracted the price of their affiliation from the political parties'.

The reasons for the development of this situation go beyond organisational and leadership problems. In the final analysis, scheduled-caste leaders and candidates depend on substantial Hindu votes to win elections. At the same time, they must be able to mobilise their own constituents. This leads to alienation and role conflicts that sometimes produce crises of identity. If scheduled-caste candidates assume a posture of radical struggle against discrimination and exploitation, they may alienate caste Hindu voters; but if they do not appear continuously and deeply concerned about injustice to their people, they risk loss of support from them, and even from some caste Hindus. The problem has been 'solved' by identification with the recognised political parties.

Given the system of reservations, such identification, particularly with the ruling party, is the only path to political success. Scheduled-caste leaders find it difficult to generate or sustain 'inter-caste alliances' under their leadership. This was well illustrated in 1937 by the fate of Ambedkar's Independent Labour party. 'Non-untouchable labourers are unlikely to follow untouchable leadership', said Ambedkar; 'the successful labour movements and political parties have been led mostly by the non-untouchables'. That scheduled-caste leaders and politicians are viewed as possessing no effective power is due primarily to their inability to aggregate and articulate class interests.

Should an independent scheduled-caste politician win in an unreserved constituency, however, there is the danger that in the next election the politician will be 'co-opted', 'accommodated' or 'absorbed' by the dominant party. All opposition groups have been exposed to this Indian political risk: if demands for change gather momentum and reach a critical point, the ruling party adopts the demands as its own, leaving to the opposition the less visible task of overseeing the rate of implementation. In the case of vulnerable, isolated political groups, to all this is added the risk of overt repression without much significant public indignation, as happened to the Dalit Panther movement in Maharashtra.

4. Scheduled-caste politicians and legislators have not produced a credible image of effective sub-organisational leadership. The expectation that they would organise into 'blocs' or 'lobbies' within the dominant parties or legislatures has not been realised. There is a loose federation of

the groups—the All India Legislators Convention of Scheduled Castes and Tribes, under the chairmanship of Jagjivan Ram—but not much is known about its concrete objectives and achievements. It has not been involved in the expressions of outrage at the continuing atrocities perpetrated on untouchables. Nor does the Convention seem to have influenced the course of vital legislation affecting the scheduled castes and tribes. At the state level, 'in so far as scheduled-caste legislators act in a bloc, they tend to concentrate their efforts on those items of the protective/discrimination system ... of [the greatest] concern to their more prosperous caste candidates—more ministries for themselves, more scholarships and reservations in higher educational institutions and, above all, more government jobs'.

5. Scheduled-caste legislators and politicians seem unable, however, to translate their power into effective political power for their constituents. As Professor Dushkin puts it, they are unable to translate their power into 'real power with voters'.

In 1978, there were atrocities in Bishrampur, Belchi, Darpu, Dharmapura in Bihar; the Villupuram atrocities in Tamil Nadu, police brutality on Harijans in Madhya Pradesh. There is a longer list for the early 1980s. There has been little evidence of political activity by scheduled-caste politicians and legislators in any of these tragedies. The same holds true for less dramatic but equally significant issues, such as the enforcement of anti-untouchability, the bonded labour elimination laws, implementation of land reform, rural credit and minimum wage legislation and the commercial exploitation of scheduled-caste women.

In sum, scheduled-caste legislators have not been conspicuous actors on the national or the regional scene, championing the causes of their constituents. What's more, scheduled-caste legislators have not even been able to do much to safeguard and promote their own interests. For example, untouchability is openly practised with the scheduled-caste members of village panchayats. This is true of most of India, though conclusive data exists only for Gujarat. In about 47 per cent of the village *panchayats*, physical contact with the untouchable members is avoided There is discrimination in the provision of drinking water to them at *panchayat* meetings. In the circumstances, it cannot simply be 'imagined that snacks would be taken together by the untouchable and *savarna* members in the *Panchayat*' (Desai). It is true that this kind of discrimination is relatively unknown as regards the scheduled-caste legislators at the state and union levels. There are enough illustrations, however, to show that there is some discrimination—often of a humiliating kind—practised towards untouchable legislators and politicians. This discrimination is accepted by some of them in the long-term interests of their political career. Some legislators apprehend loss of 'political support by upper classes' if they deliberately attempt to 'violate traditionally sanctioned proscription.' (Sachindanda, p. 45) The following responses are not untypical:

In the election of 1969, I once stayed with an upper casteman. There I was given food separately with other Harijans. I did not react to it because I was a candidate in the election and I had gone there to elicit support for myself (Sachindanda p. 48).

In the village, I do not sit in the presence of the upper castemen. Violation of this would mean the loss of [a] considerable number of votes of such persons at the time of election. In fact, the man who lost his seat to me was defeated because he could not command the majority vote of the upper castes. The upper caste people were annoyed with him because he never cared to pay deference to them (Sachindanda, p.45).

If scheduled-caste legislators are not able to struggle for their own self-respect, let alone the basic rights and needs of their people, it is because they have, more or less accepted the political system, including that of reservations, as good for *themselves*. And good for them it certainly has been. They are looked after remarkably well, compared not only with their own brethren but also with middle-class Indians. In the process, however, they 'risk becoming mere puppets of the non-untouchable leaders who dominate the political parties and local power structures' (Dushkin, p. 217).

V

If this is the position of the scheduled-caste legislators and politicians, what is the role of the electorate? Once again, studies of voting behaviour of the Indian electorates tend to ignore the attitudes and behaviour of the scheduled-caste voters. The studies that are available, however, indicate that the thesis that there has been a 'political awakening' among the scheduled-caste masses appears to be more wishful thinking than reality. A recent survey concluded:

A large proportion of Harijans are mobilised to vote, but the mobilisation is external. It has little to do with their involvement in politics or their group consciousness. A smaller group is mobilised into campaign activity, cooperative activity and contact. For them, the process of mobilisation seems to involve internalised politics (Verba *et al.*, p. 225).

Scheduled-caste populations are 'likely to be regular voters, as are the caste Hindus and indeed as are white or black Americans.' The number of scheduled-caste people, however, 'who are active beyond the vote is small' (Verba *et al.*, p. 225). Also,

Where there is mass Harijan participation, one finds that participation dominated by partisan mobilisation with no impact of group consciousness. But where there is a more active type of participation, in campaigns, and where a much thinner slice of Harijans take part, group consciousness takes over (Verba *et al.*, p. 228).

In other words, 'the sense of political relevance of one's group has no impact on Harijan voting' (Verba *et al.*, p. 235). Even where 'group consciousness increases the activity rate of Harijans, its impact on overall activity rate of the group is limited by the fact that a small proportion of the Harijans have this sense of 'political relevance of group membership' (Verba *et al.*, p. 239).

Similarly, a recent study finds that while 'the Harijan elite . . . show evidence of politicization, the scheduled-caste masses are not very much touched by this process'. National statistics on this point are not easy to obtain, but there appears to be cogency in the observation that while there are a few 'scheduled-caste members in each party', their number seems 'on the whole . . . to be quite insignificant' (Deshpander, p. 98).

Allegations of intimidation of scheduled-caste voters have always been heard in the wake of general elections; there have been a great many complaints of corrupt practices by the defeated candidates and parties. Reports on the general elections, as well as those of the commissioner of Scheduled Castes and Tribes, have made these allegations, and so have the media. In general, it is difficult to determine the extent of coercion and corruption in relation to voters of the scheduled group. Once again, no hard data are available, only judicial decisions involving charges of corrupt practices.

VI

It is in the context described above that we come to the justifications offered for continuing legislative or political reservations. Broadly, there are three justifications. Firstly, it can be said that the scheduled-caste population may not be represented effectively in the absence of a system of reservation of seats in legislatures. Secondly, one may urge that it is essential to have sufficient legislative reservations for scheduled castes if governments are to be persuaded into effective action on the implementation of constitutional assurances of development and concern for the welfare of these people. Thirdly, it can be said that the reservations system is necessary in order to generate political consciousness among the scheduled-caste population.

It is important to note, even as we consider these justifications in some detail, that nothing follows as regards the *duration* of legislative reservations from any of the three classes mentioned here. The first and third claims are *ex hypothesi* beyond validation. How is one to know whether the scheduled-caste population will receive meaningful representation in legislatures without reservations? It may be that the number of independent candidates or party candidates contesting non-reserved seats from scheduled groups is quite small. No inference, however, can be drawn from this in support of the first claim, because large numbers of reserved seats have been provided for such groups throughout India. If, upon the abolition of reservations, scheduled-caste people fail to be elected to the legislatures in significant numbers, would this be because they are scheduled-caste people or because regional and national political parties have no desire to sponsor scheduled-caste candidates in elections? These parties have hitherto developed no conventions in this matter *because* of the system of reservations. Would they fail to develop such conventions out of principle or prudence when the reservations are abolished altogether? It may be that in the initial stages, the number of scheduled-caste people who are given election tickets or who are returned to legislatures may decline somewhat from what is now constitutionally prescribed. But must the decline be so sharp as to prevent *any* meaningful representation?

On the other hand, concerning the third claim, if scheduled-caste political consciousness has not grown in the past thirty-years of reservations, will it necessarily grow in the next thirty? On the basis of evidence now available, the answer must be No. All that happens under the system of reservations is partisan mobilisation, not a fostering of political consciousness of the groups involved. Would abolition of the reservations bring this about? Who can tell? Time and again, and since Ambedkar, it has been said by untouchable and non-untouchable politicians that the system of reservations affects all concerned as an 'opiate', a 'doping'. Few today will agree with Govind Vallabh Pant, that the principle and practice of legislative reservations, in fact, serves to liberate 'the suppressed souls of the scheduled castes'.

The second claim—that reservations are necessary for the effective pursuit of programmes of compensatory redistribution mandated by the Constitution—is theoretically unsound, politically retrograde and empirically false. Theoretically, the claim, if taken seriously, must mean that, lacking legislative reservations, governments may not pursue such policies effectively. If this were so it would have to be conceded that the Indian Constitution, for a long time to come, is by its very nature, government of the majority, by the majority, for the majority. If this is the case, how can the state claim that its political system would ever respond to the social justice claims of vulnerable and depressed minority groups? Indeed, the state seldom does so. To claim that it *cannot* do so without prodding by reservations, however, is to strike at the heart of the legitimacy of power in a democratic society. It must be regarded as a paradox of Indian political history that the state frequently made this claim without at the same time generating significant crises of credibility or legitimation of political power in India.

Empirically, the claim that legislative reservations serve as a prod to ameliorative political action for the scheduled groups is shown to be false. Some evidence was reviewed in the previous section, and one must now add to this the fact that most scheduled-caste people who are elected to legislatures actually belong to the ruling parties. As B. P. Maurya once said: *'They do not represent their people to the party and the government, but represent the party in power to their people'* (Isaacs, pp. 125–6; emphasis added). This must mean that whatever pressures they could bring to bear on the party and the government for rapid change of policy, law and implementation are within the framework of the politics of the dominant political party or coalition. On the other hand, the ruling parties themselves claim that they need reservations to enable them to perform better in achieving the goals of welfare and justice for the depressed classes.

Increasingly, sane voices in the Indian political system are, in principle, protesting legislative reservations. Some scheduled-caste leaders and politicians have protested both inside and outside Parliament against the extension of legislative reservations. Their reasons are that the system of reservations fosters a new stigmatising status of 'quasi-untouchables'; that reservations are a kind of crutch thwarting development of political maturity among the scheduled castes; that reservations of this kind create over time a 'vested interest in the survival of untouchability'; that reservations create a 'dependency syndrome' among politically-conscious and active untouchable people, generating complacency and the illusion of progress; and finally, the way the system of reservations actually operates is 'just a way of keeping the weaker sections weak' (Maurya, op. cit.).

If these views are correct, legislative reservations seem necessary not for the sake of scheduled-caste people themselves but for the sake of higher-caste people. As Professor Dushkin has put it: 'political scientists of the future may look back upon protective discrimination as an efficient and expensive mechanism of social control' (Ibid., p. 217).

This must be how the system subverts social justice, how it converts revolutionary constitutional assurances into mere appeasement of the status quo. The device of legislative reservations, designed to redistribute political power as an aspect of social justice, in fact, operates as an 'efficient and inexpensive' means of social control. This is what Dr Ambedkar would have said in more trenchant terms were he with us today.

Notes

Abbasaylulu, *The Scheduled Castes Elite*, 1978.

Anonymous, *Jagjivan Ram: Four Decades of Parliamentary Career*, 1974.

Baxi, U., 'Untouchability, Constitution and the Plan: Socio-Legal Examination', in *Removal of Untouchability*, 1980.

Baxi, U., 'Political Justice, Legislative Reservations for Scheduled Castes and Social Change', Second Ambedkar Memorial Lecture, Mimeo, 1979.

Dang, S. P., 'Plight of Women Sweepers', *Mainstream* 12 (August 1974) pp. 20–2.

Desai, I. P., *Untouchability in Rural Gujarat*, 1976.

Deshpande, N., *Towards Social Integration: Problem of Adjustment of Scheduled Caste Elite in India*, 1978.

Dushkin, L., 'Scheduled Caste Politics', in J. M. Mahar (ed.), *The Untouchables in Contemporary India*, 1972.

Isaacs, H., *India's Ex-Untouchables*, 1965.

Livingston, J. C., *Fair Game: Inequality and Affirmative Administration*, 1979.

Lynch, O. M., *The Politics of Untouchability*, 1959.

Narayana, G., 'Social Background of Scheduled Caste MPs', *Economics and Politics Weekly*, 13 (1978), p. 1,603.

Nigam, S. S., 'Equality and the Representation of the Scheduled Classes in Parliament' *Journal of the India Law Institute*, 2 (1959), p. 297.

Rajeshekaria, *B. R. Ambedkar: The Politics of Emancipation*, 1971.

Sachindanda, *The Harijan Elite*, 1977.

Shah, G., *Politics of Scheduled Castes and Tribes*, 1978.

Trivedi, H. R., *Scheduled Caste Women: Studies in Exploitation*, 1976.

Verba, S.; B. Ahmed; and A. Bhatt, *Caste, Race and Politics: A Comparative Study of India and the United States*, 1974.

Notes on Contributors

UPENDRA BAXI is a vice-chancellor at the South Gujarat University, India.

SUMA CHITNIS is a professor and head of the Unit for Research in the Sociology of Education at the Tata Institute of Social Sciences, Bombay, India.

UMA O. ELEAZU is executive director of the Manufacturers Association of Nigeria and was a member of the Constitutional Drafting Committee in 1975–6.

TAI YOKE LIN is a lecturer at the Faculty of Economics and Public Administration, University of Malaya.

B. J. NDULU is a senior lecturer and chairman of the Department of Economics at the University of Dar-es-Salaam, Tanzania.

SAM. EGITE OYOVBAIRE is an associate professor of political science at the University of Benin, Nigeria.

MAVIS PUTHUCHEARY is an associate professor of economics and administration at the University of Malaya.

S. W. R. DE A. SAMARASINGHE is a lecturer in economics at the University of Peradeniya and associate director of the International Centre for Ethnic Studies, Sri Lanka.

CHANDRA RICHARD DE SILVA is an associate professor of history at the University of Peradeniya, Sri Lanka.

K. M. DE SILVA is a professor of Sri Lankan history at the University of Peradeniya and a member of the University Grants Commission, Sri Lanka.

NEELAN TIRUCHELVAM is associate director of The Marga Institute, executive director of the Asian Council for Law and Development, and a member of the Presidential Commission on District Development Councils, Sri Lanka.

MYRON WEINER is Ford International Professor of Political Science at the Massachusetts Institute of Technology.

ROBERT B. GOLDMANN is principal consultant to the International Centre for Ethnic Studies, Sri Lanka.

A. JEYARATNAM WILSON is a professor of political science at the University of British Columbia, Fredericton, New Brunswick, Canada.